MORMONS, INDIANS,
and the
GHOST DANCE RELIGION
OF 1890

Second Edition

Library of Congress Cataloging-in-Publication Data

Barney, Garold D.
Mormons, Indians, and the Ghost Dance Religion of 1890
    p. cm.
    Includes bibliographical references.
    1. Church of Latter Day Saints – Mormons. 2. American Indians –
Ghost Dance
    3. American West

ISBN 13: 978-0-9820467-5-3

Bäuu Press
PO Box 4445
Boulder, Colorado

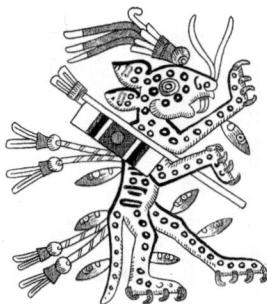

About the Author

Garold D. Barney was born and raised in western Oklahoma. In the late 1890s, his great-grandfather and grandfather were the third persons to file for Homestead land in a portion of Cherokee Strip land that would become Dewey County, Oklahoma. For their first few years the family lived in an earthen dugout in Cheyenne and Arapaho-ceded land.

Barney's mother and father were born before Oklahoma became a state in 1907. The fourth child of pioneer-tenant farmers, the pulling of broomcorn and picking of cotton were a way of life. His grandfather Durfey and Hubert Case were well-known "white preachers" in the Cheyenne-Arapaho community and his parents cared for the sick and provided sheep and goats to the Native American community during the years of the Depression and Dust Bowl.

Barney served in the U.S. Air Force during the Korean conflict, received his bachelor's and master's degrees from Central Missouri State University, and his doctorate from the University of California at Berkeley. The publication of Mormons, Indians, and the Ghost Dance Religion of 1890 represents ten years of research and writing.

Dedication

To men, women and children of all ages who have wept when they remembered Zion.

To my father and mother whose love, quiet strength, faith and vision have sustained and encouraged me through my years of wandering. Their compassion and understanding introduced me to Native American culture and values. From tenant farmers to tender-hearted parents, they taught the value of hard work and the cultivation of heart and soul. When dust, depression, and despair engulfed the land they spoke of happier days and, they too, wept.

To my son, Steven Jon, and daughter, Stacy Janette, with my deepest love.

To my grandchildren Lindsey and John Barney, Michelle, Kelsey and Jessica (Grace) Bjorland, whose lives have all taught me love.

To my sister Delphine White and her faithful and loving husband, Bob White. To our sister, Caroldene Hansen and to her faithful and loving husband, Paul L. Hansen. To Linda, Denny, Chris, and Bobby.

To my dear wife, whom I love more than words can express. To her I would give this writing and the vision of a restored earth where all creation live in harmony with each other.

To the spirit and hope of the Ghost Dance Religion—then as well as now.

Acknowledgements

Appreciation is expressed to Dr. Paul M. Edwards of Independence, Missouri and the late Enid DeBarthe of Lamoni, Iowa, for having taken time to review items and materials related to Mormon history and theology.

A special note of gratitude goes to those persons of the Mormon faith (Bernard O. Walker and Larry Coates) for their efforts to raise the level of consciousness to the many complex relationships of Mormon and Native American beliefs related to the Ghost Dance religion.

To those persons who have studied and written of the Ghost Dance Religion and Wounded Knee, we all owe a tremendous debt of gratitude.

Brodie, Fawn M. No Man Knows My History. Copyright 1945, reprinted by permission of Alfred A. Knopf, Inc.

Coates, Lawrence G. "The Mormons, the Ghost Dance Religion, and the Massacre at Wounded Knee," Dialogue: A Journal of Mormon Thought, Vol. 18. No. 4, (Winter 1985), reprinted by permission of the author.

Farb, Peter. Man's Rise to Civilization, Copyright 1978, reprinted by permission of E.P. Dutton, Inc.

Hollon, W. Eugene. The Great American Desert: Then and Now. Copyright 1966, reprinted by permission of Oxford University Press.

The following work of Michael Hittman and editor Don Lynch, University Press of Nebraska, 1990: Wovoka and the Ghost Dance, for its special contribution to the field of study.

Johnson, Edward C. Walker River Paiutes: A Tribal History. Copyright 1974 by the Walker River Paiutes, reprinted by permission of the Walker River Tribe.

Kroeber, et. al., editors. American Archaeology and Ethnology. Volume XXVIII, copyright 1965, reprinted by permission of University of California Press.

LaBarre, Weston. The Ghost Dance – Origins of Religion. Copyrights 1970 and 1972, reprinted by permission of George Allen and Unwin, Ltd., England, and Doubleday and Company, America.

Larson, Gustive O. The "Americanization" of Utah for Statehood. Copyright 1971, reprinted with permission of the Hentry E. Huntington Library.

McGavin Cecil E. The Nauvoo Temple. Copyright 1962, reprinted by permission of Deseret Book Company.

Merk, Frederick. History of the Westward Movement. Copyright 1980, reprinted by permission of Alfred A. Knopf, Incorporated.

Morgan, Dale, Ed. Overland in 1846: Diaries and Letters of the California-Oregon Trail, Vol. I and II. Copyright 1963, reprinted by permission of the Talisman Press.

Nichols, Roger L. and George R. Adams. The American Indian: Past and Present. Copyright 1971, reprinted by permission of Alfred A. Knopf.

Porter, C. Payne. Our Indian Heritage: Profiles of Twelve Great Leaders. Copyright 1964, reprinted by permission of Chilton Book Company.

Spencer, Robert F., and Jesse D. Jennings. <u>The Native Americans</u>. Copyright 1977, reprinted by permission of Harper and Row., Inc.

Starkloff, Carl. <u>The People of the Center</u>. Copyright 1974, reprinted by permission of the author.

Stegner, Wallace. <u>The Gathering of Zion: The Story of The Mormon Trail</u>. Copyright 1966 by Wallace Stegner, reprinted by permission of Brandt and Brandt Literary Agents, Inc.

Utley, Robert M. <u>The Last Days of the Sioux Nation</u>. Copyright 1963, reprinted by permission of Yale University Press.

Wallace, Anthony. <u>The Ghost Dance Religion</u>. Copyright 1965, reprinted by permission of University of Chicago Press.

Wallace, Paul. <u>The Indian Wars of the West</u>. Copyright 1954, reprinted by permission of Doubleday Company, Inc.

Foreword

In this study, Dr. Garold Barney has done an excellent job of reflecting both Mormon thought and the Indian concepts behind the Ghost Dance Religion. These two phenomena have existed in the history of the American West for a long time but it has taken Dr. Barney, following the footsteps of Dr. Coates, to make a good case for their relationship. Would recommend Barney's work to anyone interested in Mormons, the Plains Indians, the Ghost Dance Religion, or anyone with a general interest in the religious movements in the American West.

Paul M. Edwards
Baker University
Kansas City, Missouri

TABLE OF CONTENTS

Introduction:
Mormons, Indians, and the Ghost Dance Religion
of 1890 9

    Native Americans: A Chosen People 10

Chapter I:
Mormons On the Early Western Frontier 18

    Indian-Mormon Encounters: The Nauvoo Period .. 27
    The Mormon Exodus From Nauvoo 29

Chapter II:
The Mormon Frontier Moves West 31

    Garden Grove 36
    Winter Quarters 39

Chapter III:
Mormon-Indian Relations in Utah Territory 49

    Mormon-Indian Relations: The Great Basin and
    Salt Lake Regions 52

Chapter IV:
The Ghost Dance Religion: An Indian
Renaissance 66

    The Ghost Dance Religion 68
    Presbyterian Influence - The Wilson Bible 82
    The Development of the Messiah Religions 85

Chapter V:
The Paiute Restoration: Origins and Concepts ... 97

    The People: Origins In the Earth 97
    The Coming of the Whites, 1820 - 1870 102

Chapter VI:
The Ghost Dance Religion of 1890 132

    Diffusion of the Ghost Dance Religion 144
    Summary 170

MORMONS, INDIANS AND THE GHOST DANCE RELIGION OF 1890

Introduction

The Ghost Dance of 1890 was but one of many American Revivalist movements that would sweep the New World in the 19th Century. The Ghost Dance movement moved from the Great Basin to the Great Plains, from Canada to Texas, in a short span of time. Likewise Joseph Smith's new religion was to capture and inspire the hearts and minds of the inhabitants of the U.S. from New York, and Ohio to Missouri, Illinois, the Mexican Territory, and on to the British Isles and Scandinavia. The Ghost Dance and Mormonism inspired many while at the same time caused others to loathe and fear the unknown.

The revival movement known as Ghost Dance Religion was old---very old. It was as old as the stars falling from the sky at the Yellowstone[1]. Kosan, that venerable and highly respected Kiowa knew, too, of the spirit and intent of the Ghost Dance long before Wovoka was born. The Ghost Dance did not suddenly emerge in time, in a geographical location, with clearly defined beliefs, practices and rituals. Both Mormonism and the Ghost Dance sought right relationships of body, mind and soul. The Ghost Dance, while uniquely "Indian" in origin, was nevertheless a set of beliefs open to men and women of good will that centered in a belief in a Great Spirit who sought only to redeem his people, cleanse and replenish the earth. The earth was old, tired and in need of rejuvenation. The shuffle and repeated words of the dance inspired hope in the people.

The admonition given to a young Joseph Smith was to join none of the churches of his day. In adhering to this message, Joseph, like Wovoka, became a renegade—a rogue, if you will---from prevailing religious thought.

Both Mormonism and the Ghost Dance introduced their followers to new hymns and doctrines that, if followed sincerely, they believed would cause the Earth to be restored, the dead to come forth into a new age, and initiate a Millennium of peace and prosperity where the faithful would dwell in perfect peace and harmony. Zion would become a living reality for Mormon and Ghost Dancer alike.

Mormonism and the Ghost Dance were borne as a prophets' dream of peace and prosperity for all followers; however, violence, torture and wanton savagery followed the Saints and People from Hauns Mill, to Carthage, Nauvoo, from Walker Lake to Pine Ridge, and Wounded Knee.

John G. Niehardt reflected prophetically: "The victors lay buried in the snow."[2]

---

1 N. Scott Momaday, <u>The Way to Rainy Mountain</u>.
2 John G. Niehardt, <u>Black Elk Speaks</u>.

The Beginnings

Very little research has been undertaken to assess the influence, if any, that Mormonism may have had on the development and spread of the (Paiute) Ghost Dance Religion of 1890. The reason for lack of research is due, in part, to the fact that "Mormonism" has not always enjoyed the position of acceptance in literature and history that it currently appears to be gaining; perhaps it is simply because there is little actual connection between Mormonism and Indian Revivalism in the Great Basin during the closing years of the 19th Century. A third reason may be the apparent lack of unprejudiced research relating to either Mormon or Native American People for the period of 1830-1890. Typical of the attitude of the day was that expressed in Mark Twain's highly acclaimed classic, <u>Tom Sawyer</u>, in which a mixed-blood Indian was cast as its villain (p. 30 Miller, 1957). The role of 'villain' has been shared equally by Mormons and Indians on the Western Frontier. As late as the presidency of U. S. Grant, "an almost violent anti-Indian sentiment swept across the land. Whites everywhere were outraged by blood-curdling tales of Indian barbarity, both fictional and factual." (p. 30, Miller, 1957)

In a like manner blame for Indian wars and unrest was laid at the feet of the Mormon hierarchy in Independence, Missouri, (May 1830) where Mormon missionaries were "...ordered out of the Indian country as disturbers of the peace; and even threatened with the military in case of non-compliance." (pp. 54-61, Pratt, 1973)

In the late autumn of 1890, General Nelson Miles ordered federal troops on the plains and basin to mobilize, as prevailing beliefs held that Indian unrest and uprisings were all "fueled by the Mormons."

The Mormon President, Wilford Woodruff had ended his 1889 diary with the following summary:

> *Thus ends the year 1889 and the word of the prophet Joseph Smith is beginning to be fulfilled that the whole nation would turn against Zion and make war upon the Saints. The nation has never been filled so full of lies against the Saints as today. 1890 will be an important year with the Latter Day Saints and the American Nation. (p. 249, Larson, 1971)*

> *Once again, the aim of the frontiersmen was to get rid of the Indian, to get him out of the way, in order that the young nation might fulfill its "Manifest Destiny" to 'expand from coast to coast.' The image of the Indian as a Bloodthirsty Savage moved west along with the frontier. As the struggle increased in fury, Indian rights*

10

were ignored, and countless atrocities were committed
by both sides. The Indian came to be considered as less
than human, as a game animal to be hunted down and
destroyed. (p. 509, Spencer and Jennings, 1977)

Mormons and Indians became people of oppression. The question of Mormon-Indian relations will be evaluated in this manuscript and an attempt will be made to explore those traditions of Mormonism which may have influenced the Ghost Dance Religion and the Indian Prophet, Wovoka.

In the process of examining the Ghost Dance Religion, it is necessary to review at least six aspects of Mormon tradition that relate to Mormon conduct with the American Indian:

1. The Mormon belief that the American Indian represents the descendants of the lost tribes of the House of Israel. (The Book of Mormon and Mormon literature refers to the American Indian as either Lamanites or Nephites.)

2. The Mormon belief in the coming of the Messiah, the regeneration of the earth, and a resurrection of the dead. (By 1890 this belief was held by the majority of Western tribes.)

3. The teaching of Indian and Mormon revival follows a parallel of doctrine that is singularly significant in the life of the nation.

4. Both the Ghost Dance Religion and Mormonism were spawned in the midst of religious Revivalism that gripped upstate New York in 1820-30 and the Great Basin 1870-1890.

5. Both Joseph Smith and the Paiute Prophet Wovoka (Jack Wilson) were accepted by their followers as messengers of God having received marvelous revelations for their people after having been in the presence of God, heard His voice and accepted the mandate to deliver God's children from captivity and bondage and to lead them to a new promised land.

    "Wovoka then began to preach the spiritual regeneration
    of the Indians, with the promise that it would eventuate
    in the restoration of their world. He professed that God
    had directed him to instruct the living Indians that they
    should be good and love one another, that they must
    live peacefully and return to the old ways, and that
    they were to sing certain songs and hasten
    the millennium by dancing. If they did these

11

*things, the white men would disappear and the living
and dead Indians would be reunited in a renovated
world, where all would live in happiness, in deliverance
from misery, death, and disease." (p. 510, Spencer and
Jennings, 1977)*

Similarly, Joseph Smith instructed his followers "to seek to establish and bring forth the cause of Zion..."

6. Both Indians and Mormons were participants in the Ghost Dance.

   This writing will attempt to review those socio-religious conditions prevailing on the frontier that gave rise to Mormon and Indian revivalism. Meighnan and Riddell list some seven common conditions that may be present which give rise to revivalist movements. These "conditions" have been observed to have been present in revivalist movements throughout the world as well as having relevance to both the Mormon and Ghost Dance Religion.

The pattern of revivalist movements includes the following elements:

1. A contact situation between two groups, one of which is superior to the other politically and economically.

2. The appearance of a "prophet," in the less favored group, who spreads the new religion.

3. Belief in the punishment of the controlling group with the aid of supernatural means. A frequent belief is that the offending groups will be exterminated by a catastrophe of some sort: either turned to stones, drowned in a flood, or driven into the sea.

4. Belief in a return to the old life, when everyone was happy. This is commonly associated with a belief in the return of the dead ancestors of the followers, who will bring with them all material things desired by the group.

5. Belief in supernatural protection of the believers, through faith or talismans.

6. Active proselytizing of the new religion. Ordinarily there is an extremely rapid spread of the practices.

7. A community religious ceremony, usually secularized and esoteric. These elements do not always appear in the same form or in the same strength. Certain aspects may be favored over others, and some elements may be de-emphasized to the point where they are almost absent. However, some traces of all the elements given may be discerned in all the revivalist cults which are not documented at all fully. (pp. 7-8, Meighnan and Riddell, 1972)

While the listing of Meighnan and Riddell may not represent either a lasting or an all-inclusive listing of conditions that gave rise to all revival movements, the work is, nevertheless, suggestive of sufficient common ingredients shared by both the Ghost Dance Religion and Mormonism to be worthy of consideration.

An eighth consideration common to the Mormon and Indian revival movement might include the belief of the "faithful" as a chosen people having been singled out from the rest of humanity to accomplish God's will.

There is an element of ethnocentrism in the belief of a" chosen people" that has resulted in the "faithful" to fall victim to all manner of violence and persecution by those persons of the nation and state who were not considered to be members of the revival movement. The conflict at Wounded Knee may constitute one such example and the massacre of Mormon men, women and children at Haun's Mill in Missouri yet another.

Throughout this manuscript, the term "Mormon" will be used to designate the followers of the religious movement originated by Joseph Smith and whose teachings were continued through the leadership of Brigham Young in the Great Salt Lake Valley. The term "Ghost Dancers" is used to designate the followers of Wovoka and the Ghost Dance Religion and will not attempt to distinguish the Indian believers in the Ghost Dance by tribe or nation.

Native Americans: A Chosen People

The belief that the American Indians were "remnants" of the lost tribes of Israel was unique neither to Western New York nor to the Mormon Movement in 1830. Elijah M. Haines in his book, <u>The American Indian</u> credits a letter written in 1824 to contain evidence of a Hebrew origin. The letter, written by a Mr. Calvin Cushman, Missionary to the Choctaw, states: "By information received from Father Hoyt respecting the former tradition, rites, and ceremonies of the Indians of this region, I think there is much reason to believe they are the descendants of Abraham." (p. 103, Haines, 1888) Similarity of priestly office, language, and religious observances is cited by Cushman to support his belief.

Elijah Haines affirms at least two Jewish migrations: one a Tyrcon fleet under King Solomon, with a venture to Haiti and the other a voyage by "Christians and Jews" to the New World. This latter migration, he states, "... must have happened at a time when the whole of the New World was already peopled." (p. 72, Haines, 1888) Gregorie Garces in his <u>Origin de los Indies del Nuevo Mundo</u> (1607) postulates that Jewish immigrants were among the eleven groups having landed on the shores of the Americas before either the Norsemen or, for that matter, Christopher Columbus. Lord Kingsborough's nine-volume <u>Antiquities of Mexico</u> (1830-48) was written in the hope of establishing proof and credibility to the belief that the aboriginal inhabitants of Latin America were descendants of the Ten Lost Tribes of Israel.

Indians of the Americas were believed by other writers to have descended from a variety of the earth's people, including Norsemen, Chinese, Irish, Celtic and Japanese. Robert Wauchope, in an 1827 publication, <u>Lost Tribes and Sunken Continents</u>, states that:

> *...the most attention in scientific congresses of the past century was that which identified a country called Fu-Sang in early Chinese annals with prehistoric Mexico. A Frenchman, De Guines, seems to have been the first to publish his opinion in 1761 that in the Fifth century Buddhist monks were sent from China to establish religion in the New World...(pp. 90-91, Wauchope, 1962)*

Frank Waters cites work done by Cyrus B. Gordon, Chairman of the Department of Mediterranean Studies at Brandeis University as "outstanding" in its contribution to the field of research relating to early migrations. Waters credits Gordon in deciphering an inscription on the Parahyba Stone found in Brazil in 1872, as being "the record of the voyage of fifteen Canaanites across the Atlantic to the 'New Shore' of Brazil in 531 B.C." Such evidence, postulates Waters, "contradicts the present Bering Strait theory." (p. 74,   14

Waters, 1975) "It is quite probable that some of these people crossed both the Atlantic and Pacific to Mesoamerica centuries before the Christian era." (p. 74, Waters, 1975) "One thing seems certain. The American Indians were not a homogenous race. They were composed of many different sources at many different periods." (p. 74, Waters, 1975)

Mormon belief differed dramatically from these early hypotheses in that Joseph Smith was purported to have received, by divine revelation in 1830, mysterious golden plates containing the history of Jewish emigrants to the New World before the birth of Christ. The purported translation of The Book of Mormon plates was published and widely distributed and proclaimed the American Indian as being "the Blood of Israel." (p. vii-viii, Brown, 1972) The Mormon Movement, armed with its "added witness" of The Book of Mormon, declared that early wandering tribes formed nations -- "some of which flourished, some became extinct, and some corrupt. One of these groups was the Lamanite, believed by some to be the ancestors of today's American Indian." (pp. 10-11, Larson, 1971)

Mormon interpretation of The Book of Mormon, though not universally accepted by the entire body of believers, represents the Indian as being of "the blood of Israel" but "fallen and cursed with dark skin because of their wickedness." It was thought that by adherence to the "Mormon Gospel" and living by its teachings, the Indian brethren might become "redeemed and become again a white and delightsome people." (pp. vii-viii, Brown, 1972)

As a consequence of their doctrine, the Mormons believed that they should relate this message of salvation to the Indians, the Lamanites, and concentrate efforts on converting the "Remnants of the House of Israel" to Mormonism. (pp. vii-viii, Brown, 1972, and p. 704, Mooney, 1892)

> ...Orson Pratt...preached a sermon, which was
> extensively copied and commented on at the time,
> [urging] the faithful to arrange their affairs and put their
> houses in order to receive the long-awaited wanderers.
> (p. 704, Mooney, 1892)

Kulckhohn and Leighton wrote:

> ...in the early days Mormons got along a little better
> with the Indians than did most pioneers who entered
> the region. The writers inclined to connect this fact with
> Mormon teachings that Indians are descendants of the
> lost tribes of Israel. Hence, Mormons tended to show
> more respect for and interest in Indian customs; more
> than other whites perhaps, they gave Indians a sense of
> being a part and a worthy part of the world as a whole.
> (p. 78, Kulckhohn and Leighton, 1947)

15

The attitude and belief of the early Mormon Church seemed to verify the fact that a potentially unique relationship existed between the Mormons and the Indians. It was this relationship which set Mormons apart from other people on the frontier.

It is this relationship, then, which will serve as the central focus of this writing.

Arapaho Ghost Dancers - Smithsonian Photograph

CHAPTER I

Mormons On the Early Western Frontier

The Mormons, like the Indian tribes occupying the Great Plains and Basin, were "wanderers." Their original hope for a fixed-sedentary way of life, while never fully realized, was originally inseparably connected to the task of evangelizing the Indian people.[1] Less than five months after the official organization of the Church (April 6, 1830), Joseph Smith declared:

> ...*no man knoweth where the city of Zion shall be built, but is shall be given hereafter. Behold, I say unto you that it shall be on the borders by the Lamanites. (p. 93, Brodie, 1945)*

Because of misunderstanding and persecution, the Mormons were forced repeatedly by contentions both from within and without to be ever on the move in search of a suitable place to build the "Kingdom of God." In time, their search led them from New York to Ohio to Missouri, to Illinois, then on the Mexican Territory in what is now Utah, Nevada, and California. It was their wandering that kept them repeatedly in contact with Indian tribes on the Western Frontier.

The first "mission" to establish The Book of Mormon among the Indians took place in October of 1830. Parley P. Pratt, Oliver Cowdery, Peter Whitmer, and Ziba Peterson met with the Catteraugas tribe near Buffalo, (New York). They stayed part of the day and left a copy of The Book of Mormon with each of two Indians who knew English.

Late in 1830, Pratt and the others spent a few days with the Wyandottes near Sandusky, Ohio. In 1831, the four missionaries reached Independence, Missouri. Among those remembrances was a sermon delivered by Oliver Cowdery to a nameless priest of the Delawares. Pratt recorded the sermon in his autobiography:

> ...*and if the red man would then receive this Book [Book of Mormon] and learn the things written in it, and do according thereunto, they should be restored to all their rights and privileges; should cease to fight and kill one another; should become one people; cultivate the earth in peace; in common with the pale faces, who were willing to believe and obey the same book, and be good men and live in peace.*

---

1   The task of proselytizing Native American People, while still espoused, appears to be less significant among all Mormon splinter groups today than in the early formative period of the movement.

*Then should the red man become great, and have plenty
to eat and good clothes to wear, and should be in favor
with the Great Spirit and be his children, while he would
be their Great Father, and talk with them, and raise up
prophets and wise and good men amongst them again,
who would teach them many things.*

*The excitement now reached the frontier settlements in
Missouri, and stirred up the jealousy and envy of the
Indian agents and sectarian missionaries to that degree
that we were soon ordered out of the Indian country as
disturbers of the peace and even threatened with the
military in case of noncompliance. (pp. 54-61, Pratt,
1973)*

These early sermons of Cowdery and Pratt may have been motivated by
the prevailing national sentiment of "manifest destiny" as well as the teachings
of The Book of Mormon.[2]

*In some ways it is not difficult to see where the Euro-
Americans were coming from in their philosophy. After
all, their God had given them dominion over all the
earth and its inhabitants. Add to that the mission of
Christianity to bring all pagans to the One and True God,
the idea of the "White man's burden," and the concept of
"manifest destiny..." (p. 33 Bataille, 1978)*

But Mormon "manifest destiny" differed markedly from American
"Manifest Destiny" in that it generally stressed that the Lamanite people:

1. Possessed priority over even the Mormon Saints since Indians were
    regarded generally as remnants of the Lost Tribes of Israel and

2. Were to have a highly significant and worthy place in the building
    of the Kingdom of God on the earth and especially in the task of
    building the Temple in Jackson County, Missouri.

By contrast American Manifest Destiny generally held Indians as
retarders of progress and as such insisted they be removed from the land. Such
sentiments did not constitute Mormon belief. Typical of American Manifest
Destiny would be this view expressed in an 1867 Topeka, Kansas, Weekly
Leader, referring to Indians as:

---

2   A significant attitude of Mormonism still largely ignored or unobserved by writers on
Mormonism is the possible fact that Mormon teachings paralleled those of the national sentiment of
"manifest destiny."

...a set of miserable, dirty, lousy, blanketed, thieving,
lying, sneaking, murdering, graceless, faithless, gut-
eating skunks as the Lord ever permitted to infect the
earth, and whose immediate and final extermination of
all men, except Indian agents and traders, should pray
for. (p. 509, Spencer, 1977)

The editorial writings of Richard F. Burton, <u>City of the Saints</u> and
<u>Across the Rocky Mountains to California</u> (1963), similarly display the views of
American Manifest Destiny so prevalent during the preceding century:

The Sioux belong essentially to the savage, in opposition
to the Aztecan peoples of the New World. In the days of
Major Pike (1805-1807), they were the dread of all the
neighboring tribes, from the confluence of the Mississippi
and the Missouri to the Raven River on the latter. (p. 104,
Burton, 1963)

The Dakotas are mostly a purely hunting tribe in the
lowest condition of human society: they have yet to take
the first step, and to become pastoral people. (p. 109,
Burton, 1963)

Of the settled races the best types are the Choctaws
and the Cherokees; the latter have shown a degree of
improbability, which may still preserve them from
destruction; they have a form of government, churches,
theatres, and schools; they read and write English... (p.
40, Burton, 1963)

Indian agents and clergymen were troubled by the Mormon desire to
restore the Indian to "all their rights and privileges, [and that they] ...should
become one people .... to cultivate the earth ...in common with pale faces." The
Mormon doctrine of Indian "equality" caused considerable alarm to be raised
in pioneer communities such as Independence, Missouri.

From the time of earliest settlement, the European
explorers and colonists offered a confusing variety of
Christianity to the aborigines. The Protestant groups,
moreover, preached a mixture of religion and American
cultural nationalism. They assumed that tribal society
was both pagan and backward, and strove, consciously
or otherwise to replace this with their own particular
brand of civilization. The result, they hoped, would be the
extermination of native culture and the transformation of
the Indians into Christian farmers or tradesmen. (p. 120,
Nichols and Adams, 1971)

*...Like other whites, missionaries viewed the Indian as
the lowest rung on the ladder of social evolution and
believed that progress and civilization must triumph over
savagery. In fact, they felt they were in the vanguard of
the movement to force the aborigine up the ladder to the
American apex. (p. 123, Nichols and Adams, 1971)*

Nichols and Adams (The American Indian: Past and Present, 1971)
express the idea that Manifest Destiny and Christian zealousness combined to
form a curious blending of the "sacred and profane "into what "...some of them
termed...Christian Civilization."

*Therefore the only good Indian from their point of view
was a copy of a good white man, or as a Methodist
missionary wrote, "In school and in field, as well as in
kitchen, our aim was to teach the Indians to live like
white people." (p. 122, Nichols and Adams, 1971)*

*The blackcoat, on the other hand, sought not only
religious converts but the complete transformation of
Indian life. Of all the forces for acculturation between
1760 and 1860, the missionary pushed more aggressively
for change than any other white, and thus provides
important clues to the general understanding of Indian
acculturation in this period. While he led the drive, he still
acted, however, within the larger framework of contact,
especially in relation to governmental power. His
success in implementing Christian civilization depended
in the end, upon the strength of army and annuities in
thwarting tribal autonomy. (p. 123, Nichols and Adams,
1971)*

The most hostile of frontier mentality regarding Indian and Black people
is presented by Burton:

*The tribes are untamed and untamable savages... (p. 112,
Burton, 1963)*

*The warrior....is so lazy that he will not rise to saddle or
unsaddle his pony: he will sit down and ask a white man
to fetch him water, and only laugh if reproved. Like a
wild beast he cannot be broken to work: he would rather
die than employ himself in honest industry - a mighty
contrast to the Negro, whose only happiness is in serving.
(p. 114, Burton, 1963)*

Likewise:

> *The Mormons were accused by the citizenry of Missouri*
> *of plotting with the Indians for the destruction of non-*
> *Mormons ...The people of Missouri were very busy at*
> *the time driving the Indians from their heritage into*
> *unsettled land west of the Mississippi... .Indian wars*
> *were the main excitement of the country at the time, and*
> *the settlers of Missouri feared the Indians more than*
> *they admired their ancestry and preferred to suppress*
> *them rather than to trust them. Anyone who regarded an*
> *Indian as anything but an enemy could never be popular.*
> *(pp. 100-101, Werner, 1925)*

Then, too, the Mormons may have boasted too broadly that Jackson County, Missouri, "...was the land God had promised them, and that all non-Mormons would eventually be forced to leave..." (p. 97, Werner, 1925)

> *In the final analysis, relations with Indians were*
> *potentially more explosive than was the slavery issue. It*
> *is true that the Mormons were not slaveholders, "...but*
> *they never expressed themselves as opposed to slavery."*
> *(p. 100, Werner, 1925)*

The missionary excitement of the early Mormon elders notwithstanding, the attention of the Mormons was redirected in the months that followed from the Indian Mission to problems of misunderstandings and jealousies surfacing in Missouri at Independence as clashes between Mormons and non-Mormons became serious and epidemic. Thereafter the infant church, its missionary zeal and the Indian Mission moved to Nauvoo, Illinois.

Research to date fails to reveal the nature or extent of missionary endeavor among the Indians during the period 1831-1841. It is known that Sac and Fox Indians, remnants of the tribes having fought in the Black Hawk War, were living west of Nauvoo and across the Mississippi River on land that would become the state of Iowa (1846).

It appears more than reasonable to conclude that the decade of 1831-1841 was spent by the Mormon leadership in draining swampland, building homes, and the monumental task of assimilating the scores of converts trekking to Nauvoo. Little attention, it appears, was directed to the Indian Mission.

Nevertheless, Prophet Joseph Smith records that on Thursday, August 12, 1841, a meeting with the Sac and Fox tribe had taken place. This meeting is of particular significance, not so much because of its direct dealing with Indians at that time, but rather for the implications that it might have had farther west in Utah. The Mormon Prophet recorded:

*...A considerable number of Sac and Fox Indians have
been for several days encamped in the neighborhood
of Montrose. The ferrymen this morning brought over
a great number on the ferryboat and two flatboats,
for the purpose of visiting me. The military band and
detachment of Invincibles were on shore ready to receive
and escort them to the grove, but they refused to come on
shore until I went down. (pp. 541-542, Smith, I, 1910)*

The student of Mormon history, especially as it relates to the Indian
Mission, will be interested in reviewing the full text of the sermon delivered
by the prophet to the Indians; however, for our purposes, it should be recalled
with considerable emphasis that the Sac and Fox had been met by a "military
band" and a "DETACHMENT OF INVINCIBLES."

The Nauvoo historic record is not altogether clear as to the origin or
meaning of the term "invincible," but before his acceptance into the fellowship
of the Mormon community, Dr. John C. Bennett had served as brigadier
general of the <u>Invincible Dragoons</u> and quartermaster-general of the Illinois
state militia.[3] (p. 67, Taylor, 1971)

Laying aside momentarily the origin of the concept of invincibility and
its possible connection with endowment garments worn by Mormons or the
Ghost Shirt worn by the Sioux, it is important to reflect that the historical
reality of events in Jackson County, at Haun's Mill, and at Far West had so
conditioned the Mormon church population to fear or suspect outsiders that
visitors, in this case the Indians, were met with a detachment of Invincibles
and a military band rather than a hand of fellowship or, for that matter, a
copy of <u>The Book of Mormon.</u> In this case the invincibility of the cause of
God seemed to have given way to invincibility of guns, soldiers, and cultural
paraphernalia.

The cultural mind-set of Mormon invincibility is further purported to
have been seen in Carthage, Illinois, on that fateful day in June, 1844, when
Joseph and Hyrum Smith were killed by a mob.[4]

John C. Bennett, a one-time Mormon leader, a man of considerable
influence both inside the Church and in "Gentile" circles of government and

---

3   The Nauvoo Legion was commanded by Joseph Smith who served as Brigadier General.
Each of the 12 members of the Quorum of Twelve Apostles served as a chaplain of a regiment of the
Legion. Units of the Nauvoo Legion were nationalized by President Polk to serve as the Mormon
Battalion in the Mexican War. The Nauvoo Legion is theoretically, if not actually, the antecedent of
the present day Utah National Guard.

4   Considerable confusion and controversy exists among certain sects of Mormonism such
as the Community of Christ and Temple Lot Faction regarding the acceptance of the possibility
that Temple Endowments were practiced during the Nauvoo Period. The Community of Christ
(formerly Reorganized Church of Latter-Day Saints) has traditionally maintained that the Temple
in Nauvoo had never been "dedicated" and therefore that temple ceremonies, if they took place
at all, must have been practiced without the knowledge or approval of the prophet Joseph Smith.
Contemporary historians and theologians of the Community of Christ Church appear
much more accepting of the reality that, perhaps, Temple Ceremonies and
Sacraments did in effect take place in Nauvoo before the death of the Prophet.

prominence, stated that he had been present on the fourth of May 1842, when endowment ceremonies were first introduced to the church. He wrote:

> *..the lodge room is carefully prepared and consecrated, and from twelve to twenty-four sprigs of Casia, olive branches, cedar boughs or other evergreens are tastefully arranged about it. These are intended to represent the eternal life and unmingled bliss which, in the celestial kingdom, will be enjoyed by all who continued in full fellowship... (p. 76, McGavin, 1962)*

Bathsheba W. Smith was interviewed further on this subject and gave the following information:

> *...when the endowments were administered in the Prophet's office above his store, Emma Smith was in charge of preparing the room for the occasion and then washing and ironing the clothes that were used for that purpose. (p. 53, McGavin, 1962)*

Cecil McGavin states that by the time of the completion of the Temple and the exodus from Nauvoo,

> *...Emma had become out of harmony with the twelve and with the Church and never [Smith] attended an endowment session in the temple or assisted with the work in any manner." (p. 53, McGavin, 1962)*

Benjamin G. Ferris in his book, <u>Utah and the Mormons</u>, states that: "...it was believed that Doctor Richards had escaped unhurt from assassin's bullets at Carthage Jail because he possessed an endowment robe that was purported to have made him [invincible] safe from the arts of the devil, safe from shipwreck, bullets, and deceit." (pp. 311-312, Ferris, 1854, see also, Donna Hill, <u>Joseph Smith,</u> a testimony of Willard Richards at Carthage, Illinois jail)[5] Porter Rockwell, "...that long-haired, cold-nerved instrument that Joseph had created..." too had been "...blessed by Joseph with the promise of invulnerability" for so long as..."his hair remained uncut." (p. 90, Stegner, 1964, see also pg. 132, West, 1957)[6]

---

5   It is interesting to note that Doctor Richards "escaped unhurt from the assassins bullets," a fact that he attributed to the wearing of his endowment robe. Interestingly, Joseph and Hyrum Smith were killed in the same room on that fateful day; however, it would appear that the Prophet and his brother were either not aware of the protective properties of the endowment robe or were not wearing such a garment at the time of the mob action or, that it failed to provide needed protection.

6   According to some writers on the Mormons, more than one man was blessed by Joseph Smith in the early days and told that he would never be touched by an enemy bullet. Porter Rockwell, Joseph's personal bodyguard and one of the most redoubtable of the Sons of Dan, had his hair singed and his clothes pierced, and once took off his coat to shake slugs out on the floor after an affray, but the word of the prophet was good. His hide was never so much as broken by a bullet. (p. 153, Stegner, 1964)

Porter Rockwell was described during the trek west as:

> *...as dangerous a man as existed on the whole frontier,*
> *and all the more fearsome because he worked in*
> *silence, on orders, and not for his own purposes but*
> *for the Church. He was tireless, strong, a dead shot -*
> *and moreover blessed by Joseph with the promise of*
> *invulnerability. They welcomed him with joy. The man*
> *who had become the murderer of many men joined the*
> *rest of the brethren in laying hands on Clayton and*
> *rebuking his sickness in the name of the Lord. President*
> *Young being the mouth. (p. 90, Stegner, 1964)*[7]

It is of particular interest to observe that the belief that a "garment" could protect a person from harm, "even bullets of the U. S. Cavalries" was shared by Indian converts to the Ghost Dance Religion as well as by converts to Mormonism.[8]

The famous Oglala leader, "Crazy Horse," was regarded by his followers as "invulnerable." (p. 107-108, Miller, 1957) "As everyone knew, no enemy bullets could touch him, so powerful was his medicine." (p. 108, Miller, 1957)

---

7   There exists a lack of empirical evidence that seeks to establish the relationship of Masonry in influencing the teachings of Joseph Smith during the Nauvoo period. Rumor and speculation abound – evidence, however, remains limited. William J. Whalen states that Joseph "...elaborated his temple ritual..." and in so doing "...he borrowed freely from the Masonic initiations." (p. 183, Whalen, 1964)

"The Prophet began to introduce certain of the Saints to the secret rites in the room above the store. Eventually the attic of the Nauvoo temple was set apart for the administration of the new sacred endowments. Brigham Young himself took the part of Elohim in the sacred play. Thousands of Saints clamored to receive their endowments in the temple even as Nauvoo was harassed by the neighboring Gentiles." (p. 163, Whalen, 1964)

8   Stories of soldiers and warriors believing themselves to be invulnerable to bullets and injury in battle are surprisingly quite commonplace on the American Frontier. Such well-known white Americans as the infamous George Armstrong Custer were believed to have been beyond the "pale of death" from an enemy's bullet.

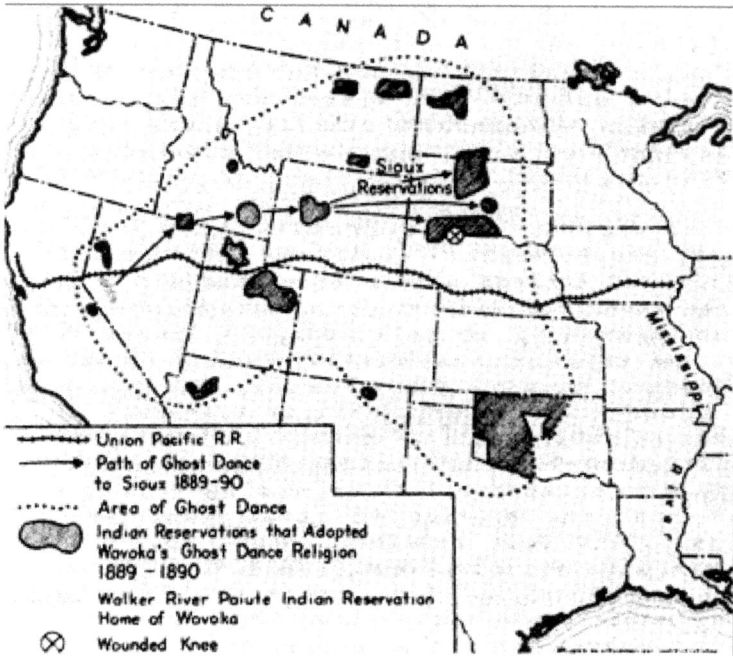

Boundary Of the Ghost Dance Religion of 1890 - Smithsonian Photograph

The courageous Cheyenne Warrior, Soldier Wolf, was said to have worn a special protective charm. "So great was the power of this war medicine that its wearer could never be touched by an enemy bullet unless the charm itself was hit." (p. 139, Miller, 1957)

Other stories, true or figment of barracks rumor-mills were circulated in North Africa during World War II. It was rumored that the German General Rommel (often referred to as the Desert Fox) was living a somewhat charmed existence based on his real or imagined uncanny skill in escaping unhurt or unharmed from dangers grip.

William J. Whalen states similarly that "stories of protection given Mormons wearing their temple garments on the battlefield or in accidents are common in Mormon folklore." (pp. 168-169, Whalen, 1964) Such garments, Whalen observes, "...provide a shield and protection..." (pp. 168-169, Whalen, 1964) Cecil McGavin reports that the Mormon endowment garments were capable of preserving their wearers from death and to "secure" for them an "earthly immortality." (p. 77, McGavin, 1962)

> *Several members of the Council of the Twelve were listed,*
> *with their wives, as having received these ordinances*
> *during the summer of 1843 under the direction of Joseph*
> *Smith. On many occasions this valiant and*

reliable witness continued to testify that the endowment
as given by Joseph Smith in his office above his store
was exactly the same as was administered in the finished
temples in Utah. (p. 54, E. Cecil McGavin, 1962)

Significant changes in Mormon mind-set appear to have taken place during the closing phase of Nauvoo history. Special garments, invincibility to bullets, and the emergence of personalities such as Porter Rockwell (bodyguard to Joseph Smith and "avenger" to the Church) all serve to illustrate the high degree of tension, apprehension, and fear that gripped the Mormon community on the Mississippi River. (p. 90, Stegner, 1964)

The fears and apprehensions of the Nauvoo period so occupied the thinking of the church leadership that no clearly articulated program of missionary outreach to the Indian people took place during the period 1835-1845. Fawn Brodie assesses the Mormon experiment of Indian evangelism as largely "a failure." (p. 110, Brodie, 1975)

The "failure" was due in part to the uneasiness with which Mormons viewed all outsiders -- Gentiles and Indians alike. The "failure" was due, in part, to the unspoken realization that while Mormonism stressed the belief that the Indians were members of the lost tribes of Israel and the chosen of the Lord, nevertheless, the Mormon hierarchy really did not know just how to "take the gospel to the Lamanites." Each effort of evangelism stressed the necessity of Indian people to take up the ways of the whites -- especially "White Mormons." The effort to convert the Lamanites into Mormon farmers, herders and craftsmen, was repeated in Utah and the West and continues to this day.

Indian - Mormon Encounters:
The Nauvoo Period

An August 1841 meeting of Joseph Smith with Chief Keokuk reflects further the uneasiness with which the Mormons would encounter Gentiles and Indians on the western frontier. Joseph admonished Keokuk and his followers to "keep peace with whites." (p. 542, Smith, J., 1888) In July, Joseph Smith instructed some Pottawattamie:

Do not kill white men; it's not good; but ask the Great
Spirit for what you want, and it will not be long before
the Great Spirit will bless you, and you will cultivate the
earth and build good houses like white men. We will give
you something to eat and to take home with you. (p. 542,
Smith, J., 1888)

Fawn N. Brodie assessed the cultural mind-set of the   27

Mormons toward the Indians as a policy of "...offering the red man, not restoration, but assimilation, not the return of his continent, but the loss of his identity." (pp. 93-94, Brodie, 1964) Assimilation was but another name for cultural annihilation and it mattered little if assimilation were the desired end of the Federal Government or as a result of efforts to "Christianize" Native American people. The end result was always the same: loss of identity, loss of a way of life.

Jacobs asserts that from as early as the colonial period, Native American people "...did not consider assimilation a solution of the problem of dealing with whites." (p. 148, Jacobs, 1972)

> *This path would have meant servitude, perhaps, slavery, educational programs, adoption of their children, and possible intermarriage (which the Indian approved, but the whites themselves generally rejected)...*
>
> *Indians who fought the English during the 1769's were fighting for self-determination in a war for their independence. For generations they had governed themselves under a complex pattern of self-government in their towns and villages. Their fortifications and buildings for families, and civic and religious affairs were impressive even to the colonists. Gardens, orchards, and grain fields attested to their agricultural skill. Indians had no desire to abandon their own culture. (p. 148, Jacobs, 1972)*

Little evidence is available that would indicate that the Mormon policy of evangelism during the period of 1830-1845 had as its goal any object other than the assimilation of Indian people into the mainstream of Mormon life. Perhaps the stress of community problems, both within the Church and without, gave little time to the Church's hierarchy to develop or articulate a plan of evangelism for Native American people. Then too, the need to articulate and formulate a workable theology for the church was of paramount importance, especially as it related to the temple ordinances and sacraments, endowments and temple garments. It is reasonable to assume that, when faced with the demands of being President-Prophet of the Church, Mayor of Nauvoo, Brigadier General of the Legion, and candidate for the presidency of the United States, that little attention was directed to just how the Native American people were to fit into the general scheme of building the Kingdom on the Mississippi.

The Mormon Exodus From Nauvoo

After the death of Joseph Smith, the concept of individual and corporate invincibility moved west with Dr. Richards, Porter Rockwell, and the First Contingent trekking into Indian Territory under the leadership of Brigham Young (pp. 34-35, Stegner, 1964). Certain beliefs and practices of the Church in Nauvoo had become firmly crystallized into dogma and fixed ritual; however, a significant change in style of leadership emerged after the death of the Prophet Joseph Smith in the personality and charismatic leadership of Brigham Young.

Wallace Stegner (p. 60, 1964), describes the demise of "prophetic" leadership within the Mormon Church after the death of Joseph Smith. Brigham Young exemplified a more pragmatic-utilitarian director-administrator then had Joseph Smith. Young appears to have emerged as a mid-1840's self-styled Moses intent upon leading the Church through the wilderness and into the Promised Land somewhere in the West.

> *Brigham Young was no seer and revelator but a practical*
> *leader, an organizer and colonizer of very great stature.*
> *He is credited with only one revelation in all his years*
> *as head of the Church, and that one is characteristic.*
> *It outlined how the Saints should be regimented for*
> *migration into tens and fifties and hundreds, with a*
> *responsible captain over each group. And when the*
> *organizational outline was completed the revelation*
> *closed with as clipped a phrase as if God were a*
> *businessman dictating to his secretary. "And so no more*
> *at this time," God said. There was no more at any time.*
> *(p. 60, Stegner, 1964)*

The assumption of the role of President-Prophet of the Mormon Church by Brigham Young could not be described as always orderly or without considerable tension and hostility within the quorums and general membership of the church.

Brigham Young had become senior member of the Quorum of the Twelve Apostles following a series of dramatic changes that took place in both the Presidency and the Twelve. Sidney Rigdon, a member of the First Presidency had been disfellowshiped from the Church, and leaders such as James Strang had begun to lead splinter groups to Beaver Island in Michigan, and Lyman Wight to Texas.[9] Such changes cleared the way for Brigham

---

9   The organization of the Reorganized Church of Jesus Christ of Latter Day Saints (present-day Community of Christ Church) under the leadership of the Prophet Joseph Smith's son, Joseph III, took place in 1853 at the Amboy (Illinois) Conference. Emma Smith fellowshipped with the Reorganization and it was here that a theological stand was taken against polygamy, Temple Endowments (including baptism for the dead) and celestial marriage.

Young to become Senior member of the Council of Twelve Apostles and, then, President of the Church.

It was into the role of leadership as President of the Church that Brigham Young, by whatever means, stepped. What Brigham may have lacked in prophetic leadership, he more than made up for in his charismatic ability to organize and direct in the life of the quorums and membership of the church. The first order of business was the preparation of the saints to leave their homes in Nauvoo and to begin a forced winter march across the prairies of Iowa. The Mormons were accustomed to persecution; indeed it appears that they accepted mob violence and torment as added testimony as to the rightness of their cause. Armed as they were with a sense of divine call and mission, the Mormon population made preparation for their exodus from the city on the Mississippi. A part of the preparation was to sell property and to secure teams, wagons and provisions for the trek into the wilderness. Still another part of the preparation was mental and emotional...a sense of spiritual oneness that seemed to bond the people together in a mutual feeling of purpose and destiny.

Of equal importance to the life of the Saints as they moved West was the assurance and stability that they found in participating in the established sacraments and ordinances of the Church. The ordinances and sacraments brought order, stability, and a sense of continuity to the rigorous demands of wilderness life and travel. On the prairie of Iowa, a few Mormons continued to receive their endowments at Garden Grove, Mt. Pisgah and Winter Quarters (near present-day Omaha, Nebraska). The published diary of William Clayton records that tents were set up for the purpose of providing shelter and sanctuary for the conducting of Mormon sacraments. The fulfillment of the sacraments appeared to be contingent upon the use of a "...borrowed ... robe and ornaments..." and that as the priesthood were "clothed" they "... offered up the signs, [and] offered up prayer..." (p. 40-41, Clayton, 1973) Those participants in the prairie sacrament service included such notables from Mormon history as: President Brigham Young, Dr. Richards, Porter Rockwell, Parley P. Pratt, Zebus Taylor, E. T. Benson, William Kimball and others whose names served as the leadership of the early Church in Utah.

> *After having arrived in Utah Territory, a few Mormons " ...received endowments in makeshift quarters...but it was nearly ten years after the end of the temple work at Nauvoo that the Old Endowment House was dedicated in Salt Lake City in 1855." (p. 163, Whalen, 1964) "These rites," Whalen stated, "differed little from those exemplified in the attic of the Nauvoo temple." (p. 163, Whalen, 1964)*

> *At a special Sabbath service in Brigham City, Utah, under the direction of President Lorenzo Snow, June 24,*

1894, Bathsheba W. Smith the widow of George A. Smith was invited to speak on the subject of temple work in Nauvoo. She related that she was the only woman living who had been endowed under the personal direction of the Prophet Joseph Smith, the few others who had received that blessing having passed away. (p. 52-53, E. McGavin, 1962)

President Wilford Woodruff was in attendance at the meeting and spoke on the same subject. He bore his testimony relative to receiving the temple endowment at the hands of Joseph Smith, emphasizing the fact that he was the only living man who was thus endowed under the direction of the Prophet. "There are many more," he said "who likewise had this great privilege, but they are all dead, leaving only these two witnesses." (p. 53, McGavin, 1962)

Garden Grove, Iowa, View of Old Mormon Trail, Photo by Jon Barney 2009

CHAPTER II

The Mormon Frontier Moves West

Missouri had become the first state (by 1820) to be carved out of the Louisiana Purchase Territory. The Missouri Compromise was significant in the Halls of Congress since the admission of Maine and Missouri to statehood allowed a favorable balance to remain in the U. S. Senate, with equal numbers of Senators from the eleven "slave" and eleven "free" states. Thus, open hostility between the North and the South had been averted for a season. It appears, however, that an anti-Indian, pro-slave sentiment prevailed in frontier communities of Missouri. The frontier mind-set will tend, in the early 1830's, to look with equal suspicion and mistrust on Mormons who came to claim lands for the building of the Kingdom of God and for the establishment of a mission to Native American Indians.

Somehow in the search for growth and expansion of the nation, the national sentiment favored strongly the overt expansion of the frontier -- ever westward beyond the ridges of the Appalachians to the western banks of the Missouri River. Growth and expansion seemed to eclipse the original thesis of President Jefferson that the land purchased from France in 1803 and known as the Louisiana Purchase Territory should be viewed as a permanent home for the Indian nations about to be caught-up in the tide of movement by white settlers into the hereditary lands of the Native American people. Stated simply, the hope of a permanent home for Native American people was somehow forgotten as the lure of wealth in the form of land, furs, and gold, began to call the restless adventurer across the Missouri, beyond the Great American Desert to the forest, streams and rich valleys of the Willamette River and to the gold fields of California.

By 1840, the decision of nearly all westward immigrants and fortune seekers was to "jump off" from Freeport Landing and Independence, Missouri, as soon as spring grass was high enough for food for livestock and the ground was sufficiently dry to allow wagon wheels to move free of the spring mud. The land between the Missouri River and the valleys of California and Oregon was dreaded and feared as a vast waterless and treeless expanse of wilderness that could be inhabited only by roving bands of Native American people. It is with more than little wonder, then, that Brigham Young selected the western limits of the Wasatch Mountains and the Great Salt Lake region as the final spot to build the promised community. For the Mormon population, the Great American Desert and the waste lands of the Salt Flats, held little fear when compared to the rewards of building the Kingdom of God and a Celestial City. For most Americans, however, the Great Plains and Basin region was a land to be feared and respected. At best, a great cloud of uncertainty covered the landscape.

Travelers contributed to further doubt and uncertainty as published letters told friends and family in the East of the rigors and dangers of western travel. One such letter, written from the Hawaiian Islands, under the pen of Jefferson Farnham, was widely published and circulated in the Eastern states. Farnham's letter painted an unfavorable image of California and the dangers of the California Trail. The lure of California was diminished somewhat and for awhile the tide of immigration dwindled to a mere trickle. However, by 1840, the Western Colonization Society was organized in St. Louis, with California as its prime objective. Farnham's letter may have been partially responsible for relatively few emigrants that rendezvoused in western Missouri in the spring of 1841. Those willing to brave the trail west elected John

Bartleson as their captain and set out in early May for the West. (p. 15, Vol. I, Morgan, 1963)

> *The Bartleson company were greenhorns such as the West has rarely seen, and no man knows what might have become of them except that a party of Catholic missionaries under Father Pierre-Jean De Smet set out at the same time for the Flathead country, guided by the experienced mountain man Thomas Fitzpatrick. The emigrants traveled with the missionaries as far as the Bear River, in that time getting a considerable education respecting the West and trail life. At Soda Springs some of the Bartleson company thought better of striking off into the unknown toward California, choosing to stay with the established trail to Oregon. But 31 men, one woman, her infant child accepted the risk and turned down Bear River. (pp. 15-16, Vol. I, Morgan, 1963)*

> *That through many vicissitudes the Bartleson party reached California is something of a miracle. They descended the Bear to the Great Salt Lake, rounded the northern and western edge of the Salt Desert to Pilot Peak, and succeeded in getting their wagons across Silver Zone Pass to Goshute Valley... (p. 16, Vol. I, Morgan, 1963)*

> *After a fashion the Bartleson party had proved that it was possible to reach California overland. That was the word carried back to Missouri in the summer of 1842 by a small party which included Bartleson himself - and more to the point, since Bartleson had had his fill of far countries, also included Joseph Chiles. This returning party took a southern route via New Mexico, hence did not encounter the small emigration of 1842 which had Oregon as its destination. (p. 16, Vol. I, Morgan, 1963)*

For most emigrants, Oregon rather than California was the ultimate goal during the years 1842-45. During the first four months of 1846, the nation's attention was directed ever so dramatically to Oregon as the clouds of war with Great Britain began to gather on the horizon.

James K. Polk had come to the presidency of the United States with a sober call of "54-40 or Fight,"

> *...and though the United States in settling the dispute with Great Britain would neither win all of Oregon nor come to blows over that far land, it was not clear until summer that the joint occupation*

*stipulated in 1818 would end with a peaceful division of
the country along the 49th parallel: There was plenty of
fight talk in the newspapers and in the bar room as the
snows of 1846 melted in the fields and along the roads (p.
88, Vol. I., Morgan, 1963)*

*There was much more fight talk in the south, where
the annexation of Texas was now an accomplished
fact despite the hostile attitude of Mexico, which had
never acknowledged the independence of the Lone Star
Republic. Mexico let it be known that war would come if
the United States forces occupied the "neutral ground"
between the Nueces River and the Rio Grande, and war
came soon after Zachary Taylor ...moved his "Army
of Occupation" across the Nueces in March: hostilities
began April 25 (1846). (pp. 88-89, Vol. I, Morgan, 1963)*

The winter of 1845-46 was a period of intense national pride that was
fanned by the fire of "Manifest Destiny" and a feeling of disdain was directed
toward any nation and religious belief that was considered either strange, or
extraordinary. These same feelings surfaced in Illinois as strong anti-Mormon
sentiment began to arise after the death of Joseph Smith. So great was the
demand that the Mormons leave Illinois, the Mormon Hierarchy agreed that
they would begin the task of evacuating Nauvoo in the spring of 1846, as soon
as grass was green and the waterways free of ice. The decision was made to
insure that the Mormon people would suffer no additional harm at the hands
of unyielding mobs.

The actual migration from Nauvoo had begun in early February when
the ice on the Mississippi River would still support teams and wagons. Still
other Mormons had left New York by ship under the leadership of Sam
Brannan. The Brannan expedition was responsible for transporting material
to California, where it was felt by some, that the larger body of Saints leaving
Illinois would eventually settle; however, it appears more than evident, that as
the first emigrants from Nauvoo passed onto the frozen plains of Iowa the final
destination had not been made clear to the Gentile community by Brigham
Young or the Quorums of the Church. The only thing that seemed clear was
that somewhere to the WEST -- somewhere beyond American law and mob
rule -- lay the only hope of establishing the Kingdom of God.

In the muddy spring of 1846:

*No one knew where they were going California, Oregon,
Vancouver Island were among the destinations proposed
- nor were the Saints themselves entirely sure though
Fremont's reports had directed their attention to Bear
River or the Great Salt Lake. (p. 89, Vol. I,
Morgan, 1963)*

34

The westward movement of Mormons in the spring of 1846 had an indirect and interesting effect upon the pattern of emigration of all travelers to Oregon and California.

> *Everybody was disposed to give them elbow room, so that for the first time since 1843 no California or Oregon-bound company undertook to cross the Missouri at the Council Bluffs and go west by the trail north of the Platte. A fruitful topic of speculation was what might be the fate of an unlucky emigrant, especially from Missouri, who might fall in with embittered Mormons in the immensities of the west. (p. 89, Vol. I, Morgan, 1963)*

For a time, Texas had been considered by Mormon leadership as a secure place to build a "Mormon Nation." Prior to the death of Joseph Smith, Lyman Wight and George Miller had been dispatched to Texas to: 1) relocate the Wisconsin Black River Lumber Company as the first step in the possible migration of the Church into this region, and 2) investigate purported ruins of Indian temples of which Joseph was to have read.

> *Joseph had seen an article in the Texas Telegraph describing ruins of Indian temples on the Rio Puerco, and traces of ruined cities and aqueducts in the Cordilleras on the Colorado. This set his imagination rocketing. What could be more appropriate than to build an empire on the site of the remnants of the vast civilizations described in his Book of Mormon? The Council of Fifty was carried away by the Texas fever and dispatched Lucian Woodworth as "minister to Texas" with orders to negotiate a treaty. He was told to secure "all that country north of a west line from the falls of the Colorado river (the Texas Colorado, not the great River of the Far West) to the Nueces, thence down the same to the in the spring of effect upon the and Gulf of Mexico, and along the same to the Rio Grande, and up the same to the United States territory.*
>
> *What Joseph was asking for was an enormous tract comprising about three fifths of modern Texas, the eastern half of New Mexico, the Oklahoma panhandle, a bit of Kansas, a third of Colorado, and a section of south-central Wyoming. Texas was to recognize the Mormon nation, which in return would guarantee to help defend the Texans against Mexico, "standing as a go-between the belligerent powers." If Woodworth brought back a favorable reply, Lyman Wight and George*

> *Miller were to proceed to Texas with the Black River*
> *Lumber Company and take possession. (pp. 359-360,*
> *Fawn Brodie, 1945)*

The exact reason why this exceedingly ambitious project was dismissed from the thinking of President Brigham Young is not known; however, it could easily be speculated that the rumors of unrest between the Texans and the Mexican Government were of sufficient magnitude as to cause a second - or third - consideration before moving forward with the plan. Then, too, there was the awareness that the land described by Joseph was already being cut in the middle by the wagon roads to Santa Fe and the west by way of the Platte River and thence to Oregon and California. Regardless of the cause, it should be remembered that only the geography of Mormon desire changed -- not the motive, i.e., to remove themselves as far as was possible from the dreaded influence of American law and mob rule.

> *...after Joseph Smith's assassination the Illinois mob*
> *spirit swiftly grew, and it was obvious the Mormons*
> *would have to move again. This was recognized*
> *by Brigham Young at once and he entered into an*
> *agreement with the leaders of the frontiersmen that the*
> *Mormons would move if they were given until spring*
> *of 1846 to dispose of their belongings. The agreement*
> *was broken by the mobs and the Mormons were set*
> *upon and driven from their homes with the same*
> *brutal applications as had marked their expulsion from*
> *Missouri. (p. 335, Frederick Merk, 1980)*

West To Garden Grove And Winter Quarters

Just how the decision to move west was made and whether the action had been in accord with a conference of the Saints or through decree is not always clear; however, it required no prophet's dream for the Mormon population and leadership to realize that their options were rapidly closing behind them.

The choices remained relatively few:

1) To remain in Nauvoo would mean persecution at best and loss of life and property at its worst. Armed hostility and open warfare was a real possibility.

2) Texas was no longer a clear option.

3) Iowa had recently been admitted to statehood and, as yet, no friction had been encountered between the Mormons and the population of Iowa. The open and largely uninhabited prairie of southern Iowa afforded the safest possible route to land of the West.

4) Travel or relocation in Missouri was out of the question since a more southerly route would have taken the Mormons through the more densely populated regions in which anti-Mormon feelings remained at epidemic state.

5) The East was never a consideration for the building of the Mormon nation.

All directions pointed west, across southern Iowa during the spring, summer and into the fall of 1846. Winter Quarters were to be set up, crops sown and provisions made for travel west as soon as was practical in the Spring of 1847.

These repeated expulsions were evidence to Brigham Young that Mormonism could not work out its mission within the borders of the United States, certainly not within the settled borders of the United States. A new migration must be made. The Book of Mormon was a prophecy of a resting place for the Lord's people in the Far "West." So to the West Brigham Young decided to lead his flock. This required more than ordinary courage. It called for a charting into the unknown. The Oregon Country and California were well-known, but they were closed to the Mormons because a population of turbulent Mississippi Valley frontiersmen was flowing into them - the very people from whom the Mormons were fleeing.

> *The choice of the valley of Great Salt Lake by Brigham Young as the abiding place of this flock is no longer a question obscured by legend. According to recent historians, both Mormon and non-Mormon, Brigham Young was already canvassing the problem of the location of the coming settlement while at Nauvoo in 1845-46. He became acquainted with John C. Fremont's Report of Exploring Expeditions to the Rocky Mountains in 1842, and to Oregon and north California in 1843-44, which had been published as a government document in 1845. Accompanying the Report was a map depicting the Wasatch Range, and just west of it the valley of Great Salt Lake and the Bear River. Of the latter Fremont wrote: "the bottoms (are) extensive, water (is) excellent, timber sufficient, soil good and well adapted to grains and grasses...mountain sides covered with nutritious grasses called bunch grass ...its*

37

*quantity will sustain any amount of cattle." (p. 335,
Merk, 1980)*

All things considered, the Mormon population had to move, fight or perish.

> *At the dawn of the new year the Church leaders were
> determined to leave the state (Illinois) and plunge into
> the wilderness. With the temple finished they had kept
> their pledge with the Lord and felt free to seek out their
> destiny in a distant land beyond the reach of their old
> enemies. While much time and money were being devoted
> to the project of the exodus, many skilled workmen were
> busy in the temple even after they started giving the
> endowments. The laying of carpets in the small rooms
> and the final endowments were given. The Lord's house
> was to be made as beautiful as possible before they
> should abandon it and hasten off toward the West. (p. 65,
> McGavin, 1962)*

The trek across the frozen prairie of Southern Iowa by foot, riding horseback, on a springboard or wagon, was undoubtedly an ordeal to test the faith of the most devoted of any religion. The rigor of travel over frozen turf, across ice covered streams and through snow and snow drifts, could only be compared to the staggering and exhausting task of pushing and pulling handcarts across the Plains and mountains to Utah.

Few travelers can begin to imagine the pain experienced as a bitter and biting arctic wind began to tear away at skin and clothing in such a way as to allow only raw nerves and moral fiber to remain. Winter temperatures in Southern Iowa are capable of hovering at near zero while winds lower the chill factor to minus twenty and thirty degrees for days and nights on end. Travel was necessarily slow to compensate for chill, fever, frostbite, and in spring, axle deep seas of mud. It was finally when the elements of nature caused travel to stop that the fiber of religious conviction could be seen and experienced most clearly. Footsore and exhausted, the Mormon emigrants were refitted, rested, and renewed in the sacraments and ordinances of the Church in sanctuaries such as those at Garden Grove, Mt. Pisgah and Winter Quarters.

The pattern of travel established at the time of the exodus from Nauvoo remained virtually the same, or with only slight modification, as that from Winter Quarters to the Great Salt Lake Basin. Advance companies were dispatched to explore the country, mark a trail, send back reports, construct shelter, provide for the repair of wagons and care for the spiritual well-being of the Saints.

The condition of western travel described by Wallace E. Stegner would remain the same, or nearly so, for each contingent of Mormon   38 people venturing forth to the "Land of Promise." It was the "faith" of a people in a concept of a righteous community that carried them where the feet of less convicted people would have faltered and fallen.

> *As early as August (1846), while Thomas Kane was desperately sick and being cared for...there was a demoralizing wave of sickness through the Mormon camps. Kane reported that in the camp that was building the bridge across the Elk Horn, more than a third were down at once, and that burial parties could not keep up with the deaths: he speaks of mass burials in trenches, and of women sitting in the doorways of tents keeping the flies off the faces of dead children whose bodies had already begun to decay. What was true of the west side of the Missouri was at least as true on the Pottawattamie side, and possible - there is less documentation in this case and though the dry plains were always healthier than the river bottoms - among the three wagon trains under George Miller and James Emmett, out on the Running Water. From the time that the Mormons gave up all thought of proceeding to the mountains, and began digging in for the winter, they worked against sicknesses so pervasive and violent that they amounted to a plague. (p. 99, Stegner, 1964)*

Winter Quarters

The Mormon refitting and resting outpost of the Winter Quarters (near the present location of Omaha, Nebraska) may have been selected for two logistical reasons:

> 1. Its location on the western bank of the Missouri River provided a vantage point from which the river served as the boundary between the State of Iowa (on the east) and the jurisdiction of the Indian tribe and government agents in Indian territory on the west.
> 2. Winter Quarters was located near the overland trail west, where the Oregon and California Trail nearly paralleled the course of the Platte River as far as Chimney Rock. The flood plain of the Platte River was a source of water and grass without which the emigrant trains could not have survived.

As Fall and Winter of 1846 neared, the population of Winter Quarters began the task of preparing living quarters, shelter for

39

livestock, and laying-in supplies to be shared with later arrivals.

> *...Near the end of the year, the Winter Quarter census
> showed 3,483 persons, of whom only 502 were men.
> About 138 other men were absent on trading trips or
> herding Israel's thousands of cattle "down to the rushes"
> in the Missouri bottoms. (p. 106, Stegner, 1964)*

By year's end the population had swelled to nearly 10,000 according to the reports of the Superintendent of the Indian Bureau to Washington. This population, he observed, was located on both sides of the river by December of 1846.

Leonard J. Arrington (p. 22, <u>Great Basin Kingdom</u>, 1958) estimates the population of Saints to have numbered nearly 16,000. The exact population figure notwithstanding, the task of providing shelter, food, clothing and education for this number of people in so little time and under such extreme and harsh conditions was nothing short of a latter day miracle. Indeed, to provide drinking water, sanitation, wood for building and fuel sufficient to care for the welfare of 16,000 persons through a winter on the plains is staggering to the intellect of even the most resourceful and imaginative of persons.

To state that preparation for "winter" was an arduous and monumental undertaking is, at best, a gross oversimplification and understatement; nevertheless, it is this sense of caring, feeling, and mutual dependence that has become the hallmark of the Mormon movement throughout its history. It is this same sense of community pride and responsibility that would be offered to Indian communities as well. The Mormon theology, as it emerged through time, taught not only a gospel of redemption for the soul, complete with rewards and punishments, but a social gospel as well. Mormonism stresses cooperation and group perfectibility in this life as well as that beyond the grave. The Mormon social gospel was expressed as the "Community of Zion" regardless of where or when it was built.

> *It being considered impractical to send a company further
> west in 1846, the 16,000 Saints on both banks of the
> Missouri were organized to prepare for the journey the
> following and succeeding years. With the permission of
> the Indians (and the Indian Agent) ...they laid out a town
> site, established a water supply system, and proceeded
> to work collectively in building a city according to plan.
> By December 1846 they had erected 621 houses, mostly
> of logs, a gristmill, a council house, and several thousand
> wagons. The houses were formed close together, and the
> space between them filled with pickets, so as to form a kind
> of fort or stockade. Although observers found their general
> condition to be pitiful, their mutual dependence made it far
> from hopeless. (p. 22, Arrington, 1958)*

The early Mormon people were certainly instructed in piety, but in the social hall or in the dying glow of the campfire, the "joy" of the gospel could be seen, heard and felt. Singing and dancing provided release from the rigors of pioneer life and travel. They may well have been essential for the survival of the people as a socio-religious body.

Dr. Perry McCandless, Professor of History at Central Missouri State University, once stated to a class in the "History of the West," that to appreciate fully the Mormon movement, the Saints should be understood as a "singing-dancing people." This truism can be seen in the songs and hymns that the people sung. Their singing and sacraments girded the people for any and every misfortune upon which they might fall.

Hymns like Come, Come Ye Saints undoubtedly caused flagging spirits to soar and an inner calm to spread across the frozen prairie as the refrain was sung,

> *...All is Well,*
> *All is Well.*

In a similar manner, the hymns and dances of the Ghost Dance Religion prepared the Native American People for the uncertainties of encounters with land-hungry and gold-crazed settlers moving onto the Plains and into the Great Basin.

The Winter of 1846-47 was a period of intense preparation for the anticipated migration to the West. There exists no evidence to conclude that the Mormon population had any intention of lingering longer than was necessary in Winter Quarters or for that matter anywhere east of the Missouri River.

In January (14) of 1847, President Young delivered to the Saints what some writers have said was his only revelation during his tenure as President of the Church. Brigham Young declared to the Saints the organizational structure and procedural plan for the westward march. It revealed that a first migration was to begin in April of 1847 followed by a second company departing in July of that same year.

On April 16, the first contingent consisting of the Presidency and Quorum of Twelve Apostles set out to mark the trail for those that were shortly to follow. The first company was:

> *...made up of 143 men and boys, 3 women, 2 children, 72*
> *wagons, 93 horses, 52 mules, 66 oxen, 19 cows, 17 dogs,*
> *and an unknown number of chickens. (p. 181, Ray B.*
> *West and also p. 22, Arrington, 1958)*

> *Ray B. West concludes they were "...as well*
> *equipped as they might be, considering the*

41

circumstances. (pp. 181-182, West, 1957)

> *The commissary of the company consisted generally*
> *of those supplies necessary for survival on the trail as*
> *well as sufficient to see the families through winter, into*
> *planting and then to harvest and on to self-sufficiency. In*
> *their covered wagons were plows, and other implements,*
> *seed grain, a year's supply of provisions.*

Some accounts say that hardly had the Mormons arrived than the earth was plowed and potatoes were planted. Some have suggested that sunflowers seeds were scattered along the trail as a marker for later travelers.

> *They also had with them the bell from the Temple at*
> *Nauvoo and a case of surveyors' instruments which*
> *Parley P. Pratt had recently brought with him when he*
> *returned from a mission. (pp. 181-182, West, 1957)*

The bell from the Nauvoo temple was looked upon by some as the continuation of temple worship that had begun in Nauvoo.

The uncertainties of travel into Indian territory as well as the Mormon cultural mind-set in an oft-times hostile Gentile environment caused the men to carry rifles and small arms and "...a cannon was taken along to overawe hostile Indians." (p. 182, West, 1957) The second company forming to depart in July was substantially larger than had been the First Contingent. The jumping-off point for the July emigrants had been Council Bluffs and Kanesville.[10] The July emigration, known as the "First emigration," consisted of 1,553 persons, 566 wagons, 2,213 oxen, 124 horses, 887 cows, 358 sheep, 35 hogs and 716 chickens. (p. 22, Arrington, 1958)

The task of each of these two companies was clear and distinct. The July emigrants were to constitute the first permanent settlement of the Saints in West; whereas the April contingent had the more arduous task of exploring the country. They "...blazed the trail, made careful notes on everything they observed, built ferries, and even earned cash by ferrying emigrants bound for Oregon across the rivers in their path." (p. 22, Arrington, 1958)

The first company reached the Salt Lake Valley in July of 1847 and the larger group "...arrived there in September and October of the same year." (p. 22, Arrington, 1958) The trail blazed by these first companies was that followed by all future emigrants venturing into the Great Salt Lake Valley, be they either "Gatherers to Zion" or the ever tide of restless humanity drawn to the gold and fortune fields of California. Stegner observes that the Mormon movement west was but a forecast of the

...continuing history of the trail, which would be the route

10   Kanesville had been named in honor of Thomas L. Kane, a non-Mormon who had become "...their most effective friend." Kanesville was a major outfitting point for the Mormon Trail. (p. 196, Stegner, 1962)

of the Gathering until the trans-continental railroad,
more than twenty years hence, would render it obsolete.
And the railroad itself, a good part of the way, would
follow the track of their laborious wheels. (p. 196,
Stegner, 1964)

The Mormon attention to detail and exactness can be seen in the records, journals and inventions made along the trail. These observations were sent back to the people in the east and undoubtedly contributed significantly to the national awareness of the lands to the "West." Among those significant observations was that recorded as the emigrants passed to the west of the 20 inch isohyet and 1,400 foot contour.

Their crossing of the Loup Fork was almost directly on
the 98th meridian, that all but mystical line at which
begins another climate, another flora and fauna, another
ecology another light, another palette, another air,
another order of being. The grass was now a variety new
to them, the short curly kind they called buffalo grass. (p.
129, Stegner, 1964)

Indeed, a new world and new experiences challenged and called the Saints to a new and better land -- a "Promised Land." However, try as they might, the Mormons could not escape the fears and hostilities that beset them on nearly every quarter. Even as preparations for the evacuation of Winter Quarters were underway, rumors spread across the frontier as far west as Fort Leavenworth, Kansas. Quite characteristic of the tension that gripped both Mormon and Gentile was that experienced when Daniel Wells and William Cutler brought news, September 24, 1846, that Nauvoo had fallen into the hands of the mob:

...arriving at a time when the camps around Council
Bluffs were hit hard with rumors of further trouble
there. It was said that a United States Marshall from
Missouri was on his way with a warrant for the arrest
of the Twelve; men heard that the Secretary of War
had instructed the Indian agent to evict all Mormons
from the Pottawattamie lands by April 1, 1847. But both
rumors, as it developed, were untrue. The United States
Marshall from Missouri was one of those embodied
fears of persecution that haunted the Mormon mind.
And there was no immediate danger that the Saints
would be thrown off the Pottawattamie lands, for the
long-awaited permission to make temporary settlements
there had finally come through. What was actually under
question was the settlements across the Missouri; the
Bureau of Indian Affairs did not acknowledge

43

the authority of either Captain Allen or Chief Big Elk to grant the permission they had given. Brigham, by now having possession, simply sent out Hosea Stout's police to establish a picket guard, and sat tight. As a Yankee guesser, he would probably have guessed that the Saints would be pretty hard for the government to move. (p. 92, Stegner, 1964)

The Mormons did not possess, concludes Stegner, sufficient "...lines of communication..." with the Gentiles to allow for the correction of rumors or for the firming up of relations with the non-Mormon population. (p. 75, Stegner, 1964)[11]

---

11   As stated previously, the ultimate destination, i.e., Texas, California, or Oregon was not public knowledge by the spring of 1846. Evidence seems to indicate that by this time, it was prudent for the Mormon hierarchy to keep this closely guarded information. Nevertheless, it should be observed that considerable confusion exists or was caused to exist, as to whether the Mormon leadership would travel to Oregon and support the British claim to the Northwest region. The following quote from Stegner, 1964, pp. 74-75, exemplifies this uncertainty of Mormon activity:

> *...Jesse C. Little, President of the Eastern States Mission, was busy offering President Polk the services of the Mormon people and delicately hinting that if the United States would not help them they might have to turn to the British in Oregon. The Mormons, Little had been instructed to say to Polk, were available for building roads or bridges, establishing ferries, transporting troops or supplies, and even for fighting. Actually, when Brigham's time of decision came on the Missouri, Polk had already made up his mind and on June 12th Little and Thomas L. Kane had left Philadelphia to carry to General Stephen Watts Kearney in Fort Leavenworth instructions about enlisting some Mormons. But Brigham did not know this, and while he struggled with the logistical problems and brought more and more Saints up to the Missouri shore, still on Pottawattamie lands, but facing the Indian lands across the river, rumors multiplied. (pp. 74-75, Stegner, 1964)*

Mormons "enlisted" by Kearney will be made up into the Mormon Battalion and will see limited service in the Mexican War in 1848.

This evident inability or reluctance to do so, continued to plague Mormon-Gentile relations into and through the period of 1890's.

Significantly, rumors that Mormons were "stirring up the Indians" swept the Missouri outposts and to Fort Leavenworth during the summer of 1846 and into the spring of 1847. The general tone of the rumors seemed to center in a fear that the Mormons were inciting the Indians to war.[1] The content of the rumors was largely unfounded, and their importance is found in the similarity of the rumors that continued to be spread about Indian-Mormon relations some forty years later after the Ghost Dance Religion had erupted along the California-Nevada border.

> *During the summer of 1846 Fort Leavenworth and the Missouri outposts heard that the Mormons were fortifying themselves somewhere up the river and preaching "Jewish powwow" to the Indians, that they were distributing arms and inciting the tribes to a holy war, that they were on their way to Oregon to join forces with the British. No one knew exactly where they were or what they were doing; therefore they seemed doubly dangerous. (p. 75, Stegner, 1964)*

Travelers on the Oregon and California Trails were by no means immune from rumors that fed on the already present fears and uncertainties of overland travel. These rumors differed from the usual fear of Indian raids on wagon trains in that they pictured Mormons seeking revenge for their ill treatment in Missouri and Illinois as the disturbers of peace and tranquility.

Among those noteworthy migrants West in 1846 was the former governor of Missouri, Lilburn W. Boggs. It was Governor Boggs who had issued the infamous "Extermination Order" in Missouri in 1838. The order had called for the forcible removal of Mormons from Missouri and if they either resisted or would not be moved, then they were to be exterminated. This order, while certainly not the first nor the last effort to practice genocide, is important to understand, for Mormons, like Indians, were faced with the very real possibility of being the victims of wanton genocide.

Having issued the extermination order years earlier, it is easy to see why Lilburn Boggs would be more than uneasy as he made plans to leave Missouri and to travel West. (The "Exterminator Order" was repealed by the Missouri Legislature in 1976.) It appears that Boggs was, like the Mormon population, uncertain at first just where it was that he was going to - California or Oregon? A part of his uncertainty arose out of the very real fact that after the Extermination Order had been issued, an attempt was made on his life at his home in Independence on May 6, 1842.

1　　　Rumors that Mormons were inciting the Indians to attack emigrant trains can be reviewed in the Secretary of War statement contained in the <u>House Executive Documents,</u> No. 2, 35th Congress, 1st Session, II, p. 2 ser. 943, pp. 1-22.

*It has always been supposed that Orrin Porter Rockwell,
a hard case among the early Mormons, did the deed
as an act of revenge for the expulsion of the Mormons
from Missouri during Bogg's term as governor. Against
all expectations, Boggs recovered, though he showed
the effects of his wound till his death in 1860. Rockwell
was jailed, but eventually released for lack of evidence.
(Footnote III, p. 761, Vol. II, Morgan, 1963)*

A published letter from one Charles T. Stanton to Sidney Stanton dated July 12, 1846, stated:

*But Governor Boggs...is afraid of the Mormons. He
has heard that they are on the route, and thinks they
will go to California. Should they do so, that will be no
place for him. You may be aware that he was shot by
(O.P.) Rockwell, and came very near losing his life;
consequently, he has something to fear. (p. 614, Vol. II,
Morgan, 1963)*

Fears and rumors notwithstanding, it should be remembered that Rockwell, in spite of, or because of, his reputation was serving as the bodyguard of Brigham Young. Young and the Saints were not on the trail in July of 1846, but will lead the First Winter Quarters in April of 1847. Regardless of Rockwell or any of the Mormon population, these uncertainties only added to the general feeling of mistrust and suspicion that gripped the frontier communities.

In Winter Quarters, increasing pressures were brought on the Mormons to leave as quickly as possible. Superintendent Thomas H. Harvey of the Bureau of Indian Affairs as early as the fall of 1846 protested to President Brigham Young the building of Mormon settlements west of the Missouri River. Superintendent Harvey is said to have informed Washington that he believed that the Mormons had no intention of leaving the Missouri River and that they "...might be planning a chain of permanent settlements from the Missouri to the Pacific." (p. 198, Stegner, 1964)

Nearly five years will have passed before all of the Mormon settlement at Winter Quarters was abandoned. From the Fall of 1846 to the Spring of 1852, Winter Quarters continued to be the jumping off place for Mormon emigrants bound for the Great Salt Lake Valley; however, during the period of Mormon occupancy in Pottawattamie lands, the efforts of the Bureau of Indian Affairs were to ensure "...that the Mormons must clear out of Winter Quarters and Cutler's Park without delay. (p. 198, Stegner, 1964)

In response to the pressures exerted by the Bureau of Indian Affairs, and to the practical need to move the membership as quickly as possible to the new permanent homes in the Salt Lake Valley, the Handcart Plan was projected in the Spring of 1852. The Handcart Plan called for the making of two wheeled carts of wheel design and size such as to allow the cart to be pushed   47 and pulled from Winter Quarters to Salt Lake. Only those provisions needed for the immediate trip were carried. Long term needs and provisions were to be provided by earlier emigrants to the Great Salt Lake Valley. This principle, too, was and is, a part of the social gospel of Mormonism. It is this social aspect of their religion that the Mormons sought, theoretically at least, to share with their Lamanite brothers and sisters. It was this sense of commonality and sharing of the land and the fruits of the land that caused many in the Gentile community to both fear and despise the Mormons.

Mt. Pisgah, Iowa Historical Marker, Photo by Jon Barney, September 2009

CHAPTER III

Mormon Indian Relations In Utah Territory

Except for one brief mission by Parley P. Pratt and three companions in 1830, the Mormons did little proselytizing among the Indian people before 1854; however, every effort was made to maintain a "hands-off" attitude toward the Indian encountered on their journey west. It is difficult to assess the motives or actions of persons of another generation, time and place. This is certainly true in the case of the Mormons in Winter Quarters and on the westward trail. It would appear that Mormon attitude toward Indian people during the early years of the Church's formation went from a position of excitement in having found the people of <u>The Book of Mormon</u> and the desire of the Saints to restore the Lamanites to their rightful place within the scheme of the Kingdom ideal, to a more tried position of pragmatism. Mormon pragmatism stressed the need to stay at peace with any tribes encountered and, perhaps more importantly, to care for and nurture the many converts to the Church who were anxious to establish new homes and opportunities wherever the Church leadership would take them.

Fear, and its companion doubt, were by no means strangers to the Mormon population. The treatment they had received in Independence, at Haun's Mill, and in Nauvoo had so conditioned the people to suspicion that anyone who was non-Mormon, including Indian people, was looked upon with a degree of distrust and uncertainty. This uncertainness was reflected somewhat in a suspicious attitude of the Mormons toward their Lamanite brothers and sisters. Both the practical needs of caring for the Saints and securing safe passage through Indian lands occupied much of the Mormon thinking. This combination of piety and secularism is described graphically in the work of Wallace E. Stegner, <u>The Gathering of Zion: The Story of the Mormon Trail,</u> 1964, in his description of Brigham Young's desire to begin sending emigrant Saints west as early as was feasible in the spring of 1847.

> *Brigham had not yet relinquished his hope of sending out a significant advance party during the current year. He had men out on the Elk Horn, thirty miles west, cutting timbers and setting piers for a bridge, and on July 22nd, the day the last company of the battalion set off for Leavenworth, 150 wagons started for the Elk Horn to catch up with the hasty George Miller and James Emmett, already well out on the Platte Valley. About August 1st they found the Miller-Emmett group camped on the west bank of the Loup Fork near modern Fullerton, Nebraska, and while they were all there counciling about their next move, a courier came from Brigham on August 8th, instructing*

49

them to go no farther that season, but organize
themselves into a branch of Zion and sit tight for the
winter. Exploration of the country along the Loup Fork
revealed no highly desirable wintering site, and that
whole region was made dangerous by the Pawnees...(pp.
84-85, Stegner, 1964)

It was hardly quite wilderness. And yet the Missouri
River, thirty miles behind them, marked what was called
the Permanent Indian Frontier, and on their whole
journey to the great Salt Lake they would come upon
only three white habitations, one of them abandoned:
the Pawnee Mission, evacuated the last autumn because
of Sioux raids; Fort Laramie; Fort Bridger. Of Indians
they would first meet the Pawnees, notorious as thieves,
blackmailers and occasional murderers, and the terror
of the dwindling and demoralized Otoes and Omahas;
then the Sioux, warlike and numerous, as fearsome to
the Pawnees as the Shoshones, deadly enemies, hunting
the Black Hills and the Wind Rivers; and finally the Utah
Indians, in unknown quantity. (p. 122, Stegner, 1964)

On the morning of April 26 (1847) the guard scared off
with gunfire six Indians who were sneaking up on the
horses. A day later, the Pawnees got away in broad
daylight with two horses, and the day after that Tom
Brown, Rockwell and others had a brush with fifteen
Indians, who fired at them without doing damage. (p.
128, Stegner, 1964)

Fortunately for all concerned, not all encounters with Indian people
were of such a potentially hostile nature. Some meetings were characterized
by an atmosphere of "geniality and good will." One such meeting took place
an estimated 425 miles west of Winter Quarters in the "...immediate area of
Chimney Rock." (p. 136, Stegner, 1964)

So far they had met only two Sioux, a man and his wife
both definitely friendly. Now they encountered thirty-five
of them - magnificent, clean, well-dressed, noble-looking,
many cuts above the demoralized Omahas or the fiendish
Pawnees. The Saints were universally impressed, and
extended overnight hospitality to the chief and his wife,
and gave them a thrill by letting them observe the moon
through Pratt's telescope. In the morning there were
more visits, some trading, much handshaking. "Truly
gentlemen and ladies," said Levi Jackman, and Thomas
Bullock wrote the chief a "recommended"
to go with the letters from Papin and other

> *Fort Laramie traders. Seven years hence, an incidence*
> *involving a lame Mormon cow would precipitate the*
> *so-called "Grattan Massacre" and send these Indians*
> *into an abrupt bloody war, but now all was geniality*
> *and good will. Stephen Markham traded a used-up mule*
> *for an Indian pony, bade his Indian friends good-bye,*
> *and hitched the pony in with his team. By the time the*
> *spooked team had run itself out...they were opposite*
> *Chimney Rock. (p. 136, Stegner, 1964)*

The published diary of William Clayton records an especially noteworthy meeting that had taken place slightly more than a year earlier (June 10th 1846) in a Pottawattamie Village.

> *Wednesday, 10th (June 1846). At six o'clock we camped*
> *in sight of the Pottawattamie Indian Village.. .before we*
> *arrived at the timber it seemed that the whole village had*
> *turned out, men, women, and children, some on horses*
> *and many on foot. Their musicians came and played*
> *while we passed them, They (came) to our wagons and*
> *asked if we were Mormons...they seemed highly pleased*
> *(p. 44, Clayton, 1973). They certainly showed every mark*
> *of friendship and kindness imaginable and treated us as*
> *brothers. (p. 45, Clayton, 1973)*

It is in the attitude of men like William Clayton, and later Jacob Hamblin (The Buckskin Apostle), that the apostolic and missionary ideal of salvation of <u>The Book of Mormon</u> people will be kept alive.

From the time of the first Indian Mission until their arrival in the Great Salt Lake Valley, no clearly discernable Indian policy existed in the Church. It was only after the Mormon population began to settle in the heart of Indian Lands in the Great Salt Lake Valley that such a policy began to emerge. The makers of Indian policy within the Mormon church ranged from those, like William Clayton, who viewed the Indian as a "brother" after all, to a more pragmatic attitude exemplified by Brigham Young in his statement: "...it is better to feed and clothe them than to fight them." It is this latter attitude, which, while reflecting a pragmatic approach to frontier life, nevertheless, undergirded an impressive degree of humanitarian concern for the welfare of people.[1]

---

1   It is this concern for frontier justice and social equality that will serve as the guide for all future efforts of winning converts to the Church.

Mormon-Indian Relations:
The Great Basin And Salt Lake Regions

Some writers have likened Brigham Young's leadership ability to that of some Old Testament Prophets; some say a modern day Moses, intent upon delivering his people into a promised land.

The analogy may, in fact, be a fair one, since few have either the opportunity or ability to give expression to such dramatic leadership. Since the Moses analogy has been suggested, it is worthy of note that unlike Moses, Brigham Young could ill afford the luxury of taking forty years to lead his people to safety. It was imperative that the emigrants, under the direction of President Young, begin immediately to break ground so that it could weather sufficiently for planting the next spring, build houses, prepare wells, and plan for sanitation, just as they had done so many times in the past.

The Mormon disposition reflected a sense of urgency in its pattern of settlement. Each setting sun brought shorter days and the knowledge that soon would come long nights of freezing temperatures. Unless everyone worked for the common good of the community, all would perish.

Probably few have been the non-Mormon travelers venturing into the Great Salt Lake region who did not ask themselves: "I wonder what in the world the Mormons wanted in such a desolate and forbidding place?" The answer to this very probing question can never be fully found in an academic explanation, but rather is best found in the somewhat hidden character of the people involved in making choices for life styles or patterns. Brigham Young was looking for:

> ...a country no one else wanted, and when, sick with
> fever, he was hauled in his carriage through the mouth of
> Emigration Canyon and looked upon the valley of Great
> Salt Lake with the Jordan River winding across the far
> flats and the late sun glittering on the waters of the Dead
> Sea, he knew that he had arrived-he had refused to listen
> to the importunities of Samuel Brannan, who had taken a
> boatload of Saints around the Horn from Brooklyn to San
> Francisco via Hawaii, and who was enthusiastic about
> the northern California Valleys. (p. 33, Stegner, 1964,
> see also p. 100, Bailey on Sam Brannan and Journal of
> History, dated entry of June 6, 1847) (pp. 26-27, Vol. I,
> Morgan, Overland in 1846, 1963)

The Valley of the Great Salt Lake became home for a "tried" and weary people. Ironically, by the time the Mormons were reasonably settled in their new home, they found themselves not in Mexican Territory, as some had wished, but still within the boundaries of the United States. The Treaty of Guadalupe Hidalgo, signed in 1848, changed radically the ambitions   52 of the Mormons to settle outside the limits of the Constitution of the United States, and certainly, far from the reach of mob rule such as that experienced in earlier times and places.

The Mormons were far from being alone in the changes that took place in the West after the treaty with Mexico was signed. The most dramatic and impactful change that took place during this time was the opening of the floodgates of migration into California and Oregon. Westward migration prior to the Mexican War had represented a fairly constant flow; it changed nearly overnight to a torrent of wave after wave of humanity sweeping to Oregon and then, after 1848, to the California Gold Fields.

The seekers for riches and fortunes had little desire to stop for long at any point between the Rocky Mountains and the Sierra's in the West. There was nothing in the barren intermountain region that caused them to want to settle down and to establish homes and communities. This was, after all, a part of the Great American Desert and it, too was unfit for white habitation.

Gold "fever" had contributed to a population vacuum in the Great Salt Lake Valley into which the Mormon population was free to move, to build and to dream. In but a few years they had built scores of villages, towns, and, fairest of them all, Salt Lake City. The Mormons cleared, fenced and irrigated the best land in the valley and laid claim to the territory for hundreds of miles in every direction from the Church's new center.

Settlement of selected regions of the Basin, in California, Oregon and Utah brought about radical changes in not only demography but in the environment as well. With each passing wagon train, the grass became more sparse. As the forage supply dwindled, horses, oxen and mules were required to be pastured further and further from the established wagon road. The shortage of grass for food for livestock was obvious -- animals, like people, became undernourished and foot-sore. Not so obvious, but equally devastating, was the impact on the economic life of the Indian people as well. Deer, antelope, fowl of all varieties, and buffalo, too, went without grass and water. Wildlife was decimated by hunger and the bullets of emigrants anxious always to fill their larder with fresh meat and fowl. Hunger, starvation and exhausted pastures rapidly took their toll on the life of animals and native populations as well. Such tragedies as these are often overlooked in the vain effort to extol the virtues of "the march of progress and civilization."

Perhaps the changes in the physical environment were more obvious to the Native American people than to the emigrants. The building of the transcontinental railroad required untold amounts of lumber -- cross ties for roadbeds and trellis for bridges. However, the cutting of forests contributed to run-off of water borne silt; the silt in turn causing a change in the ecological balance of plant, fish and waterfowl life. This loss of food base was accompanied by the demise of countless deer and antelope; the net result of which was a drastic change in the food base of many Native American people living in the basins and mountains.

Ecological changes may begin as relatively insignificant events -- the cutting of a stand of trees here, the damming of a river there -- but the effect of such activities, however, were far reaching.

As game animals became increasingly scarce, as fish died, as water became unfit for drinking, and as white men's diseases began to take their toll on Indian lives, pressures, fears, and on occasions, open hostility erupted between the Indian the white communities.

Mormon communities were by no means totally exempt from contributing to suspicions and tensions within the non-Mormon and Native American populations; however, it appears that Mormons dealt more kindly and judicially with Native American populations than did the usual run of other emigrants. Native American lands were occupied by Mormons and farming operations, timber cut and houses constructed, all at the expense of the aboriginal birthright. The Mormons, unlike many other white settlers, were anxious to exchange the acquisition of the lands for the Lamanite's inclusion in the Kingdom building task. All that was necessary for the Native American's full participation in the Mormon community was his adoption, not only of Mormon religious beliefs and practices, but of white-Mormon occupational values, honesty, diligence and, most especially, farming.

A study of the settlement patterns of Mormon communities reveals their mastery of planning and organizational skills. Their wide streets, planned gardens and planted trees, their insatiable desire for religious-political ties of the community from neighborhood to ward, to stake and to city wide involvement by all, serves as a model for city and regional planners even today. However, the settlement of all whites, while seemingly grand and glorious at the time, was, nevertheless a story of repeated encroachment and broken promises by all who cast a covetous eye on the lands of the West.

Wallace Stegner asserts:

> *Mormondom is a social and religious, not topographical entity. The Latter-day Saints imposed their peculiar institutions indiscriminately on the fertile Snake River Plains and on the arid and forbidding sand rock country along the San Juan and the Colorado. (p. 37, Stegner, 1942)*

The principle of accountability, both in temporal and spiritual affairs, has been deeply implanted in Mormon organizational schemes. The attention to priesthood quorum organization, i.e., the quorum of Deacons, Priests, Elders and Seventies all of whom are eagerly responsible to the Quorum of Twelve Apostles and the First Presidency reflects the Mormon attitude of accountability. Accountability and responsibility became inherently a part of each and every assignment made within the Church.

54

One such appointment was Brigham Young's assignment of Porter Rockwell as "Watchman" over Indian-Mormon responsibilities in the Basin. The importance of accountability can be seen in the delegation of responsibility to Rockwell to act "in the name" of Brigham Young himself.

> *On his return from California, Rockwell had been told to keep an eye on the Great Basin tribes and maintain peace in Brigham Young's name. Some months earlier a long string of skirmishes with Indians had culminated in a full-scale battle at Fort Utah on the Provo River, with the Timpanogos Utes being crushed in the encounter. Now the Saints were determined to squelch the isolated, but irritating, raids perpetrated by small bands of Utes and Gosiute, who were intent upon driving the white man from the valley, or at least upon causing him the greatest discomfiture possible. For Rockwell, the months passed uneventfully until April of 1851 when a dozen warriors attacked a settlement in Toole Valley, west of Great Salt Lake City. A Gentile emigrant subsequently lost his life because Rockwell misjudged Indian behavior. It was an error he did not repeat. (pp. 198-199, Harold Schindler, 1966)*

It would appear that Mormonism had, in spite of its desire to win Indian converts, developed its own unique type of "Manifest Destiny" that was not entirely unlike that of the American variety.

In the period of 1850-1890, Mormon settlements were established in many areas of what was to become in time the Western United States, California, New Mexico, Arizona, Utah, and Nevada.

> *Brigham Young was a colonizer without equal in the history of America. In a desert that nobody wanted and that was universally considered a fit home only for coyotes and rattlesnakes, he planted in thirty years over three hundred and fifty towns and created the technique and made the surveys for others. (p. 65, Stegner, 1942)*

> *They chiseled grindstones and millstones from the cliffs, built sawmills, woolen mills, tanneries. And though Brigham consistently refused to let his people prospect for or work deposits of precious metals, he was practical enough to know that iron and coal and lead were as necessary for a self-sufficient economy as wheat and corn. The Mormons very early found and attempted to develop all three kinds of mines. (p. 68, Stegner, 1942)*

*The morning after the scouts arrived, even before the
party under Brigham Young saw the valley, they had
potatoes in the ground. (p. 62, Stegner, 1942)*

In selecting the geographic center of his Deseret Empire, Brigham
Young:

*...considered both the Salt Lake Valley and the Valley of
the Utah Lake, forty miles to the south. His reason for
favoring the Salt Lake country were that here he had
heard that the Indians were less warlike than they were
farther south.(p. 188, West, 1957)*

*Certainly here the Saints would be safe from any enemy,
for there were only wild beasts and Indians, and what
were these to the Mormons, compared with the dangers
of civilization? (p. 190, West, 1957)*

It may be that the perceptions of Jim Bridger weighed heavily in the final decision since it was Bridger to whom Brigham turned for final information
concerning the Salt Lake Valley and the virtues of Oregon and California.

*With the exception of California, Mormons occupied
areas that were still largely inhabited by Utes, Paiutes,
and Shoshone; this fact alone necessitated a policy of
goodwill toward the Indians and caused Brigham to
reaffirm to the people. "They are the seed of Abraham,
and God is ever their God." (p. 207, West, 1957)*

In 1850, the Territory of Utah was organized. White populations were
almost entirely Mormon, therefore Brigham Young was easily appointed governor; and as governor he was the regional director of Indian policy, as well as all
other political and economic matters. Of his administration of Indian affairs,
Angie Debo writes:

*His (Brigham's) Indian policy, like everything else, was
clearly designed and executed. He and the missionaries
he sent out labored to make friends with the natives,
convert them, induce them to make peace with each
other, and train them in "civilization." They did not make
many converts, but in other ways they had fair success.
Young made peace with the Shoshonis and the Utes after
a long period of hostility but called them to a council at
Salt Lake City. (p. 128, Debo, 1970)*

Ray B. West stated that the policy of the government of the Utah Territory,
of "indulgent paternalism" was the only solution possible for the Mormon
leadership -- a solution "...which eventually became the policy of the
United States Government." (p. 209, West, 1957)   56

Much of the initial Mormon Indian activity came about as a result of an early meeting of church elders, including in time Brigham Young, with Chief Walker of the Utes. (p. 144, Anderson, 1942 and p. 18, footnote #2, Bailey, 1954)[1]

Indeed, a highly significant and far-reaching program began with Brigham Young's visit to Chief Walker in 1854. Upon first meeting, Chief Walker had refused to see Brigham Young because he feared the Mormon's intentions, and because Walker was in a state of near grief due to the illness of his son.

Upon learning of the boy's illness, Brigham Young is purported to have anointed the child's head with consecrated oil, placed his hands upon his head, and prayed for his physical and spiritual well-being. The folklore of the time indicates that Chief Walker was so pleased with the recovery of his son that he agreed to listen to the story of The Book of Mormon. Soon thereafter, Chief Walker agreed to sign a peace agreement with the Mormons, and was baptized and ordained an elder while in Salt Lake City. Three other chiefs, Sowiette, Arrapene, Unhoquitch and an interpreter, Elijah ("Barney") Ward, were baptized on this occasion (pp., x-xi, Brown, 1973). Hosea Stout recorded in his diary that upon being received into the Mormon faith, Chief Walker desired to "go and to preach to the Utahs." (p. 365, Stout, 1973) In May of the same year, Walker received his patriarchal blessing from Father Cazier with the recorder of the event concluding: "...a very good one it was..." (p. 12, footnote #14, Brown, 1973)

> *...It was two white men in particular - Thomas L. (Pegleg) Smith, and Brigham Young - who exerted the greatest force in molding the character and shaping the destiny of the renegade Indian who became the Ute Nation's most famous war chief. (p. 122, Bailey, 1954)*

> *On Monday morning, June 9, 1851, in Salt Lake City, four Lamanite chieftains - Walkara, Sowiette, Arrapeen and Unhquitch - talked words of warmth, friendship and peace with Brigham Young. It was something to be honored and appreciated as a saint. But that day President Young tendered them even greater honor. Over their heads the prayer words again were said. On that auspicious and important day all four were ordained to the higher Mormon priesthood. All four had now become elders in the church. (p. 122, Bailey, 1954, quoted from footnote #1, Journal of History dated June 9, 1851)*

---

1   "Walkara's name appears in many forms other than the anglicized 'Walker.' Among them are Walkah, Wauk, and Wah-ker. Wah-ker means 'yellow,' or 'brass.'"

> *"Because of his generalship and flawless strategy, he was known as 'the Napoleon of the Desert.'" The title he more clearly preferred, and one which he himself had consented was 'hawk of the mountains.'" (p. 14, Bailey, 1954)*

As elders, the Indians now became eligible to wear the magnificent temple garment, endowed as it was with the promises to ward off disease, deceit and even bullets.

The events connected to the peaceful baptism of Chief Walker belie his reputation as a forceful and aggressive leader. Jacob Hamblin (missionary to the Indians, one of the 12 Apostles of the Church, a man often referred to as "the Buckskin Apostle") met with Chief Walker in Cedar City.

> *Jacob quickly knew he was talking to no ordinary chief.*
> *Walker (Walkara) was a name before which lesser chiefs*
> *groveled and trembled. His guidance was not so much*
> *of a tribe, but of a tightly-knit empire, with many sub-*
> *chiefs like Sanpitch and Ammon paying tribute. Here*
> *was a man who made banditry, murder and slave-traffic*
> *an established and profitable business. Here was a man*
> *whom Mormons must either convert to their ways, or*
> *fight to the death. (p. 111, Bailey, 1954)*

In their dealings with Chief Walker, as in all relationships with the Indian People, the Mormons preferred to take the path of conversion rather than the road to war. Jacob Hamblin summarized his responsibility of attempting to bring the gospel to the Indian People in this rather short but illustrative expression: "I saw the necessity of the elders doing all they could to ameliorate the conditions of this miserable people" p. 110,

> *[Walker]...basked in the Mormon brotherhood and love,*
> *which Walkara was learning to use with advantage.*
> *There was prestige to being a Mormon Elder, he found,*
> *and the certificate of his ordination was crammed with*
> *the magic corn pollen and amulets into the buckskin*
> *prayer-bag which hung about his neck. (p. 131, Bailey,*
> *1954)[2]*

For whatever reasons, Chief Walker was not prevented some three years later from making war on his Mormon Brethren. (p. 128, Debo, 1970) The war, regardless of its cause, was short-lived and peace returned to the two peoples. Much to the credit of Brigham Young and the Mormon People, no effort was made to exterminate the Walker band. Brigham Young maintained his belief that the Lord would continue to use Walker to bring about the conversion of the Indian People. (Journal of Discourses, p. 106, vol. 1) It was Ray B. West's opinion that:

> *Nowhere was Brigham's tact and leadership better*
> *shown than in his dealing with the Indians. 'They are the*
> *seed of Abraham, and God is ever their God,' He wrote*

---

2   Paul Bailey may have taken "editorial privilege" in assuming the contents of a prayer-bag.

*of them. 'Moreover, Pacific Policy is the cheapest of any;
it is preferable to clothe and feed them than to fight them.
We make innumerable efforts to enlighten the pagan
nations of distant lands - are not the Indians, who live in
the midst of us, worth as much as they?*

*Bestow them your faith and prayers. At the same time
be on your guard against their savage nature and show
them that you are their superiors by your virtue.' (p. 207,
West, 1957)*

By the mid 1880's, the Mormons were reasonably settled in their new western home; it was then that they began extensive proselytizing activities. It appears evident that the policy of Brigham Young toward the Indian People was motivated by pragmatic as well as humanitarian desires. It is equally clear that a certain respectful distrust of Indian life can be garnered from the utterances of the Mormon leader. The admonition "...to guard against their savage nature and to show them that you are their superior by your virtue" reflects an attitude that was not altogether unlike that exhibited by the majority of all other whites of the day. The disposition to see Indian People as "savage" may have been expressed as a result of Brigham's disappointment in having to engage in the Walker War - or, perhaps, it was a mere reflection of "Manifest Destiny" after all.

Brigham Young expressed, as had Joseph Smith before him, that the "good life" for Indian People was that of the yeoman farmer and the possessors of herds of sheep, cattle and horses. Such ideas were further mirrored in the writings and speech of Mormons such as J. Cecil Alter:

*We have spared no time or expense in endeavoring
to dociliate the Indians, and learn them to leave off
their habits of pilfering and plundering, and work like
other people; but habits of civilization seem not to be
in accordance with their physical formation; many
that have tried it, pine away, and unless returning to
their former habits of living, died in a very short time.
Could they be induced to live peaceably and keep herds
of cattle, their condition would very materially be
ameliorated, and gradually induce a return to the habits
of civilization. (p. 192, Alter, 1940)*

Through their contact with Mormon People and Missionaries in particular, the Indian People learned to "...distinguish between the Mormons and Gentiles, calling the latter Amerikats and generally fearing them, while they regarded the Mormons as their friends." (p. 216, West, 1957)

Burton expressed his belief that among whites, "Mormon" had become a word to fear, whereas:

> *... the Gentiles looked upon the Latter Day Saints much as our crusading ancestors regarded "Hashshashiyun," whose name indeed was almost enough to frighten them. (p. 4, Burton, 1963)*

While such attitudes and activities as those encompassed in such events as the Mountain Meadow Massacre (1856) did cause many whites to, indeed, fear Mormon reprisal; nevertheless the attitudes of the whites toward Indians were either generally forgotten or not recorded (p. 259, Stegner, 1964). Henry A. Boller, in serving as editorial writer for Milo Melton Quaife, <u>Among The Indians: Eight Years In The Far West 1858-1866</u>, (1959), states that as

> *...far back as 1853 the whites have invariably been the aggressors. Desperados in the early immigration across the Plains leaving their record incomplete until they had killed an "injun" heedless of the consequences of their reckless acts." (p. 429, Boller, 1959)*

Garland Hurt is credited by Gustive Larson to have written in May (22) 1855:

> *The saints have either accidentally or purposely created a distinction in the minds of the Indian Tribes of this territory between the Mormons and the people of the United States that cannot be otherwise than prejudicial to the interests of the latter, and what sir, may one expect of those missionaries [Mormon] ...I suspect that their final object will be to teach these wretched savages that they are the rightful owners of the American soil and it has been wrongfully taken from them by the whites, and that the great spirit has sent the Mormons among them to help them recover their rights. (House Executive Documents, No. 71, 35th Congress, 1st Session, p. 176) (quoted in: p. 12, Larson, 1971)*

Gustive Larson stated that Brigham Young's policy that "it is better to feed them than to fight them" led the Indian People to "differentiate between their friendly neighbors and the transient emigrants who often regarded them as savages to be killed on slight provocation." (p. 11, Larson, 1971)

With the

> *...natives distinction between friend and foe extended into the Indian Administration, with Superintendent Brigham Young enjoying the*

60

> *Natives' confidence while the agents were generally*
> *regarded with suspicion, the resulting strained relations*
> *between Young and the agents were further aggravated*
> *by reports that the Mormons were inciting the Indians to*
> *attack emigrant trains. (p. 11, Larson, 1971)*

An attack by Mormons dressed as Indians did, in fact, take place, with guilt assessed and punishment administered to the guilty Mormons. Nevertheless, the Mountain Meadow Massacre would do much to tarnish credibility among Gentile emigrants. It was through events and stories such as these that campfire legends render the victims more glorious and the villains evermore terrible at each retelling. The event was tragic and from current perspective inexcusable however, like "Watergate" in our time, it will be slow in fading from the collective memory of the nation.

Rumors and fears notwithstanding, the focus of Mormon missionary work was on agricultural and practical affairs. Through these combined activities the Mormons hoped to first establish good will among the Indian populations, then they would begin evangelistic ministries. Missionary workers were sent to Santa Clara Valley in California; to the Salmon River in Oregon; to Nevada; and throughout Utah and southwestern Wyoming. (p. 145, Anderson, 1942)

Among those to whom missionary activity was directed were the Hopi in the Southwest. The expedition of Jacob (Jake) Hamblin was to serve as Brigham Young's scout and Indian Missionary; it was while in this service that Hamblin discovered an important crossing of the treacherous and highly uncertain Colorado River.

> *Exploration was a partial reason for the expedition.*
> *Another reason was explained by the presence in the*
> *company of Durias Davis, a Welshman. The mission that*
> *Davis was entrusted with was inextricably tied up with*
> *Mormon mythology; the legend of the Welsh Indians*
> *which he came to examine was part of the whole climate*
> *of superstition and speculation that had produced The*
> *Book of Mormon twenty-eight years before.(p. 146,*
> *Stegner, 1942)*

> *Because of that story [i.e., The Book of Mormon story]*
> *and the prophecy, the Mormons did their best to convert*
> *the Lamanites and make farmers of them. The Indians*
> *were not wolves to be destroyed, but souls to be saved...*
> *(p. 147, Stegner, 1942)*

> *The story also explains Brigham's curiosity about the*
> *Hopi...the Ho-ho-kim, the old people who left, were the*
> *Nephites, the ruins were the ruins of their*
> *cities. And the Hopi, whom the Mormons called*

61

the Moquis, lived in towns; they tilled the soil, raised
squash and beans and corn, showed signs of a higher
civilization than the miserable Goshutes or the thieving
Paiutes or the warlike and nomadic Utes and Apaches
and Navajo. Were the Hopi living in the echo of that long-
vanished civilization? (pp. 147-148, Stegner, 1942)

Significantly, it was to the so-called "thieving Paiutes" to whom Mormon Missionaries would go when the Ghost Dance began to spread among the tribes of the plains and basin in the 1890's.

The extent and success of missionary activities among Indian People is difficult to assess when using secondary sources. In northern Idaho, the missionary David Moore wrote that over 100 baptisms were performed in the first year; however, Jorgensen writes that many of these conversions were short-lived. (p. 79, Jorgenson, 1972)

In 1850, the Mormon settlement of Genoa was established in Carson Valley, Nevada, and by 1854, an Indian agent from the Utah Territory was sent to investigate the conditions of the tribes in the Great Basin. "For the most part he found them friendly and helpful to the whites who came into the area." However, "with large numbers of whites using the land, the People's way of life began to undergo significant changes." (p. 23, Johnson, 1975) In time, and with the discovery of gold in the Comstock (1859), and the creation of Nevada Territory (1861), the Indian People were forced to move into reservation areas within the territories.

The reservation system was seen by the whites as a geographical entity, surrounded by a well-defined boundary into which Indian People could be placed; a place in which assimilation could take place and the virtues of white culture extolled. The reservation to the Indian People, was viewed as a last repository of their "faith," a final claim to their birthright, their mother earth. The promises of the federal government were accepted as a promise by the whites that Indian religious heritage and cultural values would be allowed to exist unaltered for so long as the people would live within the confines of the reservation.

Quite typical of the white anti-Indian sentiment was that quoted by William T. Hagan:

The opinion of Commissioner of Indian Affairs Nathaniel
G. Taylor also was sought. ...the views he expressed
July 1867 resembled closely those of his predecessor,
Lewis V. Bogy. Bogy had seen the alternatives as
"total and speedy destruction of the Indians" or their
concentration on reservations to clear more land for the
whites. Commissioner Taylor saw the alternatives just as
clearly: "Swift extermination by the sword, and famine,
or preservation by gradual concentration
...and civilization." The last was achieved

*by: "consolidating them ...on large reservations, from
which all whites except government employees shall
be excluded, and educating them intellectually and
morally, and training them in the arts of civilizations, so
as to render them ...self-supporting, and at the proper
time to clothe them with the rights and immunities of
citizenship." (p. 5, Hagan, 1976)*

The alternatives to the reservation system were painfully obvious: comply or resist. Resistance to the reservation system could obviously take several forms. Indian People could fight for the retention of their hereditary lands or they could move. The options were strikingly similar to those faced by the Mormons in their exodus from Nauvoo; however, several equally striking differences appear as well. Unlike the Indian People, the Mormons could not remain in their lands even if a boundary was established between themselves and the Gentiles. On the other hand, the Indian People could not move to new lands somewhere further in the west. Richard F. Burton summarizes the Indian predicament as a "conflict" which would end finally in "...the discomfiture of the natives, who will then fast fall away."

*Those dispossessed of their lands cannot, as many
suppose, venture further west; the regions lying beyond
one tribe are generally occupied by another, with whom
deadly animosity exists. It is needless to say that many
of the Sioux look forward to the destruction of their race
with all of the feelings of despair with which the civilized
man would contemplate the extinction of his nationality.
How indeed, poor devils, are they to live when the pale
face comes with his pestilent firewater and smallpox,
followed up with paper and pen work, to be interpreted
under the general auspices of fire and steel? (p. 111,
Burton, 1963)*

Little wonder that Indian People turned increasingly to the promise of deliverance from the heel of oppression found within the Mormon Social Gospel or the promise of restoration of the Ghost Dance Religion. Little wonder, as well, that the protective hope of the Ghost Shirt seemed a reasonable alternative to the "fire and steel" of Manifest Destiny.

The rapid influx of miners, farmers and ranchers into the new lands of Utah and Nevada brought increasing problems for the Indian People who had lived in the region since time immemorial. The fact that the Indian People were the aboriginal inhabitants held little impress on the minds of whites whose concept of "Title to Land" ranged somewhere between the squatter ideal and a "Deed of Trust."

The natural resources of the area were changed or depleted rapidly since few took the time to consider the consequences that their actions would have on the landscape or on generations yet to occupy the land. To their credit, the Mormon mindset saw their response to the land as "stewards;" and as such felt responsible for the land, streams and forests. The non-Mormon miners used, with little regard to the consequences of their actions, the Pine Nut trees as shoring for their mineshafts and to burn in their mills. The Pine Nut was rich in protein and a vital link in the food chain of the Indian People. Ranchers' livestock ate the grass along the flood plains of rivers and in mountain meadows. With the increasing demand for forage came a predictable decline in the availability of game that served not only as a base of food, but clothing, shoes and warm blankets as well. With the damming of rivers to serve as a source of precious irrigation water for fields and crops came an ecological change in the availability of trout and other fishes. Increased amounts of silt in the streams accelerated the process of helping nature to change freshwater lakes into end-salt or brine lakes.

As changes took place, both in the land and in the cultural lives of the People, as disease and famine began to sweep the land, the Indian People turned increasingly to their religious leaders in anticipation of finding answers to the problems that beset them on every side. In the 1860's and 1870's, the Paiute Prophet Wodziwob prayed for the return of the dead and for the land to be restored to its fruitful condition prior to the arrival of the whites. By 1880 the Congress of the United States reported that the buffalo had become nearly extinct. The economic base of the tribes inhabiting the plains was altered beyond any hope of recovery. The hunting way of life for the Indian People was gone forever. Into this void came inadequate rations of extremely poor quantity and quality, of food, blankets and clothing. When conditions seemed desperate, government rations of beef were cut again and again.

From his agency in Carson Valley, Indian Agent Frederick Dodge, penned a report on the state of living conditions on the reservation in which Dodge claimed that '...he had met and given presents to over four thousand Indians, and never before have I beheld as much...[poverty]. (p. 27, Johnson, 1975)

Increasingly as pressures mounted, Indian People, driven to near desperation, turned again to Indian religious leaders for solutions to the problems of survival in a seemingly hostile and indifferent world of the white man.

In the midst of the social and ecological changes taking place in the environment, an obscure herder of sheep, a Paiute Prophet and heir to the role of religious leader of his people, arose and preached his new religion of renewal and restoration. Thus, the Ghost Dance Religion of 1890 began as a response of a people to a changing world. Little did anyone suspect that the teachings of peace and restoration taught by Wovoka (Jack Wilson) would result in such a dramatic change in the history of the American Nation and Indian People. The Mormons would once again, unknowingly contribute to the rapid change in America that was about to take place on the reservations and in the very shadows of the Mormon Temples.   64

The Paiute Prophet, Wovoka (seated)
Photo Taken by James S. Mooney circa 1892, Smithsonian Photograph

CHAPTER IV

The Ghost Dance Religion: An Indian Renaissance

Peter Farb, in writing of the Ghost Dance in his work <u>Man's Rise to Civilization,</u> describes the 1890 religious movement among the Basin and Plains People as being the "climax of Indian revivalism." Indian Revival Movements were not unique to only the great basin in 1870 and again in 1890, but had occupied a place in the history of nearly every tribe of North America from the very first encounter with Europeans, be they Spanish, French, Dutch, English or of whatever nationality. Indeed, the stories of the Hopi in the return of the deity Pahana indicate that revival among the American Indian was as commonplace as had been the urgings of the Old and New Testament Prophets.

The teachings of the Ghost Dance Religion, like those longings of the Old Testament Prophets, had as its central theme the recovery of lost Indian culture. It was the restoration or recovery of Indian life that characterized the desire of Indian Prophets from the Atlantic to the Pacific seaboards, from the Bering Sea to the Cape of Good Hope, to stop the inexorable advance of the whites into Indian lands. From time to time:

> ...*Native Americans produced brilliant leadership that on occasion brought the whole westward movement to a halt. The Delaware Prophet and Pontiac are examples of Indian leaders who distinctly perceived the irreversible harm that Euro-American influences had had upon Indian societies. Pontiac became such an outstanding leader because he clearly diagnosed the permanent damage his people had suffered as they bore the brunt of fierce white competition for rich Midwestern lands. (p. 7, Jacobs, 1972)*

> *If native societies reach this third stage, as the Seneca Indians did with the rise of the Prophet Handsome Lake, they usually survive as a people with their own cultural heritage. Otherwise they perish or are assimilated by the whites. (p. 134, Jacobs, 1972)*

The alternatives facing Native American People and Nations were clear: 1) to attempt to survive as a people with their cultural heritage intact; 2) perish as a people and as a cultural entity; 3) be assimilated by the whites. Of the alternatives to the Indian People, survival as a people and as a cultural entity held the only hope for the future. So it was, that in times of desperation and despair, the Native American People turned to the Ghost Dance Religion, as the source of strength,   66 courage and inspiration to guide them on their path of recovery of their lost heritage.

The Sun Dance had been declared illegal by the Congress of the United States, and the U.S. Cavalry was sent onto the plains following the Civil War to place the Indian People onto reservations and to ensure by force that they would no longer give expression to the Sun Dance. Unable to express their hopes and dreams the people turned again to teachings and urgings of their Prophets. This story was repeated time and time again, from the Iroquois to the Indian Shakers of Puget Sound, to the Prophet Dance, Smohalla cult and to the circles of the Ghost Dance. (see Leslie Spier: The Prophet Dance of the Northwest and its Derivatives: The Source of the Ghost Dance, 1935.)

The Ghost Dance Religion, like all other revival and life movements among Indian People had as its central theme the recovery of lost Indian culture. The Ghost Dance of 1870 and 1890 is unique to the history of the American frontier. Unlike the Shaker Religion, Prophet Dance and Smohalla cult, The Ghost Dance Religion of 1890 was geographically tied to the Mormon movement. The near extinction of the buffalo, short rations and broken promises and treaties caused eager emissaries of nearly every tribe in the valleys of the California, Oregon and Great Plains to gather in Nevada to hear the wonderful "Gospel of Delivery" that was being taught by the Prophet Wovoka in the Revival of 1890.

Ironically enough, the year 1890 was the long awaited year in which some of the Mormons waited for the return of Jesus as Joseph Smith was to have promised. In 1843, Joseph Smith was purported to have received several profound revelations concerning the future of the Church in America. One purported revelation concerned the movement to the West. This revelation was, theoretically at least, the basis for missions of exploration in Texas, Michigan and eventually, to the West. The second revelation concerned the return of the Messiah.

> *[Joseph Smith] ...prophesied that a new Jerusalem
> would arise in the desert, where all those with faith
> would gather, including the lost tribes of Israel. After the
> Mormons settled in Utah, it became part of their belief
> that the Indians represented the remnants of the Hebrew
> Tribes taken into captivity by the Assyrians some 2,500
> years earlier. The Mormons sent emissaries to the
> Indians, who they dubbed Lamanites, inviting them to
> join the Mormon colonies and be baptized. Joseph Smith
> was also supposed to have prophesied in 1843 that when
> he reached his 85th year, that is in 1890, the Messiah
> would appear in human form. (p. 280, Farb, 1968)*

The idea that Joseph Smith was to have given a prophecy to the Church that the New Jerusalem would be built in the west is not widely accepted among the membership of splinter groups of "Mormonism." The notion that such a prophecy was the work or inspiration of Joseph Smith is generally rejected among senior generations of splinter groups such as the Community of Christ. It is generally expressed among these persons that the "Prophecy" had not been accepted by a General Conference of the Elders and that it had never appeared in print before Joseph's death. However to the Mormons in Utah, both the movement West and the prophecy relating to the return of the Messiah are generally accepted as "matter of fact."

The scriptural reference to this prophecy is found in the scripture of the Utah Mormons and states:

> 1. *"When the Savior shall appear, we shall see Him as He is. We shall see that He is a man like ourselves."*

> 2. *"I was once praying very earnestly to know the time of the coming of the Son of Man, when I heard a voice repeat the following:*

> 3. *"Joseph, my son, if thou livest until thou are 85 years old, thou shalt see the face of the Son of Man..."*

> 4. *"...I was left thus, without being able to decide whether this coming referred to the beginning of the millennium or to some previous appearing, or whether I should die and thus see His face."*

> (Doctrine and Covenants, Church of Jesus Christ of Latter Day Saints (Mormon), Section 130, Verses 1, 14, 15, 16)

The Ghost Dance Religion

In the year awaited by Mormon Millenialists (1890), the Paiute Prophet Wovoka (Jack Wilson) appeared and preached the Ghost Dance Religion. Wovoka was, as Robert Utley suggests, "bewildered and tormented" by the flood of white settlements in the Indians traditional home.

> *As the whites poured into the western lands in swelling numbers, killing off the game animals even as they slew the Indians, many of the tribesmen lapsed into despondency. Like other frustrated, dispirited peoples in various parts of the world, whose survival and way of life was being threatened, the Indians began to yearn for supernatural deliverance from their tribulations. The situation was conducive to the rise of prophets or messiahs who would promise a withdrawal*

of the intruders and a revival of the old ways. Such
messiahs did indeed appear among North American
Indians, attracting numerous red men to their revivalist
cults. (p. 509, Spencer & Jennings, 1977)

The Ghost Dance Religion among the Paiute in 1890 arose in response
to the teachings and visions of the Prophet Wovoka; however, "...its roots lie
deeper in the past."

The customs, beliefs, and values of the white people
had crushed the old Indian life. Traditional views of
the universe were not satisfactory either. In groping
for basic explanations, in longing to roll back the
years, Wovoka differed from few of his race. but he had
determination coupled with the ability to do something
about the conflict. (p. 66, Utley, 1963)

It was a rare combination of "determination" and "ability" that enabled
Wovoka to step from obscurity into the mainstream of American History by
proclaiming himself to be the new Prophet of the Ghost Dance Religion. In
January of 1889 an eclipse of the sun is said to have darkened his vision; however, Wovoka was convinced that during those moments of darkness he "..ex-
perienced a wonderful vision." (p. 64, Utley, 1963)

Wovoka proclaimed that he " ...went to heaven and saw God and all the
people who died a long time ago." (p. 64, Utley, 1963) He returned to earth
with a...religion and mandate from God to rescue his people from the darkness
that awaited them." (p. 64, Utley, 1963) Robert Utley expresses the belief that
the Ghost Dance Religion " ...was by no means unique..." to the cultural landscape of North America.

...On the contrary, it bore striking resemblances to
earlier primitive religious movements. Wovoka was but
one of a long line of Aboriginal mystics who sought to rid
their people of an alien oppressor and lead them into the
Promised Land. By such teachings the Tewa Medicine
Man Pope united the pueblos of the Rio Grande to expel
the Spaniards in 1680. The Ottawa Chief Pontiac used
a like doctrine to forge the confederation that in 1763
nearly drove the English from the Appalachian frontier.
Early in the nineteenth century Tecumsah and his
religious ally, the prophet, built a similar confederation
that wrought destruction in the old northwest until
shattered at the Battle of Tippecanoe. In 1881, the
Apache medicine man Nakaidoklini stirred up the White
Mountain Apaches with such teachings, and as late as
1887 the prophet Sword Bearer excited the Crows with
promises of an approaching millennium. (pp.
70-71, Utley, 1963)

69

Jacobs expresses the belief that. "...the Indian frontier of the North was alive with religious prophets hostile to white culture." (p. 89, Jacobs, 1972) As early as 1762, an Onondaga leader had preached that "...the Great Spirit would punish the whites if they persisted in seizing lands in Indian country." "Certainly there is no doubt that Pontiac's war had deep religious overtones; it was almost a religious crusade against white man's culture and his religion." (p. 89, Jacobs, 1972)

It is significant that the White Man's material culture and religion was rejected in such resistance movements. It would appear that rarely did the American Indian take exception to theological beliefs of the white man's re-ligion, i.e., belief in God, Jesus as his Son, or in the state of spirits and souls after death and in a resurrection. The native American people seemed over-whelmed by the controversy that existed between Christian churches as they tried, however, vainly, to win converts and how each church claimed doctri-nal superiority over the others.

Native American religion not only accepted, but encouraged, commu-nication with the Great Spirit, and with those forces of the unseen spirit world that resided in the wind, thunder, in the soft incense of pine, in the warm breeze of a July afternoon. The message of the prophet was sure and certain. Confirmation of the Prophet's word was found in nature itself, in the animals, in the grass, an eagle's soar, free and unfettered by things of the earth. The Prophets spoke, and the people listened. Indeed, the "...gift of prophecy has of-ten been claimed by individuals in native America." (p. 89, La Barre, 1975)

> *The first well-known [Prophet] ...Pope of the Pueblo*
> *revolt in 1680, but his successors were many:*
> *Wabokieshiek, or "White Cloud," the Winnebago-Sauk*
> *Prophet of the Black Hawk War; the Delaware Prophet of*
> *Pontiac's conspiracy (1762); Tenskwatawa, twin brother*
> *of Tecumseh, and the well-known "Shawnee Prophet"*
> *(1805); Kanakuk, the Kickapoo reformer (1827);*
> *Smohalla, the Sokulk dreamer of the Columbia (1870-*
> *1885); Tavibo, the Paiute; Nakaidoklini, the Apache*
> *(1881); Wovoka, or Jack Wilson, the Paiute Prophet of the*
> *Ghost Dance of 1889 and ...Skaniadariio, or "Handsome*
> *Lake," the Seneca teacher, etc. (p. 89, La Barre, 1975)*

The work of the Indian Prophet was made somewhat easier by the In-dian belief that God was, like lesser spirit beings, vitally concerned with the welfare and wellbeing of humankind...God was always thought of as being "up there" and ready to be addressed by man." (p. 32, Starkloff, 1974) It requires very little stretch of the imagination to observe that the Mormon people shared a common belief and acceptance for the role of the prophet in their lives. The Prophet, to the Indian and Mormon alike, was one to whom the pression and to whom they looked as the "law giver" in their uncertain search people turned to point the way to deliverance from the heel of opfor the peace and tranquility of the promised land.

Important, as well, to Mormon belief was the principle of the "Social Gospel," a gospel of good works in the name of the community of believers and directed toward the welfare of the body of believers. No other unit in Mormon life is as important as is the family. Family welfare was and is to be strength-ened so that the entire body of saints could prosper in a persons' good fortune. The social gospel, while certainly not known by that name, was inherently a part of native American life as well.

> ...For the traditional Indian, personal individual
> morality is social morality. There is no boxing-off of two
> separate categories. Even the celebrated individualism
> of the plains warriors or hunters was entirely taken
> for granted as conducive to the tribal well-being. If an
> individual performed well, the whole community would
> benefit, and if he was selfish, not only would the tribe
> suffer but he, too, as virtually an organic part of the body
> would suffer. As should be evident, the pauline notion
> of the Body of Christ is very close to such a doctrine of
> solidarity. (p. 83, Starkloff, 1974)

The Ghost Dance Religion emanating from the northern Paiute was dif-fused among the Indians of the Western United States in two distinct waves (one in 1870, the second about 1890). That the dead would return and peaceful and prosperous conditions be reestablished if the Ghost Dance were performed was the essential doctrine of both movements. The second movement, that of 1890, instigated by Jack Wilson (Wovoka), is well known for its far-reaching political and psychological effects upon native life. Of the earlier movement which began in 1870, little is known save that it was originated by an older relative of Jack Wilson, who instituted the doctrine, dreams, and dances oc-curring in both phases of the cult, that its diffusion was largely westward into southeastern Oregon and California... (p. 57, Gayton, A.H., "The Ghost Dance of 1870 in South-central California") quoted in Kroeber, et al., 1965)

> The doctrine of the Ghost Dance, which promised the
> return of dead relatives, absolution from sickness
> and death, a continuous life of peace and prosperity,
> is ubiquitous in its human appeal. This, together
> with the fact that the cult had no complex features of
> belief or intricate taboos and was open for collective
> participation, made it uniquely suitable for a rapid
> diffusion regardless of the type of culture encountered in
> its travels. The framework and stimulus of the revivalist
> cult was supplied, the details were filled in according
> to the individual taste of varying culture
> patterns. (p. 82, Gayton, A. H., "The Ghost

71

Dance of 1870 in South-central California" quoted in
Kroeber, et. al., 1965)

Peter Farb, in his description of the Ghost Dance of 1870 states "...no
benefits ever resulted from these dances, and they were abandoned." (p. 280,
Farb, 1968) It may be that the "Dance Ritual" was abandoned after 1870, but it
is obvious that the beliefs of the Prophet continued to live on in the subsequent
teachings of prophets of numerous tribes and nations.

Wovoka (Jack Wilson), the Ghost Dance Prophet of 1890, lived until 1932.
It appears historically correct to say that the "Dances" of 1890 died with the
fallen at Wounded Knee, nevertheless, it is equally true to conclude that the
teachings and belief of the Ghost Dance did not die in that December snow.
The beliefs and longings of a people to be free and to be allowed to live and
worship as they see fit can never really die nor can they be totally "stamped
out" of the collective consciousness of a people or nation. If mankind has
learned but one lesson from all wars and holocausts of history, it should be
that the spirit of a race or people can never totally be erased from the face of
the earth.

The communal burial ground of Wounded Knee, the Sand Creek, and
the Cherokee removal all have their counterparts in the Warsaw Ghetto, in
Austerwitz and in the Bataan death marches. Regardless of the time or place,
the spirit of humankind speaks from the earth and beckons each new generation to take its place in the struggle to maintain home, life, families and the
right to worship as a people sees fit. Carl Starkloff admonishes that: "There are
Wovokas and Handsome Lakes today on nearly every reservation and in many
urban groups." (p. 130, Starkloff, 1974)

> Ruth Underhill divides modern Indian prophets into
> "hostile prophets" and "prophets of co-existence." Among
> the "hostiles" she includes Smohalla, Wodzuwob, and
> Wovoka, while among the "co-existents" are Handsome
> Lake (Ganioda'Yo) of the Iroquios, the Indian Shakers,
> and the Peyote followers. Generally the lines seem to have
> been drawn inasmuch as the Indian People experienced
> either hypocrisy or genuine love and valiant effort and
> personal witness at the hands of white missionaries.
> However, it is important to note that many of the hostile
> prophets were more Christian in their basic inspiration
> and teachings than some of the prophets of coexistence.
> Thus, Wovoka employed far more Christian beliefs in
> his Apocalyptic than did Handsome Lake in his reform,
> a fact which confirms the view that often the common
> denominator of these prophets was not the faith but
> the foreign culture involved in its transmission. (p. 131,
> Starkloff, 1974)

Somehow, in time, the "cataclysm" concept evoked fear in the minds of the whites, especially among those interlopers into the Black Hills and into the regions of the Pine Ridge and Rosebud Reservations. Here the whites did not see the remotest possibility that perhaps, only perhaps, the cataclysm that was to swallow them was the same as that taught by so called "Christian fundamentalist ministers" as they preached sermons of hell-fire and damnation based on the Book of Revelations. To the whites of the day, the circles of the Ghost Dance may well have taken on the form of some feared expression of "war" rather than, as it was, an expression of religious ritual. The Ghost "Dance" was not unlike the religious "Dance" of the ancient Hebrews; it was an expression of religious belief etched in the form of a dance.

Strange as it may seem, the open-trench graves of Wounded Knee and the rust colored earth of the Sand Creek Massacre, never struck at the moral consciousness of the nation as did My Lai in Viet Nam. Perhaps, it was that a young nation had yet to develop a sense of guilt and collective conscience. For whatever reason, the admonition of the Ghost Dance Prophet: "You must not fight the white man" was either not heard or was ignored. The Ghost Dance was not a call to arms, it was a call to surrender to the will of the Great Spirit.

To speed the recovery of the earth and the return of the dead, the Indian People were to sing the songs and do the dance that Wovoka had learned in his vision experience. If the People were faithful to the promise:

> *...to bring about a millennium on the earth with the*
> *Messiah, in the presence of the Great Spirit, the Indian*
> *must be industrious, honest, virtuous, peaceful. In fact,*
> *although not stated, they must follow a code of conduct*
> *almost identical to the white man's Ten Commandments.*
> *The admonition against fighting was stressed. This was*
> *indeed a revolutionary doctrine... (p. 66, Utley, 1963)*

> *"You must not hurt anybody or do harm to anyone."*
> *"You must not fight."*
> *"Do not tell the white people about this, Jesus is now*
> *upon the earth. He appears like a cloud."*
> *(Important statements from the "Messiah Letter" credited*
> *to James Mooney and quoted on p. 510, Spencer, 1977)*

The James Mooney, 1892 Smithsonian Report, continues to stand alone as the single most important attempt to understand the significance, genesis, and spread of the Ghost Dance Religion. The effort of Mooney to understand Indian people, to appreciate the deepness of their religious tradition and to allow greater latitude for the People to be free to express self-determination in all aspects of their cultural life, is nearly unequaled in the literature and ethnological research efforts of that day. A highly significant work expressed among writers of Indian religion and culture is the highly sensitive and thought provoking work of Carl Starkloff, People at the Center.   73

While it is true that Carl Starkloff devotes relatively little attention to the specifics of the Ghost Dance Religion, he does, nevertheless, look beyond the "shuffle" of the Ghost Dance Circle and attempts to peer deeply into the sacredness of the "Hoop." His search reveals, for those wise enough to listen, a People attempting to find in a religious dance, a communion and a longing to find at-one-ment with the Great Spirit, nature, earth, the People, and to find that which the modern world so desperately needs if we are to survive as a race, nation, and world -- peace. The Ghost Dance was a religious desire for peace of the soul, a release from the human condition of waste, war, and the wanton destruction of the resources of the earth.

Thus, the Ghost Dance Religion can only be seen fully when an attempt is made to push aside a preoccupation with the ritual and form of the dance and to see the teachings of Wovoka as a religious longing of a people to "...restore the spirit of hope that sees humankind of every tribe and tongue and nation assembled before the throne" (p. 19, Starkloff, 1974). Starkloff continues:

> *My own experience of reservation social and religious*
> *gatherings is of an intense desire to be at one with other*
> *tribes and white people. This is especially true of the Sun*
> *Dance in some instances, where Christian elements have*
> *already entered and transformed much of the ceremony,*
> *or where Christian clergymen are invited to give opening*
> *invocations. For the most part, Indians are willing*
> *to return to the early spirit of hospitality that existed*
> *between Indians and the Whites as we read of it in early*
> *New England accounts and eighteenth and nineteenth*
> *centuries. (pp. 19-20, Starkloff, 1974)*

Starkloff's sensitive approach to the "life" of the Indian People is portrayed in a reflection of his personal contact with the "People at the Center:"

> *...I am suggesting we look to find an opening to achieve*
> *for all Americans what the Ghost Dance strove for*
> *vaguely and with confusion. We must try to restore the*
> *spirit of hope that sees humankind of every tribe and*
> *tongue and nation assembled before the throne. Some*
> *current Indian movements evidence a desire for this, and*
> *white and Indian leaders are trying to join the spirit of*
> *Indian vision-quest, Christian prophecy, and the Peyote*
> *cult in a search for global unity. We can read many*
> *Indian religious lodge prayers that, although lamenting*
> *the Indian lot, also pray that all may live together in*
> *peace. (pp. 19-20, Starkloff, 1974)*

With this contemporary blending of Christian-Indian theology, must come a reassessment of just what it was that the Ghost Dance attempted to teach in 1890. Many writers agree that:

74

*Wovoka's teachings were a curious blending of
Christianity and native religious beliefs and practices.
How this amalgamation took place is a mystery and the
detail of their coming together may never be fully known.
(p. 44, Johnson, 1974)*

*It was the Great Ghost Dance of 1890, however, that
provided the crashing climax to the collapse of American
Indian culture. Tavibo, the messiah of the Ghost Dance
of 1870, is said to have left a son when he died, a boy
named Wovoka, "The Cutter." Some students doubt the
relationship, but the two messiahs did come from the
same area. As an adolescent boy, Wovoka is thought
to have witnessed the ceremonies in Tavibo's tule reed
wickiup, and he certainly saw the many visitors from all
over the West who came reverently to hear the prophet's
revelations. Like many other Paiute, Wovoka worked
for the white ranchers of Mason Valley in Nevada. He
became attached as ranch hand to the very religious
family of David Wilson, from whom he learned some
English and at least a smattering of Christian theology.
He also got from them the name Jack Wilson, under
which he had almost legendary fame all over the West.
Even far-off tribes knew he was omniscient, spoke all
languages, was invisible to white men, and was direct
messenger from the Great Spirit. (p. 229, La Barre, 1972)*

   Considerable confusion exists as to not only the origins of the Revival
movements in the Basin and Pacific Northwest but as to just who Wovoka's
father was and what the relationship was that existed between Wovoka as the
Ghost Dance Prophet of 1890 and that of the Ghost Dance Prophet of 1870.
Weston La Barre expresses a belief held by some that Wovoka was the son of
the Ghost Dance Religion Prophet (1870) whose name was Tavibo. Others, like
Edward C. Johnson in writing the tribal history of the <u>Walker River Paiutes</u>
(University of Utah Printing Service, Salt Lake City, Utah, 1974), states that indeed, Tavibo was the father of Wovoka, but that Wodziwob had been the Ghost
Dance Prophet (1870). Tavibo had been a follower of Wodziwob. Obscure as
names and persons appear to be to the English speaking public, it is important
that both the Ghost Dance of 1870 and 1890 were begun in the same geographic area of Nevada, and undoubtedly the teachings of the earlier (1870) prophet
did much to influence the movement of two decades later. It appears equally
obvious that Wovoka's father -- either Wodziwob or Tavibo -- had participated
in the revival movement in 1870 and that these teachings were shared with the
younger Wovoka.

   The degree and extent of influence that Wovoka's father had   75 on the training and education of the Prophet is difficult to assess since the details of Wovoka's childhood were not collected and put to some form of analysis. It would be especially difficult to establish the extent of influence of any father for a youth, in this case a boy, that was being raised in a matrilineal society in which the mother's brother, an uncle, might have been more influential in the training and discipline of a child than would have been his natural father.

It is sufficient for the present to recognize that the influences that shaped and formed the life of Wovoka were, like that for most humans, considerable. While certainly Tavibo and Wodziwob yielded considerable influence, evidence is very great to suggest that the David Wilson family, their brand of Presbyterian Christianity, and their Bible all contributed greatly to Wovoka's education. In a similar way it has been suggested that the influences of Mormonism, Catholicism and "native pageant" are all evident as well.

The fabric of the Ghost Dance is interwoven with a lifelong set of experiences that deeply influenced the man, the movement, and of course, the events of history. The details of "influence" are to be observed more in the teachings of the Prophet than those that can be found in establishing his parentage. The Ghost Dance Movement is a classic study of cultures, white and Indian, in conflict. The conflict did not, necessarily, take the form of open or hostile acts, but was a conflict based not on how things were but on how they were perceived to be. For example, to the "Fundamentalist" of Christian America in 1870-90, a "dance" may have been considered not only inappropriate but immoral and even sinful; whereas to the ancient Hebrews religious dance was a legitimate expression of belief, of faith and of hope.

To the whites in 1870-1890, "dances" of Indian people, regardless of their nature or purpose, were more than likely equated with "war." The equation was in the cultural mind set of people whose food, housing, clothing, hair and eye color and religious practices differed from those strange new people called by the Sioux as Was-ichu -- "the greedy ones." To most whites of that day, the chants of songs sung during religious gatherings were viewed as expressions of a decadent and "lost" people. The aesthetic value of silence, prayer, fasting and the ritual of endurance were foreign to the materialism of Manifest Destiny. Manifest Destiny encouraged an atmosphere to prevail in which success was equated with the accumulation of wealth, land, oil, cattle, railroads, mines, fences and cities. Success to the Indian was living in harmony with the "sacred space" -- a space given ever so generously by the Great Spirit. It was the sacredness of space that gave to the People a unique sense of belonging.

> *In song and narrative, the Center-image tells the Indians*
> *that the Creator has given them a sacred place. The*
> *Arapaho account tells how the Giver assigned this tribe to*
> *live in "the middle place." Their original name,*

Hinaneina, means simply "The People" as do many other
original tribal names, each tribe seeing itself as chosen to
hold fast to its own sacred space. Hence the great value
placed on land and the devastation wrought among
Indians when they found out that white men could not
share it with them equitably. Even now, so I am told,
Indians of the Wind River Reservation recognize four
sacred shrines enclosing this restricted piece of land, as
the place wherein the Creator will protect His people. The
acceptance of sacred space, of a cosmos, is the doing of
the will of God. (p. 49, Carl Starkloff, 1974)

Material culture fails to comprehend the power of the psyche and spirit
to find intense satisfaction in solitude, in fasting, in the communal expression
of religious dance, in communion with nature and with the Great Spirit. It was
through the communion of dance and song that the Indians sought to achieve
an individual and corporate vision. It was the blending of the individual will
to the needs of the community that would point the direction of the people to
"...a source of light and hope for the future amid the decay and disaster of..."
the time. (p. 102, Starkloff, 1974)

An example of the collective vision as a source of peace and guidance is
seen in a song sung by a Pawnee singer "...upon awakening from a trance during the Ghost Dance."

It was a dream of a yellow star coming to give him
a yellow feather, saying, "All the stars in the sky are
people." It was a highly favored vision, frustrated by
events of 1890, but still a source of light and hope for the
future....

The yellow star has noticed me, Furthermore it gave me a
standing yellow feather, that yellow star. (Pawnee Ghost
Dance Song)

Then I saw a new heaven and new earth... (Revelation
21:1, RSV).

The selection from Revelation is part of the apocalyptic
vision of the seer, who saw the new dispensation arising
out of the destruction of the old order of things, and it is
remarkably like some of the visions of Black Elk. (p. 102,
Starkloff, 1974)

Little understood and less appreciated was the desire of the Indian community to experience a state of mental, spiritual and physical -- equilibrium
-- a universal desire for at-one-ment.

*In other words, that man needs redemption seems to
me a constant element of Indian belief. I would venture
to say that there has never been a group of people more
ready to face the reality of moral evil as well as good,
and so prayerfully desirous of doing that good. (p. 82,
Starkloff, 1974)*

The Indian People, like those of the Mormon community, looked to the
singing of songs (hymns) as a vehicle of expression of one faith, one hope, one
redemption. The Ghost Dance songs (hymns) spoke of the unity of the people.

*...there is the power of music to open the heart...Indians
experience singing as power and as communion with
the spirit world: music pleases the Powers as well as
human beings, and a special rapport is thus created in its
performance. Experience bears out how much traditional
music means to Indians when one sees how they can
listen or sing for many hours on end, caught up in a near
trance, while most whites, even music lovers, will grow
tired of their favorite music after two or three hours. (p.
111, Starkloff, 1974)*

Prayer, fasting and exposure to sun's heat and the cool night air, were
utilized by the Indian People to quicken and sharpen all of their senses.

*Among North American Indians, except for the late-
nineteenth-century arrival of Peyote, a state of higher
consciousness was not achieved through drugs. It came,
as with Zen training and yoga, through severe self-
discipline and self-emptying. The latest Roman Catholic
alterations in fast and abstinence requirements were
no doubt needed reforms of a type of legalism or empty
ritualism for many. But the downplaying of personal
asceticism in the name of social and charitable actions,
however laudable, can possibly cause Roman Catholics
to lose their awareness of the importance to individuals
of silence, solitude, fasting, and bodily and mental
discipline. All of these values were sought in North
American Indian religious experience. (p. 108, Carl
Starkloff)*

The values sought in a religious experience are often difficult, if not impossible, to communicate to non-participants or non-believers. It was difficult,
certainly, for whites who observed the shuffle of the Ghost Dancers to appreciate fully that all the Indian People really desired was the recovery of their culture and the return of their dead ancestors. Word of the new
religion spread rapidly from tribe to tribe on the East, West,

78

South, and North. With equal fervor "stories" of the Ghost Dance spread from one white community to another. The story of a dance that would result in the return of the dead Indians fired the imagination of the whites to such a degree that soon the followers of the Ghost Dance doctrine were thought to have a preoccupation with death and dying. It was perhaps this misunderstanding that contributed to the further belief that the Ghost Dance was "some form of war dance."

Without a doubt the Ghost Dance was a protest movement, but it was non-violent in that it taught repeatedly that Indian People should not fight the whites. It appears, however, that the teaching of non-violence was ignored by whites, and instead stress was placed upon the beliefs in "ghosts" and the re-turn of the dead.

An analysis of the concept of death and the resurrection shows that while it is at the very heart of Christian faith, it is undoubtedly a cause of con-siderable conflict in the mind of a material culture. Death to the materialist is the end of all. Death to the ascetic is the great equalizer of the human condition -- an end to suffering and the acceptance of the principle of the brother and sisterhood in the family and in the abode of God (the Great Spirit). "There is no death, only change," proclaims the Indian Visionary.

> *This death mythology is not irrelevant to the various theologies of death which have been recently developed. Such theologians suggest that death is the ultimate determinant of the individual human "existence." Death is an ever-present "event" in the light of which one makes his life decisions - in fact, the one event that is always at least subconsciously present at every moment. The attempts of Indian mythology to give some meaning to the decision to accept death without despair indicate a similar understanding of its nature. The last description traditional Indians would give to death would be that it is merely "separation of body and soul." (p. 45, Carl Starkloff, 1974)*

The Ghost Dance, might well have been described as a "spirit dance" since it sought the literal resurrection of the body and souls of humankind and animals as well. It sought a perfect harmony and blending of matter and spirit that may have characterized the human condition in that primordial state de-scribed as the "man's original nature" that was believed to have existed in the fabled Garden of Eden. The Ghost Dance was an attempt by the People to ar-rive once again at this sublime condition.

> *Hartley Burr Alexander, who was poet and philosopher as well as anthropologist, entitled one of his books The World's Rim. The title derives from a depiction of a Plains Indian standing astride the earth, with*

79

arms outspread and held aloft, in communion with the powers and the winds that move about this rim. His skeletal frame, upright as opposed to that of four-legged creatures, is the measuring rod of the universe: his arms rotate to a point in the four sacred directions, his head is to the heavens, and his feet planted on Mother Earth. We might even see here another version of the imagery of the Rabbis of the Hellenistic period who called Adam the image of universal man - his name in Hebrew meaning "man" and derived from adamah, "earth," and the Greek letters of his name being the first letters for east, west, north, and south. (p. 47, Carl Starkloff)

One of the tragedies of our world is that the manifestation of God has been fragmented. The scientist passionately pursues the truth as he measures, weighs, and evaluates physical and mathematical data. In our world his labors are unrelated to the supreme manifestation - Jesus. Likewise the artist and even sometimes the saint, keen on their own apprehension of the divine, fail to relate what they do to the Spirit of the whole, and in so many instances even their art and their goodness become the occasion whereby their separateness from others is emphasized. And as the man is divided within himself, so are men antagonistic to each other. The fundamental spirit of the age is wrong, and all are affected by it. Our age is one of plenty, but 70 percent of us live in perpetual hunger. Our age has the language of the redeemed - we talk of liberty, of equality, and fraternity - but we are in danger of total destruction. We look for security and find only uncertainty. Science teaches us of the unity of nature, but in our behavior that unity is shattered. Armageddon, is in the making, for our modern world presents the scientific embodiment of nature's resources in two antagonistic idea systems. One centers in Washington and the other in Moscow. Even the historical revelation of Jesus Christ has been fragmented and the fragments embodied in institutions and transmitted by tradition and practice. What men need is not more science or better art, nor even more religion. Men need a new spirit in which to view life, a spirit in which there is power and motivation to reorient life around the divine purpose. The spirit men need is the testimony of Jesus - the Spirit of prophecy. (p. 151, Oakman, 1961)

And the end shall come, and the heaven and the earth shall be consumed, and pass away, and

> *there shall be a new heaven and new earth; for all things*
> *shall pass away, and all things shall become new, even*
> *the heaven and the earth, and all the fullness thereof,*
> *both men and beasts, the fowls of the air, and the fishes*
> *of the sea; and not one hair, neither mote, shall be lost,*
> *for it is the workmanship of mine hand. (Doctrine and*
> *Covenants, 28:6b, c, d –Community of Christ)*

The study of eschatology, the study of last things, has occupied the mind of humankind since earliest times. The Ghost Dance Religion had an eschatological base that was not unlike that taught by Mormon missionaries in the Basin Region. Both the disciples of Mormonism and the Ghost Dance Religion have accepted, nearly without question, the role of the Prophet not only as the instrument through which the divine message was received and transmitted to people, but have ascribed to the prophet as well, the role of "mediator" between matter and spirit, man and God.

> *The Jewish and Moslem traditions have always insisted*
> *that God needs no mediator, but is intimately close to*
> *humankind and loves it. Yet, even in these religions there*
> *are accounts of angels and divine messengers who speak*
> *to man for God, apparently because men may find the*
> *presence of divinity too awesome to bear. To whatever*
> *degree the believer may wish to be friendly with God, he*
> *always acknowledges that God is Holy, and that there is*
> *a tremendum about His presence. This awareness seems*
> *in general to be the Indian attitude. It is possible that*
> *this sense of awe made it more natural for Indians in*
> *many cases to identify so quickly and closely with Jesus*
> *Christ, to acknowledge His presence through rites added*
> *to the Sun Dance, the Peyote Tipi, the Sweat Lodge, and*
> *other services of worship. The figure of a holy mediator*
> *is very real to these people, and for Christian Indians*
> *today, Christ has become "the one mediator between God*
> *and men," symbolized by different forces in nature and*
> *ritual like the Thunderbird and the lodge pole. It is an*
> *attitude encouraged by St. Paul, who could both insist*
> *on the uniqueness of Jesus Christ as mediator and still*
> *speak reverently of the created powers on earth and in*
> *the heavens, as they profess their subjection to Him. (pp.*
> *33-34, Carl Starkloff, 1974)*

The dance form of the Ghost Dance lacked much of the stereotyped drama of a "war dance" and it certainly demonstrated far less "drama" than did the Sun Dance; nevertheless, it was in the silence of the Ghost Dance that the greatest "power" could be felt. It was the muted silence of shuffled feet and muffled chants that gave to the dancers a sense of sacred-

81

ness. It was a sacredness that was swallowed up in the immensity of star filled, silent night. Indian People have, through time, learned not only to cope with, but have encouraged the presence, of silence. Silence speaks to the soul in just the way that the form of the Ghost Dance Circle was transformed into the "Sacred Hoop." It was this same bending of self-will by the Indian that Saul of Tarsus experienced as he became "Paul" ...an Apostle of Christianity.

> *Over the centuries of their lives in the northern climes,*
> *silence and solitude have seeped into the very spiritual*
> *marrow of the forest and plains peoples. This has nothing*
> *to do with a negative attitude toward speech, which is*
> *enjoyed and treated with reverence, but rather, with*
> *a respect for the mystic void that waits to be filled up.*
> *Even though the Indian known to the white person in*
> *history is silent toward him largely out of caution, and*
> *far more outgoing at home with his own people, most*
> *Indians do seem to have a natural capacity to be silent*
> *and to listen. This is part of a long history that is both*
> *practical and religious. On the practical level, it is easy*
> *to see how a hunting or gathering or agricultural people*
> *would be free of addiction to talkativeness. The nature*
> *of the work of hunting, fishing, and gathering calls for*
> *quiet concentration and silent use of the senses. If one*
> *lives long enough in the wilderness, especially in the*
> *giant expanses of the North American West, the sheer*
> *overwhelming dimensions of the landscape become*
> *a wordless command of silence. (pp. 108-109, Carl*
> *Starkloff)*

Perhaps it is this silence and harmony of man-nature-spirit that the Oglala, Black Elk, desired for the People as he mourned for the return of the Sacred Hoop, which he feared had been forever broken. "Everyone who lived within this circle seems to have seen it as a sacred hoop, and knew that if one violated one's proper role, the hoop might be destroyed." (p. 85, Starkloff, 1974)

Presbyterian Influence – The Wilson Bible

Stories told by white settlers, generally describe the influence of Wovoka's father (Tavibo?) as negative. At least one description of the father is that Tavibo was "surly and treacherous; he could run a deer down." (p. 44, Johnson, 1974) The chances are very great that he did not care for he whites who had squatted in Mason Valley and this in itself was enough to contribute to of surliness and frustration. Indeed, if man's homeland were being invaded, his food source taken by strangers, and if he should resist, his resistance to domination could cause him to "strike out at the intruders" in such a way as to appear to the whites as being somewhat treacherous.

Somehow the literature describing Tavibo as an athlete and hunter uses analogies more animalish and brutish than human. (The ability to run down a deer may be the envy of many a hunter and Olympic athlete.) Regardless of the cause of his surliness and treachery, Tavibo appeared to be sufficiently caught-up in the teachings of the Ghost Dance Religion that he took his son to hear the teachings of the Prophet Wodziwob.

> *His son, Wovoka, was born in the 1850's. By the time*
> *Wodziwob conducted his first ceremonies in the late*
> *1860's, Wovoka was old enough to journey with his*
> *father to the reservation and, at least, observe what was*
> *happening. (p. 47, Johnson, 1975)*

History is silent as to the impression that Wodziwob's message made on the youthful Wovoka; nevertheless, we do know that the Ghost Dance Religion of 1890 closely paralleled the teachings of Wodziwob in 1870. Thus it can only be concluded that the impressions of Wodziwob's teachings were extensive.

After the death of Tavibo, other influences of equal or greater impact came into the life of Wovoka. After the death of his father, Wovoka went to live with David Wilson, a white rancher in Mason Valley. Robert Utley states that Wovoka was adopted into the Wilson family and was given the name of Jack Wilson -- a name by which he would be known by whites through the Mason Valley region.   It is not totally clear as to whether or not the "adoption" was a "legal" adoption or a matter of Wovoka's becoming a foster child in a very concerned white-Christian home.

> *...Wovoka came under Christian influences. The Wilsons*
> *read aloud the family Bible, and Wovoka learned about*
> *the white man's God and about his son, Jesus. He learned*
> *that Jesus was a great medicine man who could heal*
> *the sick and control the elements, and he noted how the*
> *whites had killed Jesus by nailing him to a cross. These*
> *stories deeply marked the youthful mind of the future*
> *prophet. (p. 64, Utley, 1963)*

It was in the Wilson home that Wovoka came under the impress of strict Presbyterian teachings. Here Wovoka learned about the crucifixion and resurrection of Christ and of his prophesied return to earth. (p. 60, McKern, 1970) The Wilsons read aloud the family Bible, and here he learned of the life, ministry and resurrection of Jesus.

83

Robert Utley states that:

> *By 1890 Mormon families had spread out in all directions*
> *from the Great Salt Lake Valley, and many had settled*
> *in Nevada. In the theology of the Church of Jesus Christ*
> *of Latter Day Saints, Indians occupied a place of special*
> *significance, and the Mormons took special interest in*
> *them. Wovoka was exposed to Mormon teachings but*
> *rejected them. Nevertheless, they were almost certainly*
> *among the factors that shaped his mind. (Underscore*
> *added) (pp. 64-65, Utley, 1963)*

The statement made by Robert Utley that Wovoka had been exposed to Mormon teachings is vital to any research effort that would seek to establish connections between the Endowment Robe and the Ghost Shirt; however, the simple statement without documentation contributes only speculation to a body of factual knowledge. Utley does not cite evidence to demonstrate a positive link between Wovoka and Mormon-Christianity (i.e., names and dates of visitation by Mormon Elders). Supporting evidence that Wovoka "rejected" Mormon teachings is equally difficult to establish conclusively.

In an attempt to establish the Wovoka-Mormon connection, this writer received a letter from the Office of the Church History Department (Church of Jesus Christ of Latter Day Saints, Mormon) which stated that the records of the Church do not show that Jack Wilson (Wovoka), circa 1880-90, was accepted into the fellowship of the Mormon Church.[3]

In an interview with a venerable woman, Mrs. Mary Wilson, in the Walker River Paiute Hospital, in June of 1984, Wilson told the writer that, indeed, Wovoka was not a member of the Mormon Church, but that his daughter was.

Yet another sect of Christianity exerted influence on Wovoka's mind; this one taking place in the hop fields of California, Oregon and Washington.

> *On Puget Sound he [Wovoka] learned of the Shaker*
> *religion, which since about 1880 had swept the tribes of*
> *the region. This religion reflected the influence to which*
> *its founder ...John Slocum, had been subjected. It was a*
> *strange combination of Catholic pageantry, Presbyterian*
> *austerity, and pagan witchcraft. Significantly, trances*
> *formed an important part of its ceremonies. Despite*
> *the efforts of the agents to suppress it, the Shaker*
> *religion held powerful sway over the tribes of the Pacific*
> *Northwest. Wovoka learned the doctrine, participated in*
> *some of its rituals, and observed its regenerating effect*
> *upon converts. (p. 65, Utley, 1963)*

---

3   A review of literature supports that Wovoka's stepdaughter Alice Vidovich and grandson Harlyn Vidovich were receptive to the Mormon theology and doctrine.

The Development Of The Messiah Religions

It is out of this cultural backdrop of varied experiences that Wovoka moved into history. His rise from a Paiute sheepherder to "obscure shaman" to Prophet of the Ghost Dance Religion was, as Utley says, "spectacular." "He came with a new religion and with a mandate from God to rescue his people from the darkness that awaited them." (p. 64, Utley, 1963)

Historically, some observers of the Indian religious revival movement have been tempted to establish the origin of all movements, such as the Shaker Religion and the Ghost Dance, in the life and personality of a single person rather than viewing revivalism as a collective experience whose form and function was the work and thought of several individuals representing numerous geographic locations. The attempt to unravel the many lines that have connected Indian Revivalism in the West was ably undertaken by Leslie Spier in 1935 (The Prophet Dance of the Northwest). In his work, Spier seeks to establish the Ghost Dance Religion as having arisen out of the Shaker Religion and not as a separate and distinct movement.[4] This position is certainly worthy of considerable attention and is likely to be more correct than incorrect; however, it may well be that each movement, i.e., Shaker Religion, Ghost Dance of the Paiute, Ghost Dance of the Pawnee, Sioux, and Cheyenne needs to be seen as an important segment of the vastly larger panorama of an Indian revival movement that was begun when the first whites entered the Basin and Inter-Mountain west.

The Ghost Dance circle may well have begun in the psychic unconsciousness of the Indian People when the first beaver felt the pain of a cold, steel trap since the beaver, like the Indian, was caught in the deadly jaws of white expansion and Manifest Destiny. With the sinking of mine shafts, denuding of forests and the pollution of rivers, streams and lakes, the Revival Movement intensified; and the intensity of the desire to return to former ways was expressed by the indigenous people as they saw their cultural environment so radically changed. Perhaps, without too great a danger of being oversimplistic, it may well be said that the Ghost Dance began when the vanguard of European colonialism first set foot on the Atlantic seaboard. The Revival Movement intensified as the inexorable tide of land and gold hungry pioneers pushed increasingly and unceasingly westward. Perhaps it was that only the form of the Revival Movement varied as whites encountered Indian people at Fallen Timbers, in the Black Hawk War, or on the Pine Ridge Reservation.

It is vastly more significant to grasp the meaning of the Revival Movement as a longing of many Indian People to return to the traditional ways, rather than to see it as an expression of regional or tribal in origin. Where or

---

4   To avoid much of the confusion that results in an attempt to establish a "first cause," Leslie Spier sought to isolate and identify those characteristics of the revival movement that was unique to the Northwest and in so doing applied the name "Prophet Dance" for it.

when the Revival Movement began, is of less significance than what the Revival Movement taught or what was the impact that the teachings had on the cultural life and pattern of living on Indian and whites alike.

Apart from the generalization that can be made regarding the regional expressions of the Ghost Dance, it is, nevertheless, important to attempt to follow the multiple trails of the Indian Revival Movement to some place, to some event in the time and life of the People. In addressing the origins of the Ghost Dance the Leslie Spier work purposes that the:

> *...ultimate origin of the two Ghost Dance movements was not with the Paviotso but in the Northwest among the tribes of the interior plateau area. It can be shown that among these peoples there was an old belief in the impending destruction and renewal of the world, when the dead would return, in conjunction with which there was a dance based on supposed imitation of the dances of the dead, and a conviction that intense preoccupation with the dance would hasten the happy day. ...This Northwestern cult agrees precisely with the case of the Ghost Dance religion among the Paviotso, and the circumstances of its appearance among the latter parallel those of earlier date in the Northwest. (p. 5, Spier, 1935)*

> *It is possible to show that the Northwestern cult was not only the source of the two Ghost Dance movements, but also of the Smohalla cult of eastern Washington-Oregon and its modern form, the Pompom or Feather Religion, and perhaps of the pseudo-Christian sect of Shakers now flourishing in adjacent coastal territory. (p. 5, Spier, 1935)*

> *The term Ghost Dance, by which the movement was known to the whites, was given the name by the Sioux. The Paiutes themselves called it Nanigukwa (Dance in a Circle), the Shoshone termed it Tana Rayun (Everybody Dragging),to the Comanches it was A Panekara (The Fathers Dance), and to the Kiowas it was Manposo ti guan (Dance with the Clasped Hands). Because it was concerned with the return of the spirits from the world of the dead, the Sioux called it Wana ghi wa chipi (Spirit Dance or Ghost Dance), and since the dramatic and powerful Sioux was the prototype of the Western Indian in the popular mind (and still is), this was the name by which it seized the public fancy. (p. 166, Porter, 1964)*

Leslie Spier observes that the Prophet Dance of the Northwest and the Ghost Dance were "identical in doctrine" and "much alike"   86 in ritual. Spier suggested that a "new form" of the Prophet-Ghost Dance was in evidence as late as 1934. James Mooney, on the other hand, portrayed the Ghost Dance of 1890 as a phenomenon separate and distinct from all other revivalist movements, including the Ghost Dance of 1870. It was Mooney's feeling that the spread of the 1890 Ghost Dance Religion throughout the plains was a wholly new development generated by the longings of a new set of people looking to a "Messiah" for a new sign of deliverance. (p. 5-7, Spier, 1935)

> *By the latter quarter of the 19th century all the tribes had undergone some exposure to the Christian religion, and many of them related Wovoka to the Christ of whom they had heard. The white man had not, in their eyes, followed the teachings of the Bible; this time Christ had returned as an Indian to His chosen children. So Wovoka became to scores of thousands the true Son of God, despite the fact that he, himself, stated many times that he was merely a prophet of divine revelation who had talked with God and who had returned with a message of peace and promise. (p. 166, Porter, 1964)*

It was Spier's opinion that the belief in the tenets of the Prophet Dance were antecedent to the arrival of Christian missionaries, and that, in fact, it had been the acceptance of the Indian People to the teachings and doctrine of the Indian Revivalist that had opened the way for the later Christian exposure. (p. 30, Spier, 1934)

> *It is well to reiterate at this juncture that the Prophet Dance complex is old, clearly anterior to 1870 when the first Ghost Dance impulse spread north and west from the Paviotso. There is ample evidence both from native and documentary sources that its elements were present at least as far back as the opening of the nineteenth century. (p. 13, Spier, 1934)*

> *At the period of...second and third decades of the last century, Christianity had not yet reached this quarter. This is evidenced by the complete silence of the whole group of explorers and traders who traversed the country at the time: Lewis and Clark, the Astoria party, Thompson, Henry, Ogden, and others. Yet, when their successors of the early thirties arrived in the middle Columbia-Snake area they discovered elements of Christian ritual already present among these inaccessible Indians. The significant fact for our purpose is, however, that they found these Christian elements integrated with pagan rites which were none other than those of the Prophet Dance Cult. (pp. 19-20, Spier, 1934)*

87

It is probably very correct that the riddle of the origin of the Ghost Dance-Prophet Cult will never be totally accepted or understood; social scientists and researchers of ethnology simply were not present in frontier America in sufficient numbers to either record or appreciate the cultural mindset of the Native American People. Those few observers with a scientific background were, more often as not, engaged in the study of the climate, soil, rainfall, flora and fauna of this remarkable new land.

The following quote is taken from Bernard De Voto, <u>The Year of Decision: 1846,</u> and describes graphically the attitude of the majority of whites who traversed the Basin Region. Totally lacking in this observation is any degree of compassion, let alone any degree of understanding of other peoples, places or times.

> *And here, ...you encountered the Diggers, their half-gram brains vibrating with the remembered murders of hundreds of kinsmen and with desire for oxen and other plunder.*

> *The term "Digger" is an epitaph, not a classification. It was properly applied to Indians who, being unskillful hunters or residing in a country where game was scarce, lived on roots. But it came to mean certain degenerate bands of various tribes who can be exactly described as the technological unemployed. Unable to stand competition with hardier Indians, they had been pushed into the deserts and, living there on the subsistence level, had lost their culture. Many of them were physically decadent. The weapons of all were crude. Mostly they lived in caves or brush huts. Some had lost the use of fire. Some "Diggers" were Bannack or Shoshoni in origin; those in the Great Salt Lake Valley were Paiute and Gosiute; fragments of other neighboring tribes also degenerated, and the Indians who harassed the Donners probably belonged to the Kuyuidika band of the Paviotso. But the whites who used the term meant no particular tribe; they meant only that they hated skulking, theft, and malicious mischief. From Ewing Young and Joseph Walker on, they had massacred Diggers idly, for fun, or in punishment for theft. The Diggers remembered.. .If they had not, they might have succored the Donners in the snow. (p. 347, DeVoto, 1942)*

The whites saw them as sulking "Diggers." Jedediah Smith expressed the opinion (1827) that the Diggers were "the most miserable objects in creation."

> *Mark Twain, riding the overland stage west of Great Salt Lake in 1861, reported coming*

*across "the wretchedest type of mankind I have ever
seen up to this writing." He went on to describe the
Gosiute, one of those groups commonly called Diggers,
who "produce nothing at all, and have no villages,
and no gatherings together into strictly defined tribal
communities - a people whose only shelter is a rag cast
on a bush to keep off a portion of the snow, and yet who
inhabit one of the most rocky, wintry, repulsive wastes
that our country or any other can exhibit. The Bushmen
and our Goshoots are manifestly descended from the self-
same gorilla, or kangaroo, or Norway rat, whichever
animal-Adam the Darwinians trace them to." (p. 16,
Farb, 1968)*

"To the whites, here were people who lived at the lowliest state of humankind, no better than the apes." (p. 17, Farb, 1968); however, to the Indian
prophet of the day, these were the children of the Great Spirit and this was a...
time of despair, and in such a time new religions are born." (p. 332, Brown and
Schmitt, 1968)

*These were Wovoka's people. They had looked for years
to his father Tavibo to interpret the world of the spirits
to them. The son had the gift of the Dreamer, and he had
been instructed in the old, old rites by his father. He was
a natural heir to the role of medicine man, dreamer,
visionary, and teller of prophecy. His great prophecy
would be twisted beyond all recognition by the other and
fiercer tribes of the plains to a point where it is doubtful
that Wovoka could identify the germ of the movement
as his own. But his it was, and none other. (pp. 162-163,
Porter, 1964)*

Many Indian delegates who journeyed to Nevada in 1890-92 heard Wovoka
talk of the Son of God, the Messiah, and heard Wovoka say that the Messiah
would return to save his Indian Children.

Stanley Vestal observes that the Ghost Dance had at its center, the
doctrine of the imminent return of the Messiah. The advent of the return, he
asserts, was rooted in Christianity, since the "return" of the Messiah had a pre-
supposition that the Messiah had, indeed, visited the earth at some previous
age. The promise of Quetzalcoatl to return had captured and fired the imagination of the Mayan centuries before the Ghost Dance circles formed in Nevada
or on the Pine Ridge Reservation.

*Thus, overnight, Sitting Bull's band became
Christianized. Of course the missionaries of long
established sects would not admit that the
Ghost Dance was a Christian church. But*

their claim is absurd. For you cannot believe in the
Second Coming of Christ unless you believe in the First.
The Ghost Dance was entirely Christian - except for the
difference in ritual. However, it taught non-resistance
and brotherly love in ways that had far more significance
for Indians than any the missions could offer. No wonder
the missionaries became alarmed; they were no longer
sure of their converts. (p. 272, Vestal, 1934)

Many Indian delegates who journeyed to Nevada in 1890 heard Wovoka talk of the Son of God, the Messiah, and heard Wovoka say that the Messiah would return to save his Indian Children. James Mooney talked with Wovoka in 1892 and concluded that Wovoka did not claim to be the Son of God.

But as the delegates of 1889-90 universally conceived
him as the Messiah, and they all told of the scars on his
hands and feet, I have chosen to use the term Messiah
freely. It is possible that by 1891, when Mooney went
west, Wovoka had modified his story from that of 1890.
The important point, however, is that whether Wovoka
actually represented himself as the Messiah or merely as
a prophet, the delegates believed he was the Messiah. (p.
71, Utley, 1963)

By the time of European infusion into the New World, it was estimated that there were at least 200 mutually unintelligible languages among the native peoples north of Mexico, at least another 350 in Mexico and Central America, and considerably more than 1,000 in the Caribbean and South America." (p. 12, Josephy, 1968) By the time of the Indian Wars, scores of these mutually unintelligible languages were still spoken on the Plains, Great Basin, and Pacific Seaboard. Little wonder, then, that considerable confusion resulted from the telling and retelling of the vision experience of Wovoka.

Oral history is a most valid expression of the history of a people; however, the details of the story often changed, or were lost, in the process of translation from one language to another. A simple illustration from English language may suffice. The word "lead" must certainly cause non-English speaking persons considerable difficulty in their effort to communicate. Standing alone the word can be either a verb or a noun. It can refer to an action, such as "to lead the horse," or it can refer to a metal sinker often used at the end of a fishing line. Because of this multiplicity of languages spoken among Peoples of North America, and in order to communicate accurately, the Native American People developed and used a "lingua franca" with the Plains sign language. Even then, it is reasonable to assume, misunderstandings arose.

At its best, language itself is an imperfect tool of communication. The ancient Hebrews recognized the difficulty of their own language as they attempted to communicate fully their hope and dream of the "deliverer" who was to carry them from danger and whose influence would recreate their heaven on earth. Consider the following use of the words "Christ" and "Messiah."

> *Actually two riddles need to be considered. Christianity arose first among Jews living in Palestine. Belief in the coming of a savior called a messiah - a god who would look like a man - was an important feature of Judaism at the time of Christ. The earliest followers of Jesus, almost all of who were Jewish, believed that Jesus was this savior. ("Christ" is derived from drystos₁ which was the way Jews referred to their hoped for savior when speaking Greek.) (p. 134, Harris, 1978)*

> *David, the founder of the first and largest Jewish empire, claimed to be in divine partnership with the Jewish God, Jahweh. The people called David messiah (Hebrew: mashia), a term which they also applied to priests, shields, David's predecessor Saul, and David's son Solomon. So messiah probably meant any person or thing possessing great holiness and sacred power. David was also called the Anointed One - the one who, by collaboration with Jahweh, was entitled to rule over Jahweh's earthly domains. (p. 134, Harris, 1978)*

Alexander Lesser reinforces the belief that Wovoka did in fact proclaim to be the Prophet of the Ghost Dance, but that he did not assert to be the "Messiah."

> *...the people of the various Nevada reservations made their own interpretations of Wovoka's purpose and doctrine; they spread the word that Christ himself had come... Wovoka never claimed to be the Son of God; he sincerely believed he was a prophet with divine revelation to impart. (p. 54, Lasser, 1933)*

> *Just as the words of eternal life from a man named Christ led to the establishment of scores of divergent beliefs, so the words of eternal life from a man named Wovoka were subject to many interpretations. As the pilgrims carried the words back to their own people, each tribe saw the movement in a different light and worked the teachings of their messiah into their own lore. The facets into which the basic belief broke up were multitudinous, but most of them revolved around one central thought - time was coming when the whole Indian race, living and dead, would be brought together upon an earth which had grown new again. There would be no disease, no want, and no death, and the regenerated earth would provide, out of her great bounty, for the needs of the Indians. (pp. 165-166, Porter, 1964)*

Robert F. Spencer expresses the belief that Wovoka did not attempt to spread his teachings broadly; however, the doctrine was spread rapidly by his followers among the Paiutes. Soon, Spencer records "...emissaries began to come from faraway Plains tribes to learn of this teaching." (p. 510, Spencer, 1977) The speed with which the word of the new Prophet and his religion was shared throughout the Pacific region, the Basin, the Southwest, the Great Plains and into Oklahoma Territory was, indeed, spectacular.

> *Broken Arm, Elk Horn, and Kicks Back left their*
> *comrades at Walker Lake and visited some tribes in*
> *the Pacific Northwest. The rest of the apostles turned*
> *homeward, the Sioux reaching their agencies in March of*
> *1890. At Pine Ridge, Rosebud, and Cheyenne River they*
> *told the wonderful story. The Messiah had indeed come*
> *to earth to save his Indian children. He had scars on his*
> *hands and feet, evidence of treatment many centuries*
> *ago by the white men. There was other proof of divinity*
> *.... (p. 71, Utley, 1963)*

The account recorded in Robert Utley's work does not refer to any of the physical features of the purported Messiah other than the reference to the wounds and scars in hands and feet. Paul Bailey, in his work, <u>Wovoka, The Indian Messiah,</u> wrote that the Messiah "was an Indian and that he spoke as an Indian." (p. 119, Bailey, 1957) The inference of Bailey is that Wovoka "passed himself off" as the Messiah and that, furthermore, he did little to discourage the stories that he as Prophet of the Ghost Dance, was the Messiah and the Christ.[5]

No historical reference is cited to demonstrate that, for example, Wovoka appeared before emissaries of the Basin or Plains tribes either wearing or attempting to grow a beard. A beard among the Paiute, or for that matter, the majority of North American People, would be extremely rare. The confusion as to the story of the Christ-Messiah and the Ghost Dance Prophet is further compounded by the stories that some delegates told to their people after having visited Wovoka, i.e., that they had seen a "Christ" figure. It can be speculated that this confusion may be, indeed, attributed to misunderstandings that result from translations from one language to another. Given the historical setting of 1890 and the rapid spread of the Ghost Dance Doctrine, it is highly likely and reasonably certain that the story of the return of the Messiah would have been uncertain and confused.

Confusion and uncertainty was by no means restricted to the Indian communities. Because of the Mormon Millenialists' belief in the immediate return of Christ to the Americas, a belief reinforced by the purported prophecy of Joseph Smith that the Messiah would return in Joseph's 85th year (1890), some Saints, too, anxiously waited to see and experience the Messiah's pres-

---

5   It should be observed that in Bailey's work documented - footnoted references are extremely rare. The work of Bailey is fictionalized but does not contribute greatly to documented information.

ence in human form. The Mormon President, Willard Woodruff, told his people that the Christ of the New Testament had not returned in 1890, but that, perhaps, one of the Three Nephites had.[6] This statement probably did much to lay at rest the concerns of some Saints after 1890, but those hearing the story of the return of the Messiah to the Indian People in 1890 were electrified by the news. There is no evidence, however, that the thought occurred to the Mormon community that the returned Messiah would be anything other than Anglo-Saxon, and more than likely, dressed in the then contemporary Mormon clothing.

It is of importance to note that some Indian observers of the Ghost Dance were equally convinced that the Messiah of whom Wovoka spoke was bearded, and had a fair countenance. Such was the vision experience of Little Horse as interpreted by Weasel.

> *Two holy eagles transported me to the Happy Hunting Grounds. They showed me the Great Messiah there, and as I looked upon his fair countenance I wept, for there were nail-prints in his hands and feet where the cruel whites had once fastened him to a large cross. There was a small wound in his side also, but he kept himself covered with a beautiful mantle of feathers that only could be seen when he shifted his blanket. He insisted that we continue the dance, and promised me that no whites should enter his city nor partake of the good things he had prepared for the Indians. The earth, he said, was now worn out and it should be repeopled.*

> *He had a long beard and long hair and was the most handsome man I have ever looked upon. (p. 332, Jan. 1891, The Illustrated American, "The Ghost Dance in the West")*

The preponderance of studies hold to the belief that "Wovoka never claimed to be the Son of God; he sincerely believed he was prophet with divine revelation to impart." (p. 54, Lesser, 1933)

> *Everywhere now [by 1890] the Indians of the West were locked within the reservation. The great chiefs were shorn of their power. Many of the mighty warriors were dead. Those who lived spent their days in idleness.*

---

6   The Three Nephites were personalities that emerge from the pages of the Book of Mormon and represent men of such extraordinary righteousness that they were given the choice of "not accepting the taste of death" but were translated from human to spirit forms. It was, according to present day Mormon belief, the spiritual manifestation of the Nephites that appeared among the Indian People in 1890.

> *The buffalo and the antelope had vanished; the old*
> *ceremonies of the tribes had become rituals without*
> *meaning. The Great White Father doled out food and*
> *clothing through his agents, and it was not necessary*
> *for one to think of the changes of the seasons, the moons*
> *of the snow and cold, the moons of greening grass, the*
> *moons when the buffalo bulls are fat, the moons of the*
> *ripening chokecherries and the falling leaves. (p. 331,*
> *Schmitt and Brown, 1948)*

This was a time of despair, a time in which new leaders of religion appeared from among the People to carry them to a new and promised land. Word of the Prophets was carried across the Basin and Plains as quickly and dramatically as the chill of an Arctic wind. It was the message of deliverance that the People heard, and their hearts were warmed by the tradition of their religion that said that the Great Spirit would be ever mindful of His children, the Indian people.

> *The Sioux speak of a son of the Creator known for many*
> *ages. Whether this is actually a Christian addition is not*
> *clear, but the famous Dakota Sioux myth of the coming*
> *of the White buffalo Woman to protect the nation and*
> *bestow the Sacred Pipe indicates a definite belief in*
> *the Supreme Being who sends messengers to do His*
> *bidding. Harley Burr Alexander writes of the myths of*
> *the southwest, which tell of the many personified powers*
> *present at the creation dawn - like the Old Testament*
> *personifications of Wisdom, "there at the making of the*
> *world." (p. 34, Starkloff, 1974)*

In the spring of 1890 the Sioux began dancing the Ghost Dance at the Pine Ridge Reservation in South Dakota. "By June they were wearing ghost shirts made of cotton cloth painted blue around the necks, with bright colored thunder birds, bows and arrows, suns, moons, and stars emblazoned upon them." (p. 333, Schmitt and Brown, 1948)

1890 was to be an eventful time for Mormon Millennialists and Indians alike. Both peoples anxiously awaited the return of the Messiah. The cultural mindset of the Mormon community was such that it was perfectly understandable that the Messiah would return and show himself to the Indians since they were descendants of the Jews and were the "Chosen" people.

The Mormon Millenialists anxiously directed their attention to the religious activities of the Indians in an effort to determine if the Ghost Dance Religion was really an expression of the Indian People having received the "fullness of the gospel," and as a sign of the imminent return of the Messiah. These events were believed by some to begin with the appearance of spirit beings such as the Three Nephites.

How or to what extent the Mormon belief in the appearance of spirit beings, such as the Three Nephites, would influence "stories" of visitation to arise among Indian communities is not clear; however, James Mooney wrote:

> *From oral information of Professor A. H. Thompson,*
> *of the United States Geological Survey, I learned some*
> *particulars of the advent of the new doctrine among*
> *the Paiute of southwestern Utah. While his party was*
> *engaged in that section in the spring of 1875, a great*
> *excitement was caused among the Indians, by the*
> *report that two mysterious beings with white skins...*
> *had appeared among the Paiute far to the west and*
> *announced a speedy resurrection of all the dead Indians,*
> *the restoration of game, the return of the old-time*
> *primitive life. Under the new order of things, moreover,*
> *both races alike were to be white. A number of Indians*
> *from Utah went over into Nevada, where they met others*
> *who claimed to have seen these mysterious visitors*
> *farther in the West. On their return to Utah, they brought*
> *back with them the ceremonial of the new belief, the chief*
> *part of the ritual being a dance performed at night in*
> *a circle with no fire in the center - very much as in the*
> *modern Ghost Dance. (p. 703, Mooney, 1982)*

The Ghost Dance doctrine reflects the general feeling that in promising to the Indian people, a new re-generated world, a recovery of their culture and religion, the return of the dead and a new age of fulfillment for the People, that Wovoka had "...given these people a better religion than they had before..." (p. 783, Mooney, 1892) Mooney further expressed the belief that if the Indian People could give practical application to the things that Wovoka taught that they would, as a natural consequence, live in better accord with their white neighbors. The Ghost dance was, according to Mooney, a step to their "...final Christianization." (p. 783, Mooney, see also p. 69, Utley, 1963) "The message they heard was truly revolutionary. Deeply rooted in Christianity..." (p 68, Utley, 1963) The message:

> *...demanded attitudes and practices leading inevitably*
> *to progress in civilization, and as a stimulus to such*
> *progress it was worth a thousand reform policies devised*
> *in New England drawing rooms. This truth, however,*
> *escaped the architects of Indian policy, who regarded*
> *the Ghost Dance Religion as a monster of paganism that*
> *would stamp out the progress of a decade. (p. 68, Utley,*
> *1963)*

Mormon Trail Marker, Cemetery in Background
Mt. Pisgah, Iowa
Photo by Jon Barney Sept. 2009

CHAPTER V

The Paiute Restoration: Origins And Concepts

If a people loses or forgets the heritage and traditions of its past, then the future may often appear cloudy and uncertain. It was this preoccupation of knowing the future that caused many Native American People to turn to the Sun Dance, and later to the Ghost Dance to find the solution to the everyday problems that beset them. The Revival Movements came at the climax period of white intrusion -- an intrusion that spelled the end of the way of life that the People had known. Change can often be frightening, especially as it destroys the values, way of life, and religion of a people, and when it fails to give to them a reasonable substitute for those things that were once held to be most valuable and worthwhile. The Ghost Dance Revival sought to restore the People to a former condition of living in harmony with nature, with others and with the Great Spirit.

The catalyst of change had formed with the arrival of the first white fur trappers. The white ways were neither understood nor wanted. The earth became tired and weary, and the recovery of the Old Way seemed to offer the only reasonable solution to the People. But recovery did not come. The past was too distant to recover and the white material culture was too difficult to resist with bows, arrows and slings.

What was it that the People desired to recover that would be more powerful than the white man's gun, disease, lust for gold, iron horse, cattle and wood frame houses? The answer: Harmony and balance between man, nature, and the Great Spirit. The only way to lasting peace was the recovery of the past and a rejuvenated earth. So the People looked to their past.

The People: Origins In The Earth

The Dawn Myth of any people is often shrouded in the primordial mist from which life itself has sprung. The Judeo-Christian Dawn Myth says: "In the beginning God created the heaven and the earth," and "The earth was without form and was void." In time God moved to create the earth and divided it into the sea and the dry land. He made all life -- including man, having formed the parents of the human race from the elements of the earth -- our Mother Earth.

The Dawn Myth of the People was not altogether unlike that of the Old Testament writers. It too, lacked the specificity of detail to make it a scientific treatise and in so doing made it, nearly, an article of faith. So it had once been with the People, the Numa (or as they are known today, the Northern Paiute). The Great Spirit had breathed upon the face of the land and waters and brought life to earth. It was the same breath of life that He blew into the nostrils of the first People. The Father of the People, Numa na ah, came from the south. The Mother of the People, Ibidsii, followed closely behind. For those wise enough to see, the huge footprints of Numa na ah can still be seen in the area in and about Agai Pah. Finally Father and Mother came to live in a cave in the mountains near Carson Sink, to the land east of the Toi Ticcutta. (p. 15, Johnson, 1975)

In a time long before the arrival of the white intruders, many ages before even the People, the entire surface of the earth was covered by water. Quite suddenly a mountain began to appear above the surface of the water. This sacred mountain was called Kurangwa (Mt. Grant) and heralded its arrival by spewing fire and ash from its peak.

Cold north winds began to blow across the water with such force that they threatened to put out the fire and thus return the earth to cold. Fortunately for the People, the sagehen flew to the sacred mountain and held back the wind and waves with her wings. In her concern to protect the fire she nestled so close that her feathers were singed, and even today the feathers of the sagehens breasts are still black from the fire of Kurangwa. Diligently and bravely she fanned the water back as Kurangwa lifted itself high above the reach of the great water that was left behind. The water that was left was called Agai Pah (Trout Lake) or Walker Lake as it is known today.

It was Rabbit that received the gift of fire from the sacred mountain, thus he gave to the People before Kurangwa began his long slumber. The rabbit, like the sagehen, is sacred to the People. (p. 15, Johnson, 1975)

So it was that the People had been given the elements necessary for life -- fire, water, earth. In this setting the Father, Numa na ah, taught his two sons the art of hunting. He demonstrated the best way for them to construct nets, bows and arrows for hunting. Numa na ah instructed them in the ways of the deer, the antelope, the mountain sheep. He showed them where they lived and what foods they ate. Ibidsii, too, was a great teacher for she taught her two daughters which plants to eat, which to use for medicine and how to find them in the earth. She showed her daughters how to use the digging stick and how to construct willow, tule and river grass houses.

As the children of the Father and Mother grew to maturity, they began to quarrel among themselves. The Father wanted everyone to live in peace, and in order to stop the quarrels, he sent two of the children to the north where they settled in an area today that is part of Idaho. These people are known today as Koo-tsoo Ticcutta (buffalo eaters) or Bannocks. The second set of descendants settled in Agai pah, and are known today as the A ai Ticcutta (trout eaters ?). Agai Pah is known today as Walker Lake.

When the waters receded, the People moved down from the mountain and named the plants and animals and gave to other People names that represented the places where they lived and the 98 food they ate. Here they met the <u>Pugwi</u> <u>Ticcutta</u> (Fish Eaters), <u>Toi</u> <u>Ticcutta</u> (Tule Eaters) to the north, the <u>Tubusi</u> <u>Ticcutta</u> (Grass Bulb Eaters) to the west, and <u>Cozabee</u> <u>Ticutta</u> (Fly Larvae Eaters) who lived to the south around the Mono Lake region. (p. 7, Johnson, 1975)

Generally the Paiute People lived in units of the extended family. While there was a division of labor by sex and age, there were, nevertheless, several activities that both men and women shared cooperatively. Among these was the rather enjoyable task of fishing and the very necessary work of constructing grass houses or temporary shelter of brush or tree branches. The children and grandparents performed tasks of gathering seeds, pine nuts, firewood and some less demanding aspects of hunting and fishing.

Characteristic of a hunting-gathering people is their uncanny knowledge of their environment and the rhythmic design for living that keeps them continuously in touch with the seasons of ripening of nuts and berries and the migration of fish and fowl. These were non-material people, intent upon merely the necessity of providing sufficient food, clothing and shelter to see them through to a new harvest. They had no desire to possess or accumulate large quantities of food or weapons. These are the overt choices that a people seek to make and are made in light of their own perceptions of what is permanent and lasting in life. The decision to accumulate nothing, to build no great cities or cathedrals is a cultural choice and is in no way related to the intelligence, resourcefulness, or ambitions of a people. It is a cultural awareness of what is and what is not important and lasting to a people. By the standards of Manifest Destiny, these were people that lived at the lowest scale of human existence. To the Paiute, the whites desire for gold or preference for cattle made little or no sense whatsoever. It is in the perception of culture that conflict arises between persons and nations.

The <u>Agai</u> <u>Ticcutta</u> were on good terms with each of the other tribes and clans. Often as not, the People shared hunting, fishing and gathering areas. Great skill and dexterity were required of the sexes as they carried out their tasks. Wovoka's father was described in earlier references as "sulky" and "treacherous," and acknowledged as evidence of his kinship to lesser animals was his ability to "run down deer." Actually, this skill was shared by many hunters in the Basin and reflects an unusual athletic ability rather than a trait somewhat less than human. What Olympic hopeful has not wished for such speed and endurance. It is of such drive and determination that athletes the world over seek to achieve. Among the Paiute People, hunting was generally an exclusive responsibility of men, especially true of the large game, the making of hunting implements (bows, arrows, nets, weirs) and the making of rabbit-skin blankets (as many as 50 skins could be used in the making of a blanket). Women were primarily responsible for seed gathering, preparing of food, the weaving of baskets and making clothing.

Each season, in its time and in its own rhythm, yielded its abundance for the welfare of the people. There were periods of   99 drought and hardships as well, but it was usually true that sufficient nourishment could be found until the next chain in the food link could ripen. It was only after the whites came that the severe effects of drought could be felt, since the wild rice grass was gone, water diverted by irrigation, and entire stands of Pinon Pine were destroyed. There was simply no part of the physical environment or ecological balance that was left untouched by the white advance into the Basin. It was the return to ecological balance that the Ghost Dance Prophets sought for their people. They had once been able to rely with reasonable surety on the ripening of plants and the migration of fish and fowl. Now all that had changed.

The Paiute knew that when the winter snows began to melt new plants would soon appear along the streams and lakes. The tender new growth yielded many new foods for the diet. Then, too, migratory birds returned on their way to the north country. The Paiute knew from experience and from observation just when it was that the birds would return, and they listened anxiously to hear their call. Some species of waterfowl nested in the lakes on the eastern fringe of the Sierra Nevada Mountains. The Paiute constructed baskets and boats of tule in which the eggs of birds were collected and transported from shore to shore. An intricate system of construction of nets allowed the People to catch quantities of ducks and mudhens. The usual preparation of the birds was to roast them in the coals of the fire or to bake them in an earth-pit oven.

As the season of spring continued its advance, the People moved down the streams and into the desert floor where a variety of seeds were collected, boiled and eaten. The cultural role during this time of the year provided that the men hunt and the women set about gathering squaw-cabbage leaves, seeds and edible roots. The gathering tools were relatively simple and light weight. The choice of implements and baskets was necessitated by the highly mobile nature of a people moving across large expanses of land in order to collect ample quantities of food. The tools of hunting included a rich assortment of bows, arrows, spears, snares, baits, pitfalls, deadfalls, nets, and blinds. Among the more ingenious tools was the decoy. The hunters used a variety of bark to construct an outline of a bird. The web construction was then covered with the feathers of the birds being hunted. Great attention was given to the exactness of scale and likeness -- attention that was characterized by a highly intelligent and resourceful people. (p. 9, Johnson, 1975)

In April and May festivals occurred that centered around the abundance of food that resulted from the spring run of trout. People gathered from many tribes and clans to fish at the mouth of the Agai Hoop (Trout River). Here a variety of methods for catching the fish was employed: platforms, weirs, harpoons, not the least of which included hooks made of greasewood or bone that were strung on lines of hemp. The feast that followed the "fish run" was an annual social event that included dancing and games.

In June many of the desert plants and berries would ripen -- mustard seeds and metzelia plants. The men hunted birds and

100

ground squirrels. In July it was the season of the harvesting of the rice grass (wai). When the mudhens began to molt and were no longer able to fly, they too provided food for the people. The lakes, it is said, were the nesting place of "thousands, perhaps millions of birds..." (p. 10, Johnson, 1975) The buckberries ripened in August. This fruit, when dried served as a source of winter food and when mixed with pine nuts and dried meat constituted a rich source of vitamins and protein.

Pine nuts were a basic staple of the food chain. The harvest of the fruit of the Pinon Pine took place in early fall and was accompanied by five days of, celebration and ceremony. Prayers were offered for the harvest -- prayers not only for thanksgiving but abundance of the crop as well. It was not unusual for a mature tree to yield up to 200 pounds of protein rich food; however, the Pinon Pine was a very sensitive tree and is endowed by nature with unusual properties that protected it during times of drought and the' irregularity of frost, snow or rainfall. The pine nut harvest was among the least certain of crops since it did reflect radical climatic changes. As a result, the People would suffer during the winter if the crop was scarce.

In November, the rabbit drives took place. The rabbit hunt was a spectacular event that employed the work of the entire community. Nets were made of cattail, sagebrush, and Indian hemp. Often the nets were 100 feet long with many net sections used to form a circular arrangement into which rabbits were driven. Rabbit meat was roasted for eating or dried for use during the winter months. The hides of the rabbit were used in the construction of capes and blankets. Deer, antelope and mountain sheep were hunted throughout the year. (pp. 10-12, Johnson, 1975)

The list of foods and the enumeration of activities is by no means an effort to establish a final or total listing, but is given as a partial inventory that is intended merely to show the relative abundance of food in the "food chain" and to demonstrate a small sampling of activities and skills possessed by the People that were essential to their survival. The importance of this review is to establish the fact that the Paiute lived and worked in close association with each other and in nearly total harmony with nature in such a way as to allow them to live adequately in their arid environment that they called "home." Both the ecological and social balance changed radically with the arrival of the whites. It was the radical changes imposed upon the environment and the people that contributed in a most significant way to the rise of the Ghost Dance Religion of 1870 and 1890. It is reasonable to conclude that had no whites entered the Basin, the Indian Revival Movement called the Ghost Dance would never have taken place, since the Revival was a response of the Paiute to the radical changes that took place in the physical and social environment -- changes that were the result of white intrusion into the Basin.

Coming Of The Whites 1820-1870

A rather interesting observation of the Spanish period of exploration and colonization in the region along the Pacific seaboard in California was their desire to secure gold and silver and to lay claim to the land in the name of the Spanish throne. In their search for wealth, the Spanish generally held close to the coastal waterways and valley low-lands and knew nothing of the fabulous wealth that lay in the mountains of the Sierra Nevada Range. By 1769, missions had been established along the coast and into the Central Valley; however, virtually nothing was known of the People who lived to the east of the Sierras.

> *In 1776 Escalante's party had touched the southwestern tip of the basin and in 1813 another Spanish party visited the Ute's territory, but present day Nevada was probably not visited by whites while the area was claimed by Spain. (p. 18, Johnson, 1975)*

The first, and perhaps, most dramatic change that took place in the Plateau and Basin Region was the tremendous infusion of "white men's goods" through contact with fur traders. This change, Alvin Josephy says, brought "further degenerations of native cultures ...brought about by missionaries, miners, and settlers." (p. 136, Josephy, 1968) The fur trade had both economic and political consequences, the results of which could never have been fully anticipated, and once realized, were difficult to countermand and overcome. In the Northeast,

> *The new [fur] market stimulated trade with the Indian* tribes, and the natives, in turn, began to war against each other for exclusive rights to barter furs to the Europeans for the goods the whites gave them. It was the start of a pattern of savage rivalry for monopoly trade privileges that spread disastrously, from tribe to tribe, across the continent during the next three hundred years. (p. 298, Josephy, 1968)

In the Basin, the fur industry served as the catalyst for international claim to lands desired by both England and the United States -- land claimed by right of conquest by Spain!

> *Peter Skene Ogden was the first white man to spend a considerable amount of time in the western Great Basin. He was under orders from the British government to trap beaver, and in fact, to attempt to deplete the beaver supply in order that the American/British competition over the area would cease. This policy became known as the "scorched stream policy."*

102

Besides the destruction of the beaver supply in the
territory there were other effects, as well. Hunting by the
trapping parties had depleted the buffalo herds in Idaho
and Utah by the 1830's. The trappers with large herds of
horses overgrazed many of the best camping spots in the
territory. The People in the Great Basin always took care
to leave some of the seeds they were gathering for food so
that the plants would return the following season, but the
trappers' stock devoured everything. (underscore added)
(p. 18, Johnson, 1975)

During the era of the War of 1812, the region from the Great Plains west
to the Pacific Ocean was claimed by three nations -- Spain, Great Britain, and
the United States. An American, Robert Gray, had discovered the mouth of the
Columbia River, and by so doing established claim to the Columbia River Basin
for the United States. The claim was further strengthened by the expedition of
Lewis and Clark in 1804-06, and by the building of a trading post in 1811 by
John Jacob Astor. Interestingly enough, the same area had been claimed by
Great Britain with the basis of their search for title being the voyages of Drake,
Cook, Vancouver, and Broughton, and the overland exploration by Mackenzie.
Spain held the vast interior regions that constituted the Texas Territory (in-
cluding the Basin and Range regions) and the region west to the Pacific Coast,
including the area that would become California. The Spanish claim was rein-
forced by the occupancy of a number of trading posts, forts, and missions.

In each case, British, Spanish and American, the lure of exploration had
not been necessarily a need for additional land, but rather had been a national
greed for wealth. By 1812, the principal wealth was that which came from furs
and pelts. Regardless of the relatively high prices and demand for fur products
in Europe, there remained, it appears, an unconscious desire by men of nations to discover rich deposits of gold and silver. The Lost Dutchman Mine, the
Seven Lost Cities of Cibalo, and other places of fact and figment, fevered many
imaginations.

The fur trade was perceived, correctly by a few, as a means of getting
rich; however, the most significant reason for the fur trade was to serve as a
"cover" for rivalries between nations. The area sought included the Oregon
Country (extending from Alaska to California, from the Rocky Mountains to
the Pacific), all of California and the intermountain plateaus, constituted a vast
expanse of untold resources -- an area nearly half the size of Europe and vastly
richer in terms of resources.

If ...the leaders of trapping parties [from England or
the United States] were disposed to overreach each
other, or a meeting occurred in an area where trapping
by any was out of bounds, episodes occurred in which
all the venom of territorial rivalries rose
to the surface. An instance was a hostile   103

*encounter which occurred in the valley of the Bear River
in present-day Utah. The Bear Valley was Mexican
soil, but boundary lines were not drawn and, even if
they had been, would not have been observed by the
mountain men. A Hudson's Bay company party, under
the command of Peter Skene Ogden, appeared there in
the spring of 1825. Its trappers were partly "engages,"
partly "freemen," ex-servants of the company, and
Indians equipped by the company. The freemen were
sullen because of years of exploitation by the company.
A party of Americans -- Ashley trappers headed by
Johnson Gardner -- appeared in the area and contacted
the freemen. Gardner offered them a price for their furs
eight times that which they had been receiving. The
freemen and Gardner's party joined, moved on Ogden's
camp, and made off with the freemen's furs, horses,
and equipment. Gardner raised the American flag and
denounced Ogden as an intruder on American Soil. A
battle in the wilderness was narrowly averted, which
might have escalated into an Anglo-American conflict.
(underscore added, pp. 254-255, Merk, 1980)*

Peter Skene Ogden followed his orders from the British officials to trap
and kill the beaver. The order he carried out with ruthless skill and efficiency
with little thought or consideration being given to the impact that such drastic
action would have on the environment or the People.

With calculated determination, Ogden moved in late 1828 into the region of present day Winnemucca, Nevada. There Ogden reported that four
of his steel traps had been stolen. Immediately he announced to the small
gathering of People (about 10 in number) that if the stealing did not stop that
he would kill the next person caught tampering with his traps. There is no evidence that Ogden -- or any other white -- ever asked permission of the People
to hunt beaver on their land. Such was not the thinking of the fur trading companies or the countries that they represented.

Moving onto the site of Battle Mountain, Ogden came upon an encampment of nearly 150 People.

*The trappers report the banks of the river are now lined
with Indians. It appears on our arrival on this river they
apprehended we were a war party, but they are now
convinced we come merely to wage war on the beaver,
and this I trust we shall do most effectually, but they
continue to annoy us having stolen two traps and by
following along the banks of the river make the beaver
very wild. (p. 19, Johnson, 1975)*

The irritation of the British fur trappers was obvious and vo-

104

cal at the bold actions of the People to steal two of their traps and to frighten the beaver so badly that they became elusive to hunters. No consideration was given as to the irritation that the Indian People must have surely felt as they saw fur bearing animals disappear one by one from the rivers and streams. The People had every reason to resent and to resist the actions of the whites. Somehow the literature of that day would lead the reader to believe that the People were doing their duty to obediently stand placidly by as the whites destroyed the environmental landscape.

In 1833 the Americans under the leadership of Joseph Redford Walker made their way down the Humboldt River to its sink. Here the Americans experienced what the British under Ogden had encountered -- missing traps! So angered was Walker over the supposed loss of two traps that he ordered "several" peaceful Indians to be killed. Just how this execution of reprisal took place is not certain; however, it is known that shortly thereafter:

> ...a large gathering [of Indian People] surrounded the
> camp, Walker ordered his men to arm themselves and
> attack. Almost forty People were killed, with the wounded
> being executed at Walker's command. From all its
> appearances, the People wanted to hold a council with
> the trappers. (p. 21, Johnson, 1975)

By the late fall of 1833, Walker's group had crossed the Sierra Nevada Mountains after having traveled up the East fork of the Walker River. Walker's group spent some time in California and then returned to the Great Basin over the route presently known as the Walker Pass. Their travels brought them back to the region of the Carson Sink -- very near the spot where the trappers had murdered the forty Indians the year before. Once again the trappers met a group of Indian People -- just how many were in the group is not known. Nevertheless,

> Walker believed he had to strike the first blow so he
> attacked again, and it is reported that fourteen Indians
> were killed and many others wounded. "We drew up
> in battle array and fell on the Indians in the wildest
> and most ferocious manner as we could, which struck
> dismay throughout the whole crowd." The chroniclers
> of the expedition give no evidence that the People were
> threatening to attack. (p. 21, Johnson, 1975)

Sarah Winnemucca is quoted by Edward Johnson as having recorded in her book, Life Among the Paiutes, that the "...people whom they called their white brothers were killing everybody that came in their way, and all the Indian tribes had gone into the mountains to save their lives." (p. 21, Johnson, 1975)

By 1841 a significant change began to take place in the mi-   105 gration patterns of whites moving across the Basin -- no longer were there small groups of "explorers," trappers and adventurers, but now entire families began crossing the landscape. As early as 1830 the primary trails west had been laid out by game, Indians, and trappers. "The Santa Fe traders had developed the technique of travel by wagon caravans in semi-military fashion." (p. 78, Hollon, 1966)

> *...the way west was long and dangerous and the*
> *desert plains and mountains swarmed with ...Indians.*
> *Nevertheless, there were always men and women willing*
> *to gamble on the odds of getting through. Tales of fertile*
> *valleys beyond the mountains, of streams teeming with*
> *fish, forests with wild game, and grasslands where*
> *cattle could be fattened quickened the pulse of thousands*
> *of western frontiersmen and Yankee farmers. And the*
> *missionaries thought they heard a distant voice crying*
> *for salvation. (Underscore added, p. 78, Hollon, 1966)*

> *...[The Missionaries] ...not only recognized the great*
> *potential that Oregon offered for farming and cattle*
> *raising, but also the unlimited opportunities for*
> *conversion of the Indians. (p. 79, Hollon, 1966)*

In 1836, Mrs. Marcus Whitman became the first white woman to ever cross the "Great American Desert." The trip was significant for yet another reason: it represented the first covered wagon to travel the length of the Oregon Trail. By 1843, 900 people made the crossing by every means available, including the use of the new prairie schooner. Within three years Oregon became a part of the United States and within another five years the population of the territory swelled to 12,000.

By the mid 1840's the migration pattern shifted radically toward California. "...literally almost overnight tens of thousands of men, women, and children were on their way west." Eugene Hollon states that by the spring of 1849, "...there was practically a solid procession of covered wagons spread out along the entire breadth of the Great American Desert." (p. 80, Hollon, 1966)

In 1843 Joseph Walker led yet another migration through the Basin on the way to California. This group was thought to be the first to travel through Nevada and then over the Sierras by wagon, their route having taken them by Walker Lake and through Walker Pass. Near Carson Sink, Walker attacked a group of Paiutes killing sixteen without, it is said, losing any of his party. Further into the Sierras, Walker continued his trail of destruction by encountering and killing twenty-five more Paiute. This second encounter, however, resulted in "several" of his group having been shot, but none appeared to have died from their wounds. Neither the encounter nor the number of deaths is quite as important as the attitude that seemed to persist from whites like Walker, who saw the People as barriers to their westward movement   106 and whose attitude was to shoot first and negotiate during the burial.

The famous "explorer," Captain John C. Fremont, reached what he named "Pyramid Lake" in 1844. "He and his party were fed and treated well by the Paiute in the region." (p. 22, Johnson, 1975) Fremont, the Trail Blazer, was then shown the way across the Sierras by Paiute guides.

The impression that Fremont received from the Paiute a year later (in 1845), was one of "sullen and defiant hostility" toward the whites. "This," Fremont correctly judged, was because the people, "either regarded us as intruders, or they had received some recent injury from the whites who were now beginning to enter California..." (p. 23, Johnson, 1975)

> *...Fremont and his party encountered some People as they traveled around Walker Lake. "Turning a point on the lake shore, the party of Indians some twelve or fourteen in number came abruptly into view. They were advancing along in Indian file, one following the other, their heads bent forward and eyes fixed on the ground. As our party met them the Indians did not turn their heads nor raise their eyes from the ground. Their conduct indicated unfriendliness." The pathfinder had been ignored. (p. 23, Johnson, 1975)*

The words of Fremont, that the Paiute were "sullen" and demonstrated "defiant hostility" are strangely similar to those used to describe Wovoka's father, Tavibo. When a people, any people, sees its resources destroyed, its population wantonly murdered, its children shelterless and hungry, then a reasonable reaction would be that of resistance. The Paiute reacted to encroachment by noncommunication. It was this unwillingness to accept the interlopers as conquering heroes that caused the Paiute to be called "sullen" and "defiant." A better description, perhaps, was "Patriot" since they acted in a vain and futile attempt to preserve their way of life, their homeland and their families.

The historical record indicates that the year 1844 saw only two additional parties passing through Nevada on their way to California. In 1845 the numbers swelled to nearly 250 persons; whereas, 1846 would be a memorable year, not so much as a result of the numbers that passed through the region, but because in that year the ill-fated Donner Party perished in the extraordinarily early snow storms that blanketed the Sierras that winter.

The year 1848 was memorable in the West: gold was discovered in California and the War with Mexico ended. The Spanish-Mexican claim to the Southwest and West was broken and the Indian People and Mormons alike found themselves living within the boundaries of the United States.

*discoveries in California and with word of the official
cession of California following the Mexican War, masses
of pioneers were ready to trek across the continent.
Migration estimates of a wave of civilization across
the Great American Desert in 1849 place the number of
emigrants at approximately thirty thousand.*

*From the first of May to the first of June, company
after company took its departure from the frontier
of civilization, till the emigrant trail from Fort
Leavenworth, on the Missouri, to Fort Laramie, at
the foot of the Rocky Mountains, was one long line
of muletrains and wagons. The rich meadows of the
Nebraska, or Platte, were settled for the time, and a
single traveler could have journeyed for the space of a
thousand miles, as certain of his lodging and regular
meals as if he were riding through the old agricultural
districts of the Middle States. (p. 101, Blouet and Lawson,
ed., 1975)*

As the population in the gold fields of California increased dramatically,
a corresponding growth began to occur in the region to the east of the Sierras and in Nevada. In 1850, the Mormon settlement of Genoa was built in the
Carson Valley. Las Vegas was established by the Mormons in 1855 as a post to
protect the overland mail and travelers. The financial crisis in the "states" in
1857 contributed greatly to a large pool of jobless workers and landless farmers. Men from nearly every region east of the Missouri River were eager to
head West in search for new wealth and a new life. For the most part, these
men were "greenhorns" and as such terribly inexperienced in the techniques
of mining and pioneering. Through great pain and frightful experiences, they
learned to survive -- often at the expense of the Indian People and their natural environment.

The fabulous Comstock Lode, discovered in the Washoe Mountains of
Nevada in June 1859, yielded $400 million in silver and gold in the succeeding
three decades. The mining population grew from an estimated 14,000 in "49"
to more than 380,000 in fewer than a dozen years. The stories of desperation
and striking it rich were repeated time and time again as the mining frontier
shifted from California to Nevada, to the Black Hills, to Colorado and to Montana. Everywhere the story was the same: A few struck it rich. Many, many
more had nothing to show for their labors; and none seemed to care or even
take notice of the Indian People.

*While the miners were hammering out their makeshift
laws, they were joined and almost overwhelmed by
an avalanche of other citizens who were not so much
interested in getting gold out of the ground as*

108

in getting it out of the miners themselves.

> *Soon after the gamblers arrived, madams and their*
> *whores would roll into town in stagecoaches or even*
> *private carriages, amid raucous shouts of delight from*
> *the miners. Then the real estate speculators would turn*
> *up, sometimes with a surveyor, and invariably with a*
> *carpet bag full of plans for laying out the perfect city and*
> *selling lots of lofty prices. And always gold, or rumors of*
> *gold, attracted professional criminals. Few were daring*
> *crooks of the sort that was glamorized in the eastern*
> *press. Most were small-time swindlers or sneak thieves*
> *and thugs -- men whose notion of a good day's work*
> *was to slug a miner in a dark alley and make off with his*
> *poke. (p. 40, Wallace, 1976)*

Progress and civilization had come to the Intermountain West. At the
same time, alcohol, some 200,000 gallons was delivered to the Comstock Mine
alone in 1880. (p. 67, Wallace, 1976) Virginia City grew quickly with a population of 20,000 in the early 1860's. "As a mining town, most of its tradesmen
were bartenders: the community boasted 100 saloons, three undertakers and
four churches." (p. 74, Wallace, 1976)

Men anxious for wealth in the gold fields often found it necessary to go
to work for large mining corporations that were financially able to drive shafts
deep within the earth to recover the ore deposits covered by thousands of feet
of nearly solid rock. It was dangerous work -- as many as 7,500 men died in the
Western mines and another 20,000 were maimed for life. Perhaps the danger
was worth it? The pay was $3.00 a day. (p. 101, Wallace, 1976)

Fortunes were to be made in other less dangerous and risky enterprises.
The price of food, clothing and tools was extremely high. For the enterprising,
wealth could be found in bread, butter, eggs, and meat. Within a short time
after the gold fields of California opened, a few Texas drovers managed to drive
small herds of cattle across the southern edge of the desert to the Pacific Coast
and then to the mine fields of the central Sierras.

> *In 1868 a Mississippi-born Texan drove a sizeable herd*
> *of longhorns all the way from the Lone Star State to*
> *the Humboldt Valley [in Nevada]. (His name was John*
> *Sparks and he later became governor of Nevada.) The*
> *hardy long-horns were excellent foragers and generally*
> *took care of themselves. They fattened well on the native*
> *grass and brought good prices in California slaughter*
> *houses and western mining towns. (p. 130, Hollon, 1966)*

The Cattle Empire was on the rise in Texas before the Civil   109

War.

Some estimates state that there were nearly 3,000,000 head of cattle in Texas in 1865. By the end of 1865, the Cattle Empire had begun to spill over into the central and northern regions of the plains; and later still, into the Basin to the west of the Rocky Mountains. In the Basin and Range Region, cattle were then driven to the gold field markets in California and Nevada. The builders of the cattle industry "...were daring, durable, and sometimes lawless individuals -- not too much unlike the men who built fortunes in mining, oil, steel, and railroads." (p. 122, Hollon, 1966)

The leadership of the Cattle Barons was both aggressive and ambitious and, as in the case of Arizona, quite productive. The census showed a tally of 5000 head of cattle in 1870 but 927,880 only twenty years later. (p. 130, Hollon, 1996) Estimates for Nevada and Utah cattle totals are as follows:

	1870	1880	1890
Nevada	31,516	216,823	210,900
Utah	39,180	132,655	278,313
			(p. 131, Hollon, 1966)

"By 1890 sheep had become more important than cattle in Idaho, Nevada, and Utah. The census lists 273,469 for Nevada, 357,712 for Idaho, and 1,014,176 for Utah." (pp. 130-131, Hollon, 1966)

Westward migration continued to be heavy during the 1850's but not on the same scale that it had been during the mad race to the gold and silver fields of California and Nevada that had taken place during the period of 1949-50. By 1860, a new breed of migrant appeared in the land to the west of the Missouri -- "the dirt farmer." The Homestead Act of 1860, followed by the National Banking Act of 1863, served to further accelerate the movement of people from the eastern seaboard states and from Europe.

The Homestead Act, passed during the Abraham Lincoln presidency, had opened the way for a 160 acre plot of land to be secured for as little as the price of filing a claim. Settlers on the public domain might be required to pay $1.25 an acre for 160 acres. The National Banking Act of 1863 subsidized the building of the transcontinental railroad in excess of the real or actual cost of road construction. Hollon suggests that the Homestead Act and the National Banking Act constituted the "...most generous 'give away' program in the history of the world." (p. 133, Hollon, 1966)

Cattlemen as well as farmers quickly took advantage
of this law, and by homesteading a tract that
controlled access to water, they secured use

*of the great ranges without owning them. The Timber
Culture Act of 1873 enabled them to acquire title to an
additional 160 acres by planting forty acres in trees.
Four years later the Desert Land Act offered another 640
acres of land at $1.25 an acre, provided a portion of it
was put under irrigation. Finally, the Timber and Stone
Act of 1878 assured a further chance to raid the natural
resources of the West. This amazing law allowed any
citizen or first-paper alien to buy up to 160 acres of land
"unfit for cultivation" and "valuable" chiefly for timber or
stone." The price was $2.50 per acre -about the price of
one good log. (p. 133, Hollon, 1966)*

A variety of inventions arose in response to the new and demanding
conditions of farming and ranching in the west: the self-polishing steel plow,
barbed wire, deep well drilling techniques, the reaper, and the use of the old
Persian windmill. Perhaps, most significant was the steel plow, since without
it the turning of the virgin prairie sod was impossible. Then, too, there was the
invention by Sam Colt of the six shooter, which when coupled with the carbine
of the Army and the Hotchkiss gun, literally gave to the whites the superiority
of arms and weapons necessary to subdue the tribes on the Plains and in the
Basin.

What the plow was to the earth, the sheep were to the grasslands. The
sheepherder, dirt farmer and drover all competed for the same land and rights
to the same water. Armed and heated conflict between each of the groups contributed to a general atmosphere of tension and, often as not, open warfare.

American folklore and legend is full of the glamour of the cattle drive,
the rugged individualism of the frontier and mountains. However, little consideration has been given to the drastic effect that was to take place in the life
of the People or the Nation as millions of head of buffalo were killed for their
hides, tallow, bones and for sport. The concept that the buffalo were killed
for food for the workers on the transcontinental railroad is so excessive as
to appear absurd. A simple division of the numbers of all people (including
Indian People, Chinese, Irish, Army Personnel, and settlers) on the plains by
the number of years required to complete the building of the railroad, and
the millions of buffalo, would reveal the superhuman effort that would be required "to eat enough buffalo in one day to match the actual decimation. That
the buffalo were killed for food for the workers was only a half-truth. The real
truth lies submerged in the national consciousness. The truth appears to lie
more in the fact that the buffalo was a most vital and important link in the
food base. The solution to the Indian problem was simply: "Kill the buffalo
and the Indian "problem" will take care of itself." No buffalo -- no Indians, or
so some reasoned. By 1880 the buffalo was nearly extinct as a species ...the
Indian People, nearly so!

The destruction of the buffalo was needless and inhumane both to the species and to the Indians as well. Misfortune seemed for a time to be the birthright of the Indian People. However, in time, even the whites would not be immune to the results of careless practices of soil conservation and the depletion of natural resources in the forests and in the mountains. Overgrazing of the grassland by too many sheep and cattle, and the turning of the prairie soil in those areas of marginal rainfall was bound, sooner or later, to create conditions favorable for disaster.

Disaster came in the spring of 1886 when the spring rains failed. Summer came hot and dry and with it clouds of dust. Overgrazing and the plow created the first agricultural disaster made by man in North America. Americans eager for wealth had unknowingly created an American legacy -- and Dust Bowl!

> *For the next two seasons, and intermittently until 1893,*
> *the soil moved back and forth with the shifting winds. But*
> *if the summer of 1886 was the poorest growing season*
> *for grass in thirty years or more, the following winter*
> *was even more severe on cattle. Snowstorms arrived on*
> *the northern plains a full six weeks earlier than usual.*
> *By the first week of November the upper two-thirds of*
> *the Great American Desert was caught in a blizzard that*
> *plunged temperatures below zero. The bad weather even*
> *froze some of the streams of northern New Mexico and*
> *West Texas into solid ice. No sooner had the blizzard*
> *spent itself than it was followed by another, and then*
> *another. They swept down both slopes of the Rockies and*
> *continued throughout December, January, February,*
> *and March, holding the temperatures to forty below zero*
> *for two and three weeks at a time. (pp. 135-136, Hollon,*
> *1966)*
>
> *Ironically, the abundance of water from the melting*
> *snow produced good range conditions that spring, but*
> *grass was no longer king. The summer of 1887 turned*
> *hot and dry like the previous one, and the following*
> *winter was equally severe. Many of the large operators,*
> *particularly the corporations, disposed of the remnants*
> *of their herds and declared bankruptcy. Whole sections of*
> *the plains and basin region were cleared of cattle. (p. 137,*
> *Hollon, 1966)*

The Paiute suffered along with the whites. Game was scarce since grazing cattle and sheep had consumed the grass, and now that the rains failed to come the earth was parched and barren. The winter of 1866 was called "Their Winter of Famine" since even the pine nuts had failed to develop during the last season. By 1869 the conditions had continued to   112

deteriorate and the reservation agent reported that...much sickness has prevailed among these Indians during the year past...between 75 and 100 deaths
occurred in the months of August, September, and October." (p. 41, Johnson,
1975)

By 1870 Lieutenant Lee, Special Indian Agent, stated that the estimated
1,200 to 1,500 Paiutes were without Pine nuts and grass seed because of a "...
total failure by reason of drought, and it may become necessary to issue some
provisions to them the coming winter to prevent starvation." (p. 41, Johnson,
1975)

Early attempts to learn white farming techniques especially those related
to irrigation were largely ineffective. Once irrigation canals were constructed,
the Paiute lacked sufficient resources to purchase plows and cultivators necessary to plant, care for and harvest a crop. The single most difficult obstacle to
their success was the fact that too often the spring floods, during good years,
washed out the ditches, and the People had only hand tools with which to
repair and maintain the canal system. During drought years, white farmers
would divert much of the needed water from the canals of the Paiute to their
own land. Often canals were dammed entirely, allowing no water to pass to the
Indian farms.

> *...the crops dried up after the ditch broke and the river
> receded. This was to be a continual problem on the
> reservation. The dams and ditches were washed out time
> after time. The crops dried up and were blown away by
> the wind. Wild hay was the only crop harvested with
> success on the reservation. (p. 59, Johnson, 1975)*

The white population of Nevada in and around Carson City to the north
and Walker Lake to the south had grown so much to depend upon the cattle
ranching and mining industry that pressures were brought upon the Paiute to
permit their land to be cut in the middle by the Carson and Colorado Railroad.
Oni April 13, 1880, tribal leaders signed an agreement with the railroad that
gave the Carson and Colorado a right-of-way "forever across the reservation."
(p. 69, Johnson, 1976) In exchange the tribe was given the sum of $750.00 and
the promise of free transportation of persons and produce to market. However,
the right to use the railroad was a long and hard fought battle. The People were
finally permitted to ride on the top of box cars or on flat cars -- but never inside
a passenger car.

> *...Governor John H. Kinkead had petitioned Carl Schurz,
> Secretary of the Interior, in February of 1880, on
> behalf of the railroad interests. He maintained that the
> reservation was the best route for a railroad. Kinkead
> also felt that a radical reorganization of Indian affairs in
> the state had to take place. Too much land was reserved
> for the "Pah Utes." The People were blocking
> progress. (p. 69, Johnson, 1975)*

113

With the coming of the railroad came a new set of cultural problems with which the People had to learn to cope -- the Chinese. The Chinese had been brought into the West to be workers on the Central Pacific Railroad. When the construction was completed in 1869, the Chinese moved into the mining camps and towns. About this time, strong pressures were exerted against the Indian People to prohibit them from associating with the whites in public restaurants and bars. The Chinese too excluded the Paiute from their restaurants. However, both the Chinese and Indian People were free to purchase all the food they wanted from the white's restaurants -- so long as they paid the full price for a meal AND used the back door. Alcohol and opium could be purchased from Chinese merchants. Race relations between the Paiute and Chinese, as well as the Paiute and the whites, were "brittle and tense" throughout the closing years of the 19th century.

Farther to the east, conditions on the Pine Ridge and Rosebud Reservations were equally difficult. Beginning in 1868 and continuing through 1890, the government in Washington had made a series of treaties with the Sioux. The Laramie Treaty in 1868, the Agreement of 1876, and the Sioux Act of 1889 provided that the federal government give specific quantities of food and supplies to the Sioux and in exchange the Sioux were to give up claim to their lands and to move onto "reservations." The 1889 agreement had radically reduced the Sioux land in half, and then specified that the remaining land be divided into five reservations. The land area of the new reservations was too small to permit the hunting of deer, elk and other game. The Sioux were repeatedly encouraged to farm and to give up their guns. The buffalo were gone, the land reduced drastically in area, and the hunters' guns taken. Life had indeed changed for the Sioux.

In its efforts to be efficient, the government required that a census of the Sioux population be taken and it would be this count that would serve as the basis for all subsequent rations. In 1885 a census was taken and immediately the ration of beef was cut.

> *This sharp cut in the meat supply preceded the severe winter of 1886 when thirty percent of the Indians' own cattle died from disease. Two years later, the Indians suffered a disastrous crop failure which contributed to illness and starvation on the reservation. By early 1890, therefore, the Sioux were angry and despairing over their hopeless situation. (p. 2, Briggs and McAnulty, 1977)*

> The Indians often went hungry when rations failed to *arrive or were of insufficient amounts to feed them all. By 1890, crop failures and diminishing rations had caused near starvation and serious illness among the Sioux. (p. 9, Briggs and McAnulty, 1977)*

114

Thomas J. Morgan, the Baptist preacher whom President Harrison had appointed Commissioner of Indian Affairs, admitted that the reduction came at an unfortunate time but denied that it reduced the Sioux to starvation or even extreme suffering. Others were sure it had. Bishop Hare, for example [declared] that the people were often hungry and died when taken sick, "not so much from disease as from want of food." Whatever the situation -- one cannot read the evidence without concluding that the Sioux were desperately hungry -- the Indians felt tricked and trapped. (pp. 320-321, Olson, 1965)

Hollon states: "The Indians of the desert plains clearly saw the end long before it came," (p. 114, Hollon, 1966) and added, "The people returned to the reservation to remain in peace and poverty as they struggled to 'follow the white man's road.'" (p. 112, Hollon, 1966)

The only hope for the Indians was a messiah, and indeed, one appeared before the close of the century. He was a Paiute named Wovoka and from the other side of the Rockies, and he preached that the ghosts of dead Indians would return to help drive out the whites and that the vanished buffalo would reappear. Soon the plains and deserts and mountains would belong to the original owners and the old way of life would be restored. (p. 114, Hollon, 1966)

The Ghost Dance Movement Of 1870

The winter of 1866 had been especially difficult for the Paiute People. Large stands of pines had been cut by whites to build houses and especially, to serve as supports for the shafts in mines. No estimate has been made of the acres or board feet required for this industry; nor has an effort been made to calculate the impact of deforestification on the food base of the Paiute. Franklin Campbell, a resident of Mason Valley, attributed the 1866 famine as having resulted from the failure of the pine nut harvest.

Other factors contributed to the lack of food -- inadequate knowledge of farming and horticulture. The Paiute were required to live within the restricted and confined reservation boundaries where they once had been free to hunt and to gather over the entire landscape. In the arid conditions of the Basin, a vast area was necessary to sustain a relatively few people. When a significant number of people are required to live in a small area in any arid environment, it becomes physically impossible to have enough food available for everyone. Logically, then, or so reasoned the In-

115

dian agents, the Indians should be instructed more thoroughly in the arts of farming and horticulture. Irrigation was a natural extension of agricultural pursuits especially when the rivers leading out of the Sierra to the east appeared to be wasted as they sank into the ground. Irrigation provides a reasonably sure source of moisture in an area of uncertain and limited rainfall (ten inches or less a year was predictable but at best insufficient for the growing of most grain crops). An irrigation ditch was dug at the northern end of the Walker River Reservation in 1866. Under the watchful eye of the agent, some oxen were used in the construction of the ditch; however, the Paiute were also engaged in the building process as well. Since "the people possessed few iron tool implements, they were encouraged to use baskets and greasewood sticks to move the earth." (p. 41, Johnson, 1975)

The ditches washed out time after time during the spring floods. By the time the repair was made, crops; were either ruined or the water table too low to carry additional water to the fields.

The Paiute were paid for their labor by providing them with wagons. Ideally, the wagons would have been well-suited for transporting goods and produce from farm to transportation sites or markets. Had the Paiute been paid in farm implements, plows, shovels, hoes, and cultivators, then they could have contributed greatly to their own support; as it was, irrigated fields were of little value if there were no seeds and implements with which to till the earth.

A great deal of sickness and death gripped the reservation area in 1869, and by the time winter began starvation faced the nearly 1,500 members of the Paiute Tribe. It was in this socio-economic environment that Wodziwob moved in the late 1860's.

The review of literature reveals that the emergence of Wodziwob among the Walker River Paiute was in no way spectacular. He came among the people as any other member of the tribe. Wodziwob made no initial claim as a religious leader or Prophet. However, as times changed and as conditions of human suffering increased more and more, Wodziwob turned to the native practice of seeking answers for the tribes and his problems -- pragmatic solutions that centered in a need for food and a desire to see an end to the sufferings and longings of his people.

It must have appeared clear to Wodziwob that the answers to his questions and the solutions to the problems that beset the Paiute, were not to be found in those things that the whites brought with them. White diseases -- the shock troops of European Invasion only created more suffering. The white rancher's cattle ate the precious grass; the deer ranged higher in the mountains. The Paiute were prohibited from leaving the Reservation to hunt. The price of killing a rancher's steer was excessive reprisal and punishment even in the event an unfortunate stray would wander onto the Reservation lands. Irrigation had not helped. White man's whiskey and Chinese opium eased the suffering -- for a moment -- and then the sickening reality of hunger and whooping cough returned. While   116 whimpers and tears could be hidden, the spattle of blood from infected lungs could not as the numbers of children's' graves increased. Wodziwob sought solutions that were rooted deeply in the cultural fiber of his people -- their religion.

The only reasonable solution to the problems of the Paiute was to be found in the discovery of principles and practices that were "spiritual" in nature. These were extraordinary times and the Paiute were in danger of total extinction; thus, extraordinary solutions were the only wonders capable of bringing healing and recovery to the Paiute . Through prayers, through fasting, through cleansing ritual, Wodziwob began to approach the realm of the Spirit. He sought the realm of spiritual awareness of which many whites spoke but few had experienced.

Like religious leaders, practitioners, and mystics before him, Wodziwob was thought, or so the whites had said, to be a magician or some type of slight-of-hand artist, who could not only work wonders and cures through incantations and sucking, but could control the weather. The powers attributed to Wodziwob, like those of many religious mystics, were nearly as spectacular as had been the staff, frogs, and rivers of blood of a Moses time. However, the purported achievements in magic and curing may have been excessively exaggerated. Wodziwob's approach to religious and spiritual concerns was to seek special guidance from spirit beings that would suggest right actions and right relationships for the Paiute to follow.

Wodziwob's desire to know first-hand from the spirit world the answer to problems was not unlike that which the Mormon people believed had motivated the youthful Joseph Smith to ask: "Which Church should I Join?" The answer that Joseph Smith received so inspired him that he sought, with divine help, to establish a new -- a restored -- church on the earth. This proclamation was believed and followed unreservedly by his disciples. So also, Wodziwob, had sought in his faith to pray, to fast and to gain for his people the final word as to what they should do and as to what the final course of their life should be.

It is impossible to know with any degree of certainty the particulars of Wodziwob's experience, i.e., whether it was a dream, a vision, a trance, or by whatever means, believed he had been permitted to visit "the land of the dead" and in the process of his experience he had learned that great changes were about to take place on the earth and that these changes would center in the lives of the Paiute people. (p. 42, Johnson, 1976)

In an effort to understand the power and workings of the Indian practitioner, Dr. Charles A. Eastman (Ohiyesa), a Sioux physician on the Pine Ridge Reservation in South Dakota, stated that the most significant influence that the Indian medicine man had was that which came through the influence of the mind of both the practitioner and patient. Eastman stated that the medicine man possessed his "...main hold on the minds of the people [and that the hold] was gained through his appeals to the spirits and his magnetic and hypnotic powers." (p. 122, Eastman, 1916)

Regardless of the means by which Wodziwob gained his power, it can only be concluded that for a time he was highly successful in his appeal claiming that he had received a marvelous message of deliverance and recovery, and that the source of this mystery had been the Great Spirit Himself. The Doctrine of the 1870 Ghost Dance was clear and relatively simple to comprehend. It taught that Wodziwob, while in a vision state, had visited the land of the dead and that soon the dead would live once again on the earth. When this event was to take place the earth itself would be renewed and transformed into "a paradise." Especially significant was his declaration that "Life was to be eternal and no distinction was to exist between the races." (p. 42, Johnson, 1975)

Some writers have suggested that the prophecy that Wodziwob had given in 1869 had great effect in establishing his credibility among the Paiute as being truly a "Prophet." It had been in 1869 that Wodziwob had purportedly prophesied that a large train would come from the east. Peter Farb wrote that Wodziwob had proclaimed it would be a train that would carry the dead back to the Walker Lake region. This belief does not appear extensively in the literature relating to the Ghost Dance of 1870.

> *The Union Pacific Railroad had recently completed its first transcontinental run, and no doubt that inspired the vision of the Prophet Wodziwob, that a big train would bring back his dead ancestors and announce their arrival with an explosion, an idea probably inspired by the steam whistle. He proclaimed that a cataclysm would swallow up all the Whites but miraculously leave behind their goods for those Indians who joined his cult. (p. 280, Farb, 1968)*

The reliability of the message that Wodziwob taught is not to be found in a vain attempt to establish that a steam whistle had either influenced or frightened the Prophet to such an extent that he went into a trance or had a vision, but in comparing his teachings to those of past revivalist movements. The message of the Ghost Dance of 1870 was strikingly similar to those of the past and was to be mirrored in nearly the same terms in the Ghost Dance Movement of 1890.

Perhaps the greatest miscalculation that Wodziwob made (if indeed, it can be said that he made any at all) was in the statement, quoted by the Indian Agent by the name of Campbell, that "...the dead would return in three or four years and that everyone would be badly frightened when the event occurred." (p. 42, Johnson, 1975) Credibility cracks occurred in Wodziwob's prophetic mantle in 1874 when the dead did not return. The pine nut crop of 1873 had been a bumper one, a factor that may have contributed greatly to a lessening of intensity of the Ghost Dance doctrine. However, the time between 1870 and 1874 had been eventful ones for the Prophet and for the People.

118

Wodziwob had come to the Walker River reservation area in the 1860's, having journeyed from the south, probably from the Mono Lake region where he may have lived in Fish Lake Valley. (pp. 42, 44, Johnson, 1975) Wodziwob was buried in the Paiute cemetery in the Walker Reservation slightly to the west of the burial spot of Wovoka, however, his head board might go unnoticed since it is marked by the original name of Fishlake Joe. "Wodziwob and Fishlake Joe were one and the same person." (p. 44, Johnson, 1975) Edward C. Johnson stated that the Paiute in Fish Lake Valley were accustomed to taking part in religious ceremonies (cry dances) that were done to commemorate the memory of the dead. "It was natural for Wodziwob," wrote Johnson, "to advocate the return of the dead." (p. 42, Johnson, 1975) The Walker River Paiute were described as being "traditionally" fearful of the dead, but that their uncertainty about the dead was overcome when they saw so many of their people dying from hunger and sickness. Then, too, the Prophet had assured the Paiute that their "...immediate family members would return." (p. 42, Johnson, 1975)

> *Wodziwob attended traditional gatherings in the Spring*
> *and Fall. The prophet instructed the People to dance the*
> *round dance. "A flat space 200-300 yards in diameter*
> *was cleared and a pole set up in the center of the dance*
> *ground; fires were lit in the nighttime at the edge of the*
> *dance circle; men and women painted their faces and*
> *other exposed parts of their bodies with bars and dots*
> *in red and white and held hands and circle-danced in*
> *counterclockwise direction for five all-night dance cycles;*
> *the ceremony was presided over by a dance leader who*
> *stood outside of the dance circle and who prayed for rain,*
> *wild seeds, fish, game, pine nuts and for good health."*
> *The round dance was a social dance of the People. (pp.*
> *42-43, Johnson, 1976)*

A search of literature relating to the 1870 Ghost Dance fails to reveal the belief in, or the use of, any garment that would render its wearer immune to white men's bullets.

For awhile, the Federal Government employed a number of Christian ministers to serve as Indian Agents and assigned them to reservations. One such agent was the Reverend George Balcom, who was assigned to the Pyramid Lake region in 1871. (p. 43, Johnson, 1976) Balcom, true to his "calling" and convictions, began to preach the gospel, as well as to administer the affairs of the reservation. Little is known of his ability as an administrator or of his pastoral concern as a Christian minister; however, by some strange set of happenings or circumstances, the teachings of the Christian ministry, i.e., that the Second Coming of Jesus Christ was near at hand, came to the attention of the Indian People. The idea of the Coming of Jesus was somewhat modified to include the belief that "God was coming."

> *Harassed, not knowing which way to turn, the Indians*
> *hearkened to the words which had been ceaselessly*
> *poured into their ears by white missionaries. They had*
> *heard of the second coming of Christ, how He would*
> *return to His own people; that the meek and lowly,*
> *the downtrodden and oppressed would be exalted*
> *and redeemed. They had also been taught that the*
> *generations before would be restored to life; and that evil*
> *would be banished from the world. But it was a strange,*
> *bizarre interpretation which the red man put upon these*
> *teachings. (p. 229, Wellman, 1954)*

The reference just quoted was made by Paul Wellman to describe the Ghost Dance Movement of 1890. It is cited here to establish the awareness that the doctrine of both the 1870 and 1890 movements was virtually the same and that the Revival led by Wovoka in 1890 was but an extension -- separated only by time -- of that movement twenty years earlier. Reference made by Wellman as to the "strange and bizarre interpretation" that the various tribes made to the doctrine is, indeed, important and highly significant. The interpretation of aspects of the movement contributed directly to the demise of the movement in 1870 and again in 1890. The effort by Wodziwob to establish a date, i.e., sometime in 1874, that the dead would return and the white culture and dominance end, was fatal to the movement when, obviously, the events did not take place. In a like manner, the 1890 Movement was to include -- especially among the Sioux -- the Ghost Shirt and the belief in the concept of invincibility to bullets. Aside from these two elements, the 1870 and 1890 Movements were principally the same. Often forgotten, too, is the similarity of the Ghost Dance Doctrine and that of Christianity -the resurrection, the cleansing of the earth, and the return of Jesus as Messiah. "It is a weird circumstance that the last hope and belief of the unfortunate red race was founded upon the doctrines of the Christian religion..." (p. 229, Wellman, 1954)

> *The...belief spread silently and swiftly. Almost overnight*
> *it was flourishing, full-blown. The Messiah was coming,*
> *they said. He had come once to save the white race but*
> *they despised and killed Him. Now He rejected them*
> *and would come to destroy the whites and save His red*
> *children. All who believed in Him were to-practice the*
> *Ghost Dance as often and as long as they could. The*
> *Ghost Dance, in common with many Indian dances,*
> *notably the Sun Dance, was a test of endurance. It was*
> *believed that if anybody died of exhaustion during this*
> *dance he would be taken directly to the Messiah and*
> *enjoy the company of those who had gone before. (pp.*
> *229-230, Wellman, 1954)*

Drought once again gripped the landscape during 1871 and 1872, and with it came the crippling effect of; undernourished bodies, sickness, and suffering, especially among the very young and the old. The Ghost Dancing reached a new height as the suffering of the People intensified. Indian Agent Calvin Bateman:

> *..reported to the Commissioner of Indian Affairs on January 19, 1872, that "a messenger has just come in from Walker River Reservation with the intelligence [sic] that large numbers of Indians from Virginia City and among the mountains near and remote had gathered upon the reservation under the impression that God was coming at an early moment to distroy [sic] the world and fears are entertained by farmer Campbell that they will distroy [sic] the Govt [sic] Stock for food unless provided for as it is impossible for them to sustain themselves but a short time..." (p. 43, Johnson, 1975)*

Whites in and around Mason Valley and the Walker River Reservation became increasingly concerned at the news of the "dancing" that was taking place and with the numbers of Indian People who appeared to be moving in and about the dance sites. It is impossible to know for certain the white's thoughts, but it requires little imagination to conjure up fears of massive uprisings. Very little concern was expressed in the literature that the white communities even suspected that the Indian People were hungry, sick and dying. Had these needs been addressed, many of the fears and apprehensions of the whites could have been laid to rest. As it was, when the People gathered together, danced long into the nights and fed upon an unfortunate steer that inadvertently wandered onto the reservation, the whites became overtly concerned -- not at the suffering -- not as much at the dancing -- but more specifically at the killing of a steer.

The edition of the <u>Reese River Reveille</u> reported that "There are more than three thousand Indians at Walker River Reservation and it is reported that they are in a starving condition..." (p. 44, Johnson, 1975) The Indian agent gave the figure as more nearly 1,500 People. Edward Johnson expressed the belief that it mattered little if the number was 1,500 or 3,000 -- the reality was that the reservation land and food supply could not begin to feed even the smaller number of People. In response to the fears of the whites and the obvious needs of the Paiutes, five tons of flour were distributed to the Paiute People. The kind and amount of other foods given to the People is not known, but by suggestion, it was only flour that was given.

As the effects of the drought spread across the land, so also did news of the Ghost Dance. The Washoes (a nearby Nevada Tribe) took up the dance in 1871. By 1872, the doctrine spread to the Snake River region in Idaho, to Utah, to Washington, California and Oregon.

121

Throughout the winter and the following spring, the circles of the Ghost Dance continued to form; however, by mid-1872 the Ghost Dance movement appeared to be losing much of its momentum. Some writers maintain that the Ghost Dance (1870) came to an end during 1872 for it was believed by a few that the Prophet, Wodziwob, died and his followers fell away.

> *Michael Hittman, an anthropologist who did field work among the Mason and Smith Valley People, has stated that the People stopped believing in Wodziwob's predictions because the Government provided more assistance for farming. (p. 44, Johnson, 1975)*

> *Other writings suggest that with the promise of good planting conditions and excellent crop possibilities in 1873, the People turned to tasks more directly related to sustaining life.*

The specific details as to why the Ghost Dance movement declined during the 1872-73 period will, perhaps, never be totally understood. Michael Hittman is quoted by Edward Johnson as stating that Wodziwob had died in 1872 and that with his death, the Ghost Dance Movement began its decline. However, Johnson states that Wodziwob did not die in 1872, but continued to live on in Mason Valley and served as a "native doctor until his death in 1918." (p. 44, Johnson, 1975)

THE INTERLUDE   1870 - 1890

Many changes took place in the United States during the period from 1870 to 1890. A number of significant inventions had begun to revolutionize industry and to bring added comforts to many of America's people. Transportation was well-established and comfort became a new way of life for those traveling across the landscape by train. In 1875 the Westinghouse air brake and automatic block signal were both in use. Steel boilers and fire boxes were used in locomotives and coal, rather than wood, served as the source of fuel. Passengers were made more comfortable still by the introduction of the "hotel" or Pullman car. By 1879-1880, cities were installing electric lights in homes, in businesses and along city streets. Charles F. Brush of Cleveland helped to make this all possible by the construction of a practical generator capable of creating electricity. Edison's incandescent lamps began to be produced on a large scale. By 1870 the refrigerator car was developed, and from that day on fresh meat and produce could be shipped quickly and easily to nearly any part of the country. The rise of big business had profound effects upon American life. Generally speaking the tremendous industrial development of the nation contributed to a steadily growing standard of living for the American population. Machines made life easier and more enjoyable. "Per capita income, in dollars of constant purchasing power, rose from $285.00 in 1859 to $482.00 a half century later." (p. 371, Fite and Reese, 1959)

In 1855 it had taken 39 hours of labor to grow and harvest 40 bushels of corn. In 1894, the time needed had been reduced to 15 hours. Because of the new skills and technology, a worker in 1850 could expect to care for only 12 acres of crops; however, by the turn of the century the acreage was increased to nearly 30.

> *The Great Plains was an ideal region for ranching. The area abounded in succulent and nutritious grasses which were excellent for putting cattle in good flesh. Moreover, the natural cuts and brakes furnished winter protection. Of great importance was the fact that there were millions of acres of government land which could be grazed without cost or obligation. The Commissioner of Agriculture wrote in 1880 that western ranchers "practically use and control millions of acres of land belonging to the government for which they pay neither rent nor tax."*
>
> *The Carey Cattle Company of Wyoming had over 32, 287 head in 1884 and valued its property at $1.2 million.*
>
> *Montana had only 36,738 head in 1870, but twenty years later her cattle population had climbed to 1,442,517. Wyoming's cattle numbers jumped from only 11,130 to 934,066 in the two decades after 1870. (p. 420, Fite and Reese, 1959)*

On July 9, 1870, Congress authorized a survey of mineral lands to be sold at $2.50 per acre. Later the price was increased to $5.00 per acre for those areas with proven mineral deposits and at the same time reduced the land containing iron ore to $1.25 per acre. In a rather dramatic endeavor to protect the landscape, Yellowstone National Park was created in 1872. By spring of the next year (March 3, 1873), the Timber Culture Act was passed and provided that any person who kept 40 acres of timber land in good condition could acquire title to a total of 160 acres; however, the protected acreage was reduced to 10 only five years later. The Coal Lands Act provided for the sale of coal lands to individuals of up to 160 acres and corporations to acquire 360 acres at 10 to 20 dollars an acre, depending upon how far the coal land was from the railroad. (p. 439, Morris, 1953)

On June 3, 1878, the Timber Cutting Act was passed, permitting settlers and miners to cut timber on the public domain, free of any charge, as long as they used the lumber for their own needs.

123

The Timber and Stone Act was made applicable to California, Oregon, Washington and Nevada. This act allowed the sale of timber and stone lands that were unfit for cultivation at the price of $2.50 an acre.

On February 8, 1887, the Native American People were given a devastating set-back in their now futile attempt to keep the Louisiana Purchase lands for a permanent home "for as long as the grass grew!" The Dawes Act was passed, and in one sweeping reform the homeland of the aboriginal landholders dwindled from all of North America, to the land west of the Appalachians, to the Louisiana Purchase Territory, to Indian Territory, and finally to Reservations. The act provided for the dissolution of the tribes as legal entities and the division of the tribal lands among individual members of the population on a basis of 160 acres to each head of family and 80 acres to adult single persons. Rights to the land were to be held by the government for 25 years, after which the person was to be free to do with the land as he/she saw fit. The most deadening aspect of the act was in its covert intent of breaking up the tribal way of life for the People. It must be remembered that by 1887 the Native American People had been given land in some of the most undesirable and unproductive regions in America. In most instances, 160 acres was inadequate, due to limited rainfall, poor soils and regional isolation for providing an agricultural way of life.

The population of the United States west of the Mississippi River increased significantly during the period 1870-1890.

1870	2,298,952
1880	3,300,378
1890	4.078,157
	(p. 443, Morris, 1953)

A variety of schemes and acts made the land west of the Mississippi especially desirable after the gold rush period in California. Among the least attractive schemes was that associated with the killing of buffalo for their hides, the price of which varied from a high of $3.00 to as little as $1.00. No immediate source is available to show the value of the bones of these animals that went into the tallow and comb industry. Beginning in 1867 and ending by 1883, a conservative estimate of the numbers of buffalo killed ranged at nearly 13 million. Some estimates put the number of beasts killed at 60 million, while others say that even this figure was too low.

Regardless of the numbers actually killed, it is far more important to see the impact of this wholesale and wanton destruction of animal life as a hideous expose of the destruction of other parts of the environmental landscape of the nation -- mineral, plant, animal and human. Human destruction followed closely in the wake of the demise of the buffalo, since the Plains Indian culture was nearly totally dependent upon the buffalo as a

124

source of food, clothing, tools, and shelter. While it may not have been a conscious attempt of the government of the United States to totally destroy the buffalo, and in so doing, allow the Indian populations to be starved into submission; nevertheless, the result was the same. The difficulty of such an action by the whites was that while the Indian People could be brought to their knees through disease and starvation, they could never be subdued psychologically or culturally.

Farming, ranching, and mining too, continued to attract whites into the Plains and Basin. Beginning in 1870 and continuing until 1880, the number of farms in Texas increased from 61,125 to 174,184. Wyoming had been organized into a territory in 1868, and almost overnight the population swelled. In 1873, the First Dakota Boom was begun, and immediately the population grew to 20,000 persons. By 1885, the Northern Pacific Railroad had begun construction through the country, followed by the Great Northern in 1887. By 1884 over 11,083,000 acres of land had been granted to settlers and the population grew to 539,583 (1890), with 142,924 in Montana alone.

The worst grasshopper plague in the history of the nation was reported in 1884 with nearly total devastation of crops in the Great Plains from the Dakotas to north Texas. However, grasshoppers soon faded from the thinking of gold seekers as the Black Hills (South Dakota) yielded up its metallic treasure. A military expedition headed by none other than the infamous George A. Custer had brought the word of gold to white communities. No sooner had the word come than 15,000 prospectors entered the region. The mining camps bore the names of such places as Custer City and Deadwood. Deadwood was the home, for awhile, of such characters of western fame as Wild Bill Hickok.[7]

The Black Hills, long a sacred dwelling place of the Sioux, was now violated by the railroads, by miners' picks and shovels, and by the carrion of civilization, the bawdy houses, saloons, and gaming wheels. The Sioux, angered and disillusioned by the breaking of their treaty, began to resist. On June 26, 1876, General George Armstrong Custer and 264 men in his command were defeated and annihilated in the Battle of the Little Big Horn.

The victory for the Sioux and Cheyenne was a hallow one. The defeat of the cavalry was a serious blow to the white man's national pride, and would only be made "right" when Custer and his men were revenged. It may be that Custer hoped that a victory over the Sioux and Cheyenne would assure his nomination for President of the United States at the Democratic Convention to be held in July of 1876. Few whites would be able to see that Custer's ambition to consider the presidency of the United States as a source of outrage against the Sioux and Cheyenne. Fewer still, would say that the Indians had been wronged in any way and that treaties were only so much paper. The white man's anger seemed to be quieted to a small degree with

---

7   In 1872 some 60 million dollars in gold bullion was taken in Tombstone, South Dakota alone.

the arrest and return to the reservation of Sitting Bull and Crazy Horse. Final revenge for the humiliation of Custer would be vented upon the Sioux at Wounded Knee in December of 1890.

The Omnibus States were admitted to the Union: North and South Dakota, Montana, Washington (1889) and Idaho and Wyoming (1890).

In April of 1884, the "Boomers" led by David L. Payne and W. L. Couch entered the Oklahoma Territory only to be forcibly removed from Indian Lands. Pressure. from people from nearly every section of the country, many having been blown out of the regions of the plains by dust and drought, all clamoring for land resulted in the "Opening of Oklahoma" to homesteaders. At noon on the April 22, 1889, the Oklahoma Land Rush was on, and within a few hours nearly 1,920,000 acres had been "staked." By nightfall it is said that "Oklahoma City" had a population of 10,000 persons.

The United States Census Director is reported to have said: "There can hardly be said to be a frontier line."

In the Southwestern region of the United States, a long and often bloody war had been waged against the Apaches. Cochise, Victorio, Nana and Geronimo were chased across Arizona and New Mexico until they were captured or run deep into Mexico. The Apache War had begun in New Mexico and Arizona on April 30, 1871, with the massacre of over 100 Apaches at Camp Grant, Arizona. The conflict came to an end finally, with the capture of Geronimo, the leader of the Chiricahua, in 1886 and the placing of the Apache People on small reservations.

In Idaho the Bannack and Sheepeater "wars" caused considerable alarm among the white settlements. Sitting Bull and several hundred of his people continued to live in Canada. Even though Sitting Bull got along well with the Canadian Government and people, he was nevertheless suspected by the United States Government of stirring up trouble inside the United States. By the summer of 1874, Crazy Horse and Sitting Bull were "...still at large, harassing soldiers and immigrants alike, and General Custer had just been placed in military command of the Dakota Territory." (p. 30, Eastman, 1916)

> _...this was September, 1876, less than three months after Custer's...command was annihilated by the...Sioux. I was especially troubled...(statement made by Charles A. Eastman (Ohiyesa), Sioux, and Physician to the Pine Ridge Reservation) (p. 53, Eastman, 1916)_

> _Captain Sword, the dignified and intelligent head of the Indian police force, was very friendly, and soon found time to give me a great deal of information about the place and the people. He said finally: "Kola (my friend), the people are very glad you have come. You have begun well; we Indians are all your friends. But I fear that we are going to have trouble. I must tell you that_

126

a new religion has been proclaimed by some Indians in the Rocky Mountain region, and some time ago, Sitting Bull sent several of his men to investigate. We hear that they have come back, saying that they saw the prophet, or Messiah, who told them that he is God's Son whom He has sent into the world a second time. He told them that He had waited nearly two thousand years for the white men to carry out His teachings, but instead they had destroyed helpless small nations to satisfy their own selfish greed. Therefore He had come again, this time as a Savior to the red people. If they would follow His instructions exactly, in a little while He would cause the earth to shake and destroy all the cities of the white man, when famine and pestilence would come to finish the work. The Indians must live entirely by themselves in their teepees so that the earthquake would not harm them. They must fast and pray and keep up a holy or spirit dance that He taught them. He also ordered them to give up the white man's clothing and make shirts and dresses in the old style. (p. 83, Eastman, 1916)

Again the Native American People turned to their own religious beliefs and traditions to find the solutions to the problems that faced them on every side. Nothing that the white men possessed or offered brought an end to the hunger that the People felt, or lessened, in any degree, the longings that they felt to return to the old former ways of hunting and living in harmony with the earth as a free people. The "Salvation" of the People of all nations and tribes was to be found in the personhood of the mysterious Ghost Dance Prophet.

His name was Wovoka, but he had lived for a time in his youth with a white family named Wilson, and the whites in the vicinity of Walker's Lake, Nevada, knew him as Jack Wilson. He was unknown and insignificant up to the time of his great vision. When the Sioux visited him, he was about thirty-five years old. He was a full-blooded Paiute, affecting white man's clothing and distinguished by tattoo marks on both wrists. He had never been out of Mason Valley in which he was born and spoke only Paiute, except for a smattering of English. Wovoka's great "revelation" occurred about two years before he talked with Short Bull and Kicking Bear. (pp. 230-231, Wellman, 1954)

Kicking Bear and Short Bull returned to their homes after a journey of more than two thousand miles among strange people. At a great council the

127

*emissaries expounded the story of the Messiah's coming.
It was received with profound rejoicing. (pp. 231-232,
Wellman, 1954)*

It was the belief of Paul Wellman that to this point in history, the Ghost
Dance Movement of 1890, had been solely a "religious mania." "The Ghost
Dance was entirely Christian -- except for the difference in rituals." (p. 232,
Wellman, 1954) Wellman suggests that the "spark" that was needed to change
the fire of religious fervor into the uncontrolled prairie fire that swept the Ba-
sin and Plains, was ignited by a "...green 'tenderfoot' agent, F. F. Royer, at Pine
Ridge." (p. 232, Wellman, 1954)

Royer became increasingly alarmed as the Sioux gathered on the Pine
Ridge Reservation to dance the Ghost Dance. He remained convinced that the
dancing was but a sign of an impending uprising by the Sioux that would result
in the wholesale slaughter of whites in the region. The person most responsible
for the spread of the Ghost Dance, a man who had to be stopped, according to
Royer's thinking was Sitting Bull.

Royer was successful in convincing General Miles that something needed to be done quickly. So in November, at Thanksgiving time of 1890, General
Miles resolved to arrest Sitting Bull and to "disarm the rest of the Indians" (p.
232, Wellman, 1954). The events that followed are now only reflections of history. A terrible reflection that need never to have taken place...but did.

*Sitting Bull was dead. Now came the more difficult of
Miles' two measures the disarming of the hostiles.*

*At news of the chief's death the whole Sioux Nation
became tense. Within three days after the killing on
Grand River, there were two fights on or near Cheyenne
River, where Big Foot's Village stood. On the other hand
many of the Indians returned to their agencies. For
example, a thousand Ogalallas returned to Pine Ridge on
October 18th. Six days later, Hump's band, numbering
two hundred and twenty-four, gave up at Fort Bennett.*

*But there was still one big band at large--Big Foot's
village on the Cheyenne. The remnants of Sitting Bull's
people had joined that chief. (p. 235, Wellman, 1954)*

Big Foot informed Colonel E. V. Sumner of the Cavalry that he wanted
peace and that he would not fight. Proof of his intent was to be the surrender of
the 333 people in his band. The surrender was to take place on December 21,
1890, at the Big Foot camp at Wounded Knee Creek.

By December 22, nearly 3,000 troops began to. encircle the camp; and
on December 28, Major Whiteside' of the 7th Cavalry called upon
the People to surrender.

> *Big Foot tried to parley.*
> *"We want peace," he said. "I am sick and my people..."*
> *"I will not parley with you," said Whiteside. "You must*
> *surrender or fight. Which shall it be?"*
> *"We surrender," answered Big Foot.*
> *(p. 236, Wellman, 1954)*

During the morning of the 29th of December, Colonel J. W. Forsyth placed 500 of his men in a circle around the Sioux camp. Four Hotchkiss guns were aimed at the central gathering point occupied by women and children. Big Foot lay in his tent suffering from pneumonia. The tension in the camp was grave and increased as Whiteside, after talking with Forsyth, brought his cavalry closer.

As cavalrymen began to search the teepees for weapons, anger among the Indian men intensified as they watched helplessly as their women and children were pushed and shoved by the soldiers.

> *A medicine man, Yellow Bird, began haranguing the*
> *Indians, calling out that the ghost shirts nearly all of*
> *them wore were bulletproof and urging them to resist. A*
> *trooper grabbed the edge of a warrior's blanket to jerk*
> *it away. Yellow Bird stooped and tossed a handful of*
> *dust into the air. Sharply a rifle shot rang out. (p. 236,*
> *Wellman, 1954)*

The action of Yellow bird, some writers maintain, was a signal for the Indian men to begin to fight. Others maintain that the throwing of a handful of dust into the air was a token of disgust by Yellow Bird and more likely than not constituted an action of contempt rather than a prearranged signal to attack.

Regardless of the intent of his actions, Yellow Birds' sudden motion caused a shot to be fired. Whether or not the Indians or soldiers fired the first round has never been fully or satisfactorily established. Regardless of the blame, the incident was, in the words of Wellman, "...what the 7th Cavalry was waiting for."

> *For fourteen years they had wanted to wipe out the*
> *Custer disaster in blood. This was too good a chance*
> *to miss. Right into the crowd of sitting and standing*
> *warriors, many of them so close to the muzzles of the*
> *carbines that they could nearly touch them, the soldiers*
> *discharged a shattering volley. Nearly half the warriors*
> *in Big Foot's band were killed or wounded by that first*
> *discharge. (pp. 236-237, Wellman, 1954)*

129

> *The Hotchkiss guns went into action. Rapid-fire shells*
> *burst among the Sioux with terrible execution. Within a*
> *few minutes the field was strewn with the bodies of dead*
> *and wounded Indians. A handful broke through and*
> *fled in wild panic down a deep ravine. The blood-mad*
> *soldiers pursued, and the Hotchkiss guns never ceased*
> *to hurl their shells into the helpless, fugitive crowd. This*
> *was massacre in all its horror. (p. 237, Wellman, 1954)*

The inhumane killing of men, women and children, many of whom had been clubbed to death several miles from the camp, was over by 9:00 p.m. Just how many of the original 333 members of Big Foot's band survived is not known. It is generally agreed that many men, women and children perished. Twenty-nine soldiers died and 33 were wounded (p. 236, Wellman, 1954). General Miles reported that "...not less than two hundred..." Sioux were killed.

The night of December 29 turned cold and gray. A blizzard spread its chilling agony across the landscape. Snow provided the only decent covering for the twisted and tormented dead. For some strange reason of providence, several small children survived for up to two days, clinging close to the dead bodies of their parents.

Thus 1890 ended for the Indian People, and for the Mormon Millenialist, much as it had begun -- with a longing for the return of the Messiah. The death songs of the dying at Wounded Knee were a far and distant cry from those songs of peace sung around the circle of the Ghost Dance. The wails of agony from the wounded and the survivors were but a dim reminder to the Mormon population of their responsibility of having attempted to take the gospel of peace and deliverance to the People. Echoes of the Mormon hymn, "All is Well -- All is Well," fell as hollow notes on a deafened ear. Mormons and Indians survived the year 1890 but, for many, their hopes in the return of the Messiah were dashed to the ground at Wounded Knee and in the shadows of the Mormon Temple.

> *...the sun had dipped behind the sharp skyline of*
> *the Omaha hills. Silence was then called, and a well*
> *cultivated mezzo-soprano voice...gave...a little song,*
> *the notes of which I have been unsuccessful in repeated*
> *efforts to obtain since...a version of the text, touching to*
> *all earthly wanderers:*
>
> *By the rivers of Babylon we sat down and wept. We wept*
> *when we remembered Zion. (p. 82, Stegner, 1964)*

It had been William Clayton who composed what "...was shortly to become the camp song of Zion:"

Come, come ye saints,
No toil nor labor fear,
But with joy wend your way;
Though hard to you
This journey may appear,
Grace shall be as your day.

'Tis better far for us to strive
Our useless cares from us to drive;
Do this, and joy our hearts will swell.
All is well! All is well!'

The Body of the Sioux leader Big Foot
Wounded Knee Massacre Site
Smithsonian Photograph

CHAPTER VI

The Ghost Dance Religion Of 1890

Because of their geographical proximity to Nevada, and because of their unique doctrine and powerful evangelical outreach, it is perfectly understandable that the Mormon Millenialists may have contributed a great deal to the enthusiasm that centered in the teachings of the Paiute Ghost Dance Religion. Unfortunately, there is little empirical evidence that would lead to the conclusion that the Mormons and Mormon doctrine were in fact the forces that produced the Ghost Dance Religion. On the contrary, there is equal speculative evidence that would cause the conclusion to be reached that the Ghost Dance, was indeed, uniquely Indian in its origin, concept and application. It is far easier to believe that Mormonism simply fanned the fire of Indian revivalism that had already begun to rage in the west.

The threads connecting Mormonism and the Ghost Dance are complicated; however, an effort to unravel the parts is vital to any attempt to understand the history of either the Mormons or the Indian People living in 1890. The story centers in the little known life of an Indian religious leader and practitioner by the name of Tavibo (sometimes spelled Tavivo -- see pp. 42-43, Johnson, 1975). Tavibo had come originally from the southern end of Mason Valley, Nevada. Tavibo was, according to Johnson, the father of Wovoka, the man destined to become the Ghost Dance Prophet of 1890. Tavibo had, it is said, participated in the Ghost Dance Movement of 1870.

Wovoka had been born in the 1850's and came under the youthful influence of not only his father, Tavibo, and was old enough to travel with his father to listen to the teachings of Wodziwob when he began to conduct his first public ceremonies in the 1860's. It is reasonable to conclude that Tavibo, like many of his kinsmen, distrusted the white encroachers into Mason Valley and into the Walker Lake region. It is also likely, and highly probable, that Tavibo openly resisted any and every effort of the whites to take over his homeland. It is equally probable that Tavibo's most effective form of resistance was in his teachings to his own people.It is reasonable to assume that since Wodziwob had begun to formulate the principles of the Ghost Dance Movement of 1870 that Tavibo would almost certainly incorporate the same philosophies into his own teachings. Tavibo was certain to have believed and to have taught that an end to white domination of the Peoples' land was to be, and that there should be a return to the Indian value system.

Like any number of religious teachers, Tavibo soon began to attract notice both within the Indian community and among whites as well. Reginald and Gladys Lauben state that "Tavibo's teachings spread to Indians in Utah, where they were considerably influenced by the Mormon missionaries." (p. 53, Lauben, 1976)

The Laubens state that Smohalla, leader of the Sahaptin of the middle Columbia River and Plateau, was also influenced by Mormonism. Smohalla, it is said, "...incorporated both Catholic and Mormon dogma and ritual into his new religion." (p. 53, Lauben, 1976) The reference to the possible influence of Mormonism on Tavibo, Wovoka's father, is among the most isolated of references. It is more likely that references will be made attempting to establish the probable influence of Mormonism in the life of Wovoka than in the teachings of either Wodziwob or Tavibo.

The exact names, dates, and location of Mormon missionary endeavors have yet to be established with any degree of credibility; however, it is said that Jacob Hamblin, missionary and Apostle of the Mormon Church, did extensive work among the Paiute. Specific reference to Wovoka and his father cannot be established from current literature in this field. Moreover, the effect of Mormon missionary endeavor would be difficult to assess totally, since the barrier of language between English and the Paiute tongue is obvious.

In a description of Wovoka, Albert S. Gatschet, says:

> [Wovoka]...is a full-blood Indian and was married
> in his twentieth year; no other language but Paiute is
> spoken by him, and he is but imperfectly acquainted with
> English. (p. 111, Journal of American Folk-Lore, from
> the article, "Report of an Indian Visit to Jack Wilson, the
> Paiute Messiah")

A review of the literature related to the early life of Wovoka tends to place greater emphasis upon the teachings of Wodziwob and the David Wilsons than it does on his father, Tavibo. Edward C. Johnson, in writing an authoritative account of the history of the Walker River Paiutes, states that not only was Wovoka influenced by his father, Tavibo, but that by the tradition and culture of the Paiute, "At least one child of a shaman often became a doctor." (p. 45, Johnson, 1975)

> One did not have to seek the powers of a religious
> leader. Dreams foretold what was to happen. Doctors
> interpreted the dreams. Power was gained from various
> creatures including deer, snakes, bears, eagles, owls,
> water babies, etc. These creatures appeared in the
> dreams. Individuals also traveled to various caves where
> power was obtained. Only the most powerful shamans
> were able to go into extended trances or deep sleeps and
> visit the other world. (p. 45, Johnson, 1975)

It is said of Wovoka that he became ill sometime during the year of 1879, and while suffering from a high fever, he sank into a coma and remained near death for several days. "Several persons report having

133

seen him in a trance about this time." (p. 45, Johnson, 1975) It is not certain that this experience constituted a visionary experience. In the minds of a few of the Paiute, this was indeed a confirmation of the extraordinary and exemplary life led by the future prophet.

This experience would have occurred while Wovoka was still in his 20's. James Mooney interviewed Wovoka in January of 1892, learned that Wovoka had never traveled more than thirty miles from Mason Valley and that he generally used an interpreter to speak to whites. Edward Dyer, a purported white friend of Wovoka's, is quoted by Paul Bailey as stating Wovoka traveled when he was in his 20's to Oregon to pick hops during at least two separate summers. It was during this time that Wovoka could have come into contact with Native American People from Oregon who had taken up the "Shaker" religion of John Slocum (Squaschtin). It may be that it was through John Slocum, or through the Smohalla religion of Washington and Oregon, that Wovoka learned to cultivate spiritual awareness through visions or trances.

It has been suggested that through the teachings of Mormonism, Wovoka may have learned of the vision experience of the young Mormon Prophet, Joseph Smith, while praying in the woods of Palmyra, New York. The experience of the youthful Joseph Smith would surely be among those favorite stories told by Mormon Missionaries since it would constitute a significant claim of Mormonism to the plates containing the record of the Lamanites in America.

The only definitive truth as to how, when and where Wovoka learned that it was necessary to communicate with the spirit world and to receive authority for its work from the Great Spirit, lies in a cemetery west of Schurtz, Nevada -- or is resident in the mind of the Ghost Dance Prophet. In either case, a great mystery still surrounds this phase of the life of the Prophet, Wovoka; nevertheless, it is no less of a mystery than the visionary experience of any Old Testament Prophet, or that of Buddha or even Mohammed ...but a mystery nonetheless!

By 1889, Wovoka had established his credibility in the Mason Valley both in the Indian Community and in that of the whites. Among the white residents, Wovoka was generally held to be hard working and industrious, virtues necessary to gain respect in the white man's world. Wovoka was unable to read and to write English; however, it is reported that his wife, Mary, could read well enough to communicate happenings of the newspapers and to read some books on religion. This contribution; of his wife undoubtedly added to his general; understanding of the stories of Jesus of Nazareth; stories of His life and resurrection that were, reinforced through members of the David Wilson home.

It has been said that Wovoka had spent a portion of the year of 1888 battling the effects of scarlet fever. At least one writer reports that he may, have even suffered delirium when the fever became excessively high; however, it would be less than objective by writers or   134 observers to conclude that the "delirium" was the cause or source of Wovoka's visions and experiences in the spirit world. It may have been that this was the case; however, there exists no evidence to support conclusively that this was true. Thus, the "fever" and delirium can only be described as an effect of illness (scarlet fever), and not as the source of Wovoka's power, vision, or experience. Whatever his power source, his teachings were epidemic among the Paiute. They came to believe in him as their Prophet, and Deliverer.

Myth and legend continue to surround the events associated with the solar eclipse that took place on January 1, 1889, for it was on this date and at the time of the eclipse that Wovoka went into a trance or vision state. It is said that he remained in this physical-mental condition for up to three days. Upon regaining consciousness, Wovoka announced that the elapsed time had been spent in the presence and in communication with the Great Spirit. The message that he brought back to his people was one of peace.

James Mooney recorded Wovoka's experience of the trance/vision as follows:

> On this occasion, "the sun died" and he fell asleep in the daytime and was taken up to the other world. Here he saw God, with all the people who had died long ago engaged in their old time sports and occupation, all happy and forever young. It was a pleasant land and full of game. After showing him all, God told him he must go back and tell his people they must be good and love one another, have no quarreling, and live in peace with the whites; that they must work, and not lie or steal; that they must put away all the old practices that savored of war; that if they faithfully obeyed his instructions they would at last be reunited with their friends in this other world, where there would be no more death or sickness or old age. He was then given the dance which he was commanded to bring back to his people. By performing this dance at intervals, for five consecutive days each time, they would secure this happiness for themselves and hasten the event. (pp. 771-772, Mooney, 1892)

Later that month, Wovoka held the first Ghost Dance at the Walker River Reservation, "about a mile above the railroad bridge near the agency." It was at this time that Wovoka announced the ritual of the Dance, introduced hymns that were to be sung, and encouraged the dancing to continue for the full five days.

News of the Ghost Dance gathering spread quickly among the Paiute People and their neighbors among several tribes. The white community was quick to learn, too, of the strange events that were beginning to take place on the reservation; and again, just as had been true twenty years earlier, stories of Indian uprisings began to surface and spread.

The Mormon missionary activities among the Paiutes in the eastern portion of Nevada seem to have been more successful than those nearer the mining centers along the California/Nevada Border. In the east a number of Paiutes had entered the waters of Mormon baptism and the story of Mormonism concerning the return of Jesus to the Chosen of the Lord, the House of Israel, dove-tailed perfectly with the story spreading from the Walker Lake Reservation -- that is, Jesus was soon to return.

Mormon missionary activities had limited success among the mining populations of Nevada and California. This may have been the result of Brigham Young's admonition to his people to refrain from entering into gold and silver mining activities. A consequence of this reluctance to associate with the mining industry carried with it an equal timidity to engage in any kind of social activity with the miners themselves. A second consideration is that while Brigham Young had sent Mormons into the Carson Valley to establish settlements, such as they did at Genoa, their efforts were, nevertheless, short lived as Brigham Young called his people back to help protect Salt Lake City in 1857. It was during this time that the clouds of the "Utah War" were gathering.

Interestingly enough, it had been in this very area of western Nevada that appeared to have been neglected by Mormon missionary activity that the messianic Ghost Dance Prophet arose.

> *His message and his promise bore close semblance to* those of Mormon doctrine. Converted Paiutes by the scores saw in Wovoka not only God's working means for their rejuvenation and redemption, but they claimed him as their own. (p. 100, Bailey, 1957)

> *In the years preceding Wovoka's translation and his* *emergence as Christ and Savior to the Indian world,* *the Mormons from Salt Lake City and their outlying* *towns in Utah and Nevada, had made their great strides* *in conversion of the Paiute nation to the doctrines and* *practices of their church. Their peculiar teachings* *regarding the Israelitish background of the American* *Indian, the Book of Mormon with its purported history of* *this fallen people, its promise of their redemption and rise* *again to greatness, its story of Christ's ministry among* *them, and His promise to return, had been assimilated* *and accepted by hundreds upon hundreds of Paiutes,* *long before Wovoka stepped in the center of the spiritual* *stage. While intrigued by Mormon doctrine, there is no* *indication that he ever personally entered the waters of* *Mormon baptism. (pp. 121-122 Bailey, 1957)*

A unique aspect of both Mormon theology and the Ghost Dance Religion was the belief that the end of the age would be characterized by a physical transformation of the earth. A belief that the earth was tired and worn, that it had yielded to the exploitation of mankind, and was now ready for renewal, was a common belief of both Mormons and Paiute Ghost Dancers. The concept that the earth, like all of humankind, must die (rest?) and be renewed before it could be the final dwelling place of the Messiah was, also, a common belief of Mormonism and followers of the Ghost Dance Religion.

Likewise common to both Mormonism and the Ghost Dance Religion was the belief that the faithful followers of the religions would be rewarded for their steadfastness by being gathered into a specific geographic location and there they would be safe from the destruction that would fall upon the despoilers of the earth and the polluters of God's law. The belief in the redemption of the elect was by no means unique to either Mormonism or to the Ghost Dance Religion. Many religious sects adhered to such beliefs; however, it is unique that Mormons and Ghost Dancers believed in this concept so totally, at the same time, and in the same region of the United States. The belief of the elect being gathered out of the four corners of the earth is by no means a forgotten theme of religious movements and revival. The same story can be found in present day Hopi prophecies concerning the end of this age, the renewal of the earth and the restoration of humankind to a proper relationship with the Great Spirit and Pahana. The Hopi represent their belief today in nearly the same terms as had the Ghost Dance Religion in 1870 and again in 1890. Hopi prophecies proclaim:

> ...the Hopis and their homeland will be preserved as
> an oasis to which refugees will flee. ...Those who take
> no part in the making of world division by ideology
> are ready to resume life in another world, be they of
> the Black, White, Red, or Yellow race. They are all one,
> brothers." (p. 408, Waters, 1963)

The sentiment expressed is nearly -- if not exactly that expressed in the Ghost Dance Religion.

Paul Bailey, in The Indian Messiah, wrote about Mormon interest in the Native American People as a fulfillment of the promises made to the Lamanites, as stated in The Book of Mormon, i.e., they were to be a chosen people, a redeemed people destined to live in a perfect community and in a position of equality with their white brothers and sisters.

> The eastern segment of the Paiute nation, spiritually
> dominated by the Mormon Church, more than ever
> turned acute ears to the sensationally new doctrine which
> had erupted as a living flame out of the area
> of Walker Lake. For one thing, redemption

137

*of the American Indian was a basic tenet of this faith.
The Book of Mormon that unique scripture said to have
been dug out of a New York hill, in the form of graven
gold plates, and translated with divine assistance by
their prophet, Joseph Smith, was an historical record
of the American Indian and his predecessors upon the
American continent. In this book, as widely accepted
by the converted of the eastern Paiutes as it was by the
white Mormons themselves, held forth the promise that
the earth would undergo a physical transformation, that
the faithful would be gathered out of all the lands of the
earth, that the American Indians would be lifted out of
their barbaric state, and would become again the "white
and delightsome" people which their Book of Mormon
ancestors had claimed to be. (p. 99, Bailey, 1957)*

*The Book told how the Christ had once visited the
American continent, set up His church, and had chosen
twelve favored disciples from among the natives. In
the Book was the heartening promise that this same
Messiah would again return, and personally hasten the
redemption of a race, which the Book claimed had its
genetic origin in ancient Judea. (pp. 99-100 Bailey, 1957)*

It is the belief expressed by Paul Bailey that the "evangelized" eastern
Paiutes, and the Utes of the Basin, listened in an attitude of total acceptance
and belief. So total was their commitment to the message of the Ghost Dance
Prophet and to the tenets of Mormonism that they quickly began to spread the
story of their new religion to other neighboring tribes. In a matter of weeks or
months, the story of the new Prophet had reached the Sioux on the Pine Ridge
and Rose Bud Reservations.

*For the first time in two hundred years of death and
oppression, a voice of hope and promise was raised to
the dwindling, beaten tribes of North America. Wovoka
himself could scarcely have realized that his simple,
unlearned words and convictive declarations would, in a
matter of months, blow themselves into a whirlwind. (p.
98, Bailey, 1957)*

News of the teachings of the Ghost Dance Religion brought considerable excitement Mormon communities as well. James Mooney states that:

*When the news of this Indian revelation came to their
ears, the Mormon priests accepted it as a prophecy of
speedy fulfillment of their own traditions, and Orson
Pratt, one of the most prominent leaders,
preached a sermon, which was extensively*

> *copied and commented on at the time, urging the faithful*
> *to arrange their affairs and put their houses in order to*
> *receive the long-awaited wanderers. (p. 75, Utley, 1963)*

Indian Agents at Fort Hall, Idaho, reported that Mormon missionaries were actively seeking converts among the Bannock. Just how effective the Mormon missionary effort was being carried out among the western Paiute at Walker River is not a well-established fact. It is Paul Bailey's belief that efforts to convert eastern Paiutes, specifically Mary and Jack (Wovoka) Wilson, had been futile: "Even though," records Bailey, "the Mormon missionaries made him think a lot, Wovoka rejected their creed. Both he and Mary utterly refused to be dipped in the Utah church." (p. 112, Bailey, 1957)

Bailey does record that the daughter, Alice Wilson Vidovich, and son-in-law of Wovoka, Andrew Vidovich, were in fact, members of the Church of Jesus Christ of Latter Day Saints (Mormon). (p. 212, Bailey, 1957) The son-in-law, Andrew, is described as an admixture of Shoshonean and Slavonian, who appears to have entered the waters of Mormon baptism and was described as a "staunch member" of the Mormon faith. The story that the Ghost Dance Prophet, Wovoka, was not a member of the Mormon Church, but that his son-in-law was, is current on the Walker River reservation. The persistence of this story through the years is most interesting from the point of view that it appears now to be fixed in both time and tradition and thus it appears to be accepted by persons interviewed as, indeed, fact.

An interesting speculation could reasonably be made that since the son-in-law of Wovoka was Mormon in name and in fact, that it would be more than reasonable to assume that Andrew Vidovich was a member of the Mormon priesthood, an Elder of the Melchisedic Order and as such quite capable of participation in the Mormon ritual known as Baptism for the Dead.

> *Baptism for the dead is first alluded to by [Joseph Smith]*
> *the prophet, who in a revelation dated January 19, 1841,*
> *declares, 'A baptismal font there is not upon the earth,*
> *that they, my saints, may be baptized for those who*
> *are dead.' It is intimated that a reasonable time will be*
> *allowed in which to build a temple and a permanent*
> *font, and that during this time a temporary substitute*
> *for the font may be employed; but after the completion*
> *of the temple, no baptisms for the dead will be of avail*
> *unless conducted within the building. See Doctrine and*
> *Covenants [Utah] 392, 395 (p. 337, Bancroft, 1890)*
>
> *Daniel Tyler says the doctrine was first taught in*
> *Nauvoo, although Joseph told some of the elders in*
> *Kirtland that it was part of the gospel, and would yet be*
> *practiced as such. Juvenile Instructor, xv. 56. He also*
> *says that before other provision was made,*

139

> *many were baptized in the Mississippi River. The first*
> *baptismal font, a temporary structure, intended for use*
> *only until the completion of the temple, was erected in the*
> *basement of that building, and dedicated on November*
> *8, 1841, Joseph being present and Brigham delivering the*
> *address. (p. 337, Bancroft, 1890)*

Baptism for the dead, as best understood by this writer, is to fulfill the scriptural command: "Except a man be born of the water and spirit, he cannot enter the Kingdom of God." The principle appears to be applied to not only the living, but to the dead as well. It is believed that as many as 5,000 persons were baptized for the dead in Nauvoo before the exodus in 1846. The teachings of the church relative to the doctrine of baptism for the dead, like the "concept" of invincibility and special protection through the use of special "endowment' garments was carried west after 1846 and was shared universally and broadly among converts -- Gentile and Indian -- to the Mormon faith. Wovoka knew, as did most Paiutes, that redemption of the American Indian was a basic tenet of Mormonism." (p. 111, Bailey, 1957) It is generally believed that it was these tenets that Wovoka had rejected; however, the work of converting the Indian People was pursued with renewed vigor.

As early as the Spring of 1875, Mormon Missionaries had begun teaching among the Bannock, urging them to be baptized into the Mormon religion.

> *A large number accepted the invitation without the*
> *knowledge of the agent, went down to Utah, and were*
> *baptized, and then returned to work as missionaries*
> *of the new faith among their tribes. As an additional*
> *inducement, free rations were furnished by Mormons*
> *to all who would come and be baptized, and they were*
> *told...they were a chosen people of God to establish his*
> *kingdom upon earth... (pp. 4 - 5, Utley, 1963)*

At other times and in other places, Native American People entered not only the waters of Mormon baptism, but the realm of spiritual marriages for eternity as well. The Buckskin Apostle, Jacob Hamblin, is said to have taken a Paiute woman, Eliza, as his fourth wife (February 14, 1863); and that this solemn occasion was witnessed by Daniel W. Wells, Wilford Woodruff and others. (p. 256, Bailey, 1948) In nearly every phase of life -- farming, establishing of homes, in education and welfare, the Mormons gave considerable attention and energy. To enter the waters of Mormon baptism meant to be totally immersed in the socio-economic and religious activities of Mormonism. The Ghost Dance stirred considerable excitement in the Mormon communities as it undoubtedly appeared to the Church membership that the Lamanites were, indeed, ready to receive the gospel and The Book of Mormon.

Mooney asserts:

> *...it is evident that the Mormons took an active interest*
> *in the religious ferment then existing among the*
> *neighboring tribes and helped to give shape to the*
> *doctrine which crystalized...in the Ghost Dance. (pp. 4-5,*
> *Utley, 1963)*

> *In the shuffling circles of the Ghost Dance throughout the*
> *Paiute nation were many of these Paiute Mormon elders.*
> *They talked to Wovoka, and he was cognizant of the holy*
> *garment they wore, and which was accepted by them as*
> *an actual physical protection against disease and death.*
> *(p. 123, Bailey, 1957)*

The Mormon population of Salt Lake City was gripped by excitement as a result of an anonymously written pamphlet that announced a series of lectures to be delivered in July of 1892, "weather permitting, at the Nineteenth Ward, 6:30 to 8:30 p.m." The lectures were to begin on the 10th of July and were to include topics centering in the life and ministry of Jesus to Hebrews and to the American Indian. The title for the lectures included:

> *"The Coming of the Messiah to the Hebrew,"*
> *"The Coming of the Messiah to the Jews," and*
> *"The Coming of the Messiah to the American Indian."*

All things considered, the topics of the lectures were rather ordinary and as such incapable of exciting too much interest in American Indians; however, the lectures took place after a number of important events were reported to have taken place beginning in March 1890. The events had been of such magnitude as to capture and fire the evangelistic heart of every man, woman and child that called themselves: "Mormon!"

> *..the people of God, were notified by the three Nephites,*
> *met at Walker Lake, Emerald County, Nevada, where a*
> *dispensation of the celestial kingdom of God -- the gospel*
> *in the covenant consecration, a perfect oneness in all*
> *things, temporal, and spiritual – was given them. Twelve*
> *disciples were ordained, not by Angels of men, but by*
> *the Messiah, in the presence of hundreds, representing*
> *scores of tribes or nations, who saw his face, heard and*
> *understood his voice as on the day of Pentecost. (p. 783,*
> *Mooney, 1892)*

The excitement of the Mormon community must certainly have been epidemic! The combination of all of these events prompted the circulation of a pamphlet declaring that the "...Mormons have stepped down and out of Celestial Government -- the American Indians have stepped up and into Celestial Government." (p. 783, Mooney, 1892) The Native American People were to be, as the Mormons came to view them, the "...chosen people of God to establish his kingdom upon the earth..." (p. 704, Mooney, 1892) To the Indian People, the religious revival of the Ghost Dance as taught by Wovoka, was the beginning of the millennial reign of Christ upon a new earth. To the Mormon Millenialist, 1890 was the long awaited year in which it was believed, that the Messiah would return. Both the Indian People and the Mormons began 1890 with a burning desire to see and feel the return of the Messiah.

It is little wonder, then, that considerable confusion reigned throughout the region when the Mormons said: "The Messiah is about to appear!" and the Indian People proclaimed that "the Indian Prophet, Wovoka" is indeed here. Somehow during this time-span the term "messiah" (not Messiah) came to be associated with Wovoka's name. He was known, therefore, as "the Prophet Wovoka" or as "Wovoka, the messiah." The difficulty in attempting to sort out details and events becomes nearly impossible as languages and dialects are encountered. Imagine, for example, the perception of the Indian Community (in Nevada) when a Mason Valley Paiute would say: "The messiah (meaning Wovoka) is here." In St. George or Salt Lake City, to the Millenialist, word from the "Lamanites" that the Messiah (interpreted to mean Jesus of Nazareth) had returned (as He said He would in The Book of Mormon) to the Lost Tribes of the House of Israel, and that the Messiah was in the Mason Valley of Nevada, was, without a doubt, electrifying news. Stories spread that the Messiah had been seen, heard and even the scars in his hands, felt.

> *After the first meeting with Wovoka it seems that he made every effort to impress them with the actuality of his being the Messiah. He would appear to them out of clouds of smoke or from the top of a rock high above the river. On one occasion he called the various delegations together, and although he talked in Paiute, the Sioux, Cheyenne, Arapahos, and Shoshonis all claimed to understand him. He said that he was the Christ, the same whom the white men had persecuted, and showed them scars on his hands, feet, and breast to convince them. Since the white people had rejected him, he was coming back to save the Indian people from their oppressors. (p. 57, Laubin, 1976)*

Some writers, as did James Mooney, maintained that Wovoka never claimed to be the Messiah; but that the notion of his "messiahship" had come from the words and descriptions of his followers. Other writers, such as Paul Bailey and the Laubins, allude to the notion that Wovoka deliberately did those things to create an image of his being Jesus.

142

Paul Bailey in his book, <u>Wovoka</u> <u>Indian</u> <u>Messiah,</u> reconstructs a conversation that might have taken place between Wovoka and Elder (Mormon) Peter Swenson of Mt. Pleasant, Utah. In this fictionalized account, Wovoka is reported to have told Elder Swenson that he, Wovoka, was the Christ. It is of such stories as these that legends are made, but they rarely contribute to factual knowledge.

Whether Wovoka innocently or with deliberate intent, passed the idea to his people that he was really the Christ Messiah is not empirically known. This writer is inclined to place more credence in the position of James Mooney, i.e., that Wovoka did not deliberately pass himself off as the Messiah; however, regardless of where, how or when, it all began, the idea was spread rapidly across the land that the Messiah (or messiah) had come to the Indian People.

Once the story of the returned Messiah fell upon the ears of the Mormon Church Officials, a series of lectures were given to discredit the story of the return of Jesus. The timing of the refutation came when the anti-polygamy sentiment of the Gentiles was at its height. A number of Church officials, including members of the Quorum of Twelve Apostles, were arrested and charged as polygamists.

A pragmatic assessment of the times may have caused the Mormon hierarchy to conclude that they could not afford, politically, to have any more bad publicity. Times were hard enough as it was without running the risk of additional unfavorable news articles about the return of the Messiah.

In response, President Woodruff advised the Mormon community that it was to be assumed that the person or persons currently visiting the Lamanites in Nevada was not, after all, the Risen Lord, but rather it was assumed that the " ...heavenly visitor had been one of the Three Nephites[8] instead of the Messiah;" nevertheless, enthusiastic Mormon men and women joined with the Indians in the dancing of the Ghost Dance.

> *So prevalent was the thought of the Christ's second*
> *coming among the people that president Wilford*
> *Woodruff, George Q. Cannon and many others took to*
> *the pulpit during the semi-annual Church conference*
> *of October 1890 to refute this notion. (Coates) (p. 24,*
> *an unpublished research paper, Bernard O. Walker,*
> *Brigham Young University, undated)*

---

8   The "Three Nephites" represent personalities that appear in Mormon folklore as <u>Book</u> <u>of</u> <u>Mormon'</u> personalities who, because of their righteousness, were allowed to be translated from mortal beings to spirit beings without "tasting of death."

Diffusion Of The Ghost Dance Religion

The Ghost Dance Religion gained converts rapidly among the tribes living on the Great Plains, on the Colorado Plateau, and in the Basin and Range region of the West. As the Ghost Dance spread and gained converts, increased alarm began to seep through white mining and ranching communities. A part of the concern and excitement generated came from a failure of the whites to understand--or even attempt to understand--the Ghost Dance as a non-violent protest movement against the whites. However, considerable excitement was undoubtedly generated--and this time with cause--as converts to the Ghost Dance Religion encouraged some Indian People to dance with renewed fervor, for to do so (it was claimed) would cause the whites to be destroyed.

> Mooney recorded that a Paiute from southern Utah
> was "inciting" the Hualapai "to dance for the purpose of
> causing hurricanes and storms to destroy the whites and
> such Indians as would not participate in the dances." (p.
> 16, Dobyns & Euler, 1967)

Word of the Ghost Dance Prophet, his new vision and the promise of the new earth spread rapidly from tribe to tribe. Soon emissaries from many regions and tribes were wending their way toward Walker Lake. The railroad helped to spread the story of the Ghost Dance by allowing Indians free passage on the newly create transcontinental line, thus reducing the travel time from months to a week. A few letters in English began to circulate, written by Indian People who had been taught to read and to write at Government Schools. Yet "Moccasin telegraph" continued to be the most effective means of spreading the story of the new Prophet and his religion.

Everywhere -- and with only minor changes -- the teachings of the Ghost Dance remained basically the same: Indian people must return to their former way of living, i.e., the Indian way, to stop eating food and wearing clothes that the whites had given them, to lay aside drinking and gambling, and most certain of all, to accept the Ghost Dance Religion, then white domination would end, the dead would come back to life, the Messiah would come, and peace would return to the Land.

The expression has often been used that the Ghost Dance Swept the Plains like a prairie fire. Perhaps this analogy is most fitting and correct, as it did describe how quickly the Ghost Dance Movement spread across the land. The first Ghost Dance had begun at the Walker Lake Reservation in January, 1889, and had begun to be fairly well-known among the Utes, Bannocks Goshutes and Pai in the early part of that same year. Significantly enough the Ghost Dance had been introduced to the Pai by the Paiutes, who lived in the immediate vicinity of the Mormon Temple and community in St. George, Utah. (p. 14, Dobyns and Euler, 1967)

144

The Mohave County <u>Miner</u> reported:

> *The Walapai are thoroughly imbued with the idea of the coming of Christ, and that it is not far distant when the Indians will have "full possession and that all the dead Indians, deer, antelopes and other game will be back,"...*
> *(p. 19, Dobyns & Euler, 1967)*

To a people in despair, the promise of a restoration of the earth and the People was, indeed, a message of deliverance, and with amazing speed the story was being told among the disheartened People of Nevada, Idaho, Oregon, and Utah. At Fort Hall, the Shoshoni and Bannocks too shared the new story.

The story, of which legends were made, told how a Bannock left Fort Hall to visit among his family among the Wind River Shoshoni in Wyoming. After hearing the story of the new Prophet, the Shoshoni decided to send their own representative to Walker Lake to see and hear for themselves. Living, too, in a portion of the Wind River Reservation were the Northern Arapahos. The Arapaho and the Shoshoni had struggled between themselves for several years prior to coming to live on the Wind River Reservation; however, tribal differences seemed to be forgotten for a time, as the excitement and promise of the Ghost Dance captured the imagination of the People. So complete was the excitement that an Arapaho by the name of Sage, joined the Shoshoni in their travels to see Wovoka.

It has been said that the Arapaho are inclined toward religious experiences in which the seeing of "signs and wonders," and listening to the words of the prophets, constitute a very important part of their meditation and communion. Following the inspiration of their traditions, the Arapaho, too, quickly followed the leadership of Sage, and began, almost immediately upon his return to the Wind River Reservation, to dance the Ghost Dance.

Spoon Hunter, an Oglala Sioux, had married an Arapaho woman and was living among her people on the Wind River Reservation when Sage began recounting the story of his adventure and in his telling of the Ghost Dance doctrine. Spoon Hunter, like many of his wife's people, began to believe in the Ghost Dance Religion and to dance as they had been instructed through the new disciple, Sage. Not merely content to pray, fast and sing, Spoon Hunter called his son from the Mission school and set him about the task of writing to a nephew on the Cheyenne River Reservation in South Dakota. Spoon Hunter's nephew, Kicking Bear, concluded Sage, was looked upon by his Minikon'ju (Minneconjou) people as not only a wise and virtuous man, but a man of extraordinary spiritual insights as well. Kicking Bear was just the man to hear the news of the marvelous new vision and religion being taught by Wovoka.

At the trading post of the Cheyenne River Reservation, Kicking Bear asked for and received help in translating the letter from Sage.

145

> *Kicking Bear was about forty-one years old, a mystic*
> *with a modest reputation as a medicine man. In the old*
> *days he had been a mighty warrior and an intimate*
> *of Crazy Horse. ...by birth an Oglala, he became a*
> *Miniconjou band chief through marriage to Woodpecker*
> *Woman, niece of the Miniconjou chief, Big Foot.*
> *Uncompromising hatred of the white man and all his*
> *ways, refusal to adjust to the new life, mystical leanings,*
> *and rank and reputation made Kicking Bear a natural*
> *leader in the quest for the old life. (p. 62, Utley, 1963)*

The story of the Ghost Dance Religion and the restoration of the Indian People and the Earth to their former way of life, was the "call" that Kicking Bear was waiting to hear. Immediately Kicking Bear started West toward the Wind River Country. The journey of some 500 miles to his uncle's lodge was made in spite of cold weather and, equally as important, in spite of the fact that Kicking Bear had left the Reservation without getting a pass from the reservation agent. His footsteps directed his course well out of reach of white settlements and ranches for fear that he might be discovered and turned back.

The curious may well ask just what it was that caused a man to set out on such a precarious journey--in the face of winter and without permission from the government to travel. The answer: Kicking Bear was totally convinced that the Ghost Dance Religion was sufficient to save his people from destruction. He had to go to see and to hear--and to teach his people.

> *...In March 1890, eleven Indians returned to Pine Ridge,*
> *Rosebud, and Cheyenne River from a long journey to*
> *the west. They told a wonderful tale. A Messiah had*
> *appeared on earth. He preached a new religion. It was a*
> *religion that offered hope for the Indian race -- hope not*
> *dependent upon promises of white men. He held forth*
> *a vision of paradise in which not only the Sioux but all*
> *Indians would at last be free of the white burden and*
> *reside for eternity in a blissful land. By simply believing*
> *in the Messiah, practicing the tenets of his faith, and*
> *dancing a prescribed "Ghost Dance," they could bring*
> *forth a new world where everything was even better than*
> *it used to be. (p. 60, Utley, 1963)*

This was, indeed, the glad message Kicking Bear shared with hir relatives among thePine Ridge Reservation. Among the Utes the story was nearly the same:

> *Keeps-the-Battle (Kicizapi Tawa) told me a few days ago*
> *that it was during the visit of the Pine Ridge Sioux last*
> *July [1890] that they first heard of the coming*

146

of the new Messiah. He related the following story:

"Scarcely had my people reached the Ute village when we heard of a white preacher whom the Utes held in the highest esteem, who told a beautiful dream or vision of the coming of a great and good red man. This strange person was to set right the wrongs of my people; he could restore to us our game and hunting-grounds, was so powerful that every wish or word he gave utterance to became fulfilled."

"His teachings had a strange effect upon the Utes, and in obedience to the commands of this man, they began a Messiah Dance. They resolved to...institute a Messiah Dance ...at Pine Ridge, and keep up this dance until the Lord himself should appear." (p. 327, The Illustrated American. January 17, 1891)

In the months that followed, the Ghost Dance Religion was taught in each of these tribes: Paiute, Bannock, Shoshoni, Gosiute, Ute, Pit River, Mohave, Walapai, Chemehuevi, Havasupai, Mission, Northern Arapaho, Southern Arapaho, Gros Ventre, Assiniboine, Northern Cheyenne, Southern Cheyenne, Teton Dakota, Yankton Dakota, Caddo, Wichita, Kiowa, Kiowa Apache, Delaware, Kitsai, Comanche, Pawnee, Ponca, Oto, Missouri, Iowa and Kansas. (pp. 53-58, Lesser, 1933)

From the Pine Ridge Reservation, Kicking Bear carried the Ghost Dance Religion to other Sioux living on the Standing Rock Reservation during the Fall of 1890. Among those to whom the new religion was brought was the famous Sitting Bull. The names of other Hunkpapa war chiefs were well known both in the Indian and white community; they included names of men such as Gall, Crow King, and Black Moon. "Their head chief was probably the greatest Indian leader of all time -- Sitting Bull." (p. 49, Miller, 1957)

A visionary and a healer, Sitting Bull was no ordinary medicine man. But it was not only his mystical power that brought red men to the Little Big Horn from every quarter. Nor was it his courage alone -- although he was a brave fighting chief whose daring and vigor in battle were known to every Indian in the Northwest. Above all others -- even the reckless Crazy Horse -- Sitting Bull stood as a clear, unspoiled symbol of the old free way of life that the Indian held sacred and that was passing so fast into oblivion. The example he set gave him dominion over the encampment. (p. 49, Miller, 1957)

147

Sitting Bull was a man to be respected, and yes, even feared. Perhaps, no one disliked him more than Indian Agent James McLaughlin. It is difficult to know what McLaughlin disliked most about Sitting Bull: Something in his personality? Was it his charismatic style of leadership? Or was it the reputation that Sitting Bull held among his people. Probably all of these and more! Whatever it was, McLaughlin wrote of Sitting Bull in later years: "I never knew him to display a single trait that might command admiration or respects." (p. 81, Utley, 1963) McLaughlin characterized Sitting Bull as "crafty, avaricious, mendacious, and ambitious."

Sitting Bull had returned to the reservation area only in 1881, after having spent considerable time in "exile" in Canada. It is more than true, perhaps, that one of the major reasons for his return to the United States had been to aid his people in the struggle to keep the U. S. Government from taking away more of the Sioux land. Sitting Bull was a strong spokesman for resistance of further encroachment by either agents like McLaughlin or his government.

The Sioux were so concerned at the reported encroachment by the whites that they sent delegates to the Standing Rock Reservation to seek the advice and council of Sitting Bull. It was in the time of the "Drying Grass Moon" (October 1890), after the break-up of the great reservation, that a group of Minneconjou Sioux came to talk and to confer with Sitting Bull. It was obvious that the future of the Sioux and the fate of their individual families stood in the balance.

Into this setting of social upheaval and unrest Kicking Bear arrived at the Standing Rock Reservation and began to teach the gospel of the Ghost Dance, and to tell his kinsmen of the wondrous works being performed by the Prophet, Wovoka. It is estimated that as many as 20,000 Sioux took up the Ghost Dance with nearly 16,000 of that number being made up of Teton Sioux. Of all the Plains Indians, it appears that the Sioux, both in numbers and in terms of land lost, were the hardest hit of most Native American People. A treaty in 1868 had taken all of their land west of the Missouri except for a portion of South Dakota, which had been set aside for reservations.

With the discovery of gold in the Black Hills, whites by the thousands swelled into the sacred places of the Sioux. Indian resistance was at its strongest point in the defeat of Custer's troop at the Little Big Horn. Significantly, the defeat of Custer only demonstrated that the whites could take through treaty that which they had been unsuccessful in securing by bullets. By 1876 the Sioux lost an additional one-third of their land -- including the sacred Black Hills. By the mid-1880's the buffalo, their principal food source, was gone. By 1890 the Congress of the United States declared the "frontier closed" no longer could vast tracts of land be taken under the Homestead Act.

In 1889 the Sioux were requested, by a variety of schemes, to give up title to one-half of their remaining land -- about 11,000,000 acres. The years preceding 1889 had been hard -- drought covered the land, rations had been cut and those provisions that did get through were often of inferior quality and, in some cases, infested with insects and worms. Crop failure, coupled with the Federal Government's failure to make payment for seceded lands, rendered the Sioux incapable of buying seed, and food. Whooping cough, a dreaded killer of children, struck without mercy. Measles and influenza, too, extracted their toll. The year of 1890 promised no relief as drought once again gripped the land. These were desperate times and it is during times of extreme stress such as these, that people look to signs and manifestations that indicate that somehow they will be fed and that peace and prosperity will return. The People longed for a time when sickness and death would cease to ravish the land.

Kicking Bear could not have planned a better time for his arrival at the Standing Rock Reservation. The people had gathered to hear the council of Sitting Bull. What better news could be heard than that the Messiah had returned to save His people from certain destruction? The land was to be restored to its rightful heirs, the Sioux and their relatives. The happy condition was to be brought about by the singing of the Ghost Dance Songs, by praying and dancing.

> But there was a price for this. The religion imposed
> a rigid moral code, grounded in Christian ethics and
> departing radically from ancient attitudes and habits.
> "Do no harm to anyone. You must not fight," Wovoka
> enjoined the disciples. A people who had fought for
> centuries, who loved to fight, whose greatest rewards
> sprang from war, were told to put away all weapons and
> trophies of war, to think gentle thoughts, and to harm
> no person, red or white. "Do not tell lies." "When your
> friends die, you must not cry." Since all dead Indians
> were to return, there was no need to cry, to mutilate and
> torture their bodies, to cut off their hair, and to destroy
> property. And finally, a blanket injunction to cover all
> else, "Do right always." (p. 70, Utley, 1963)

It was the opinion of Robert Utley that the combination of "Christianity and paganism" welded the Ghost Dance into a new moral code that if adhered to would restore the "old savage life and its dominant values." (p. 70, Utley, 1963) It was, according to Utley, just the "combination" that "... appealed strongly to the heart and mind of the American Indian." (p. 70, Utley, 1963)

The historic record seems clear that the teachings of Wovoka regarding the dance form and some of the ritual beliefs were altered and modified as the Ghost Dance was adopted by the many language families. The change or modification of the Dance, i.e., the use of a central fire, or the use of cedar boughs in the dance performance, was of minor significance when compared with the teachings of Wovoka that dealt with fighting and war.

149

*The doctrine as taught by the Paiute prophet was entirely
pacifistic. Indians need only follow his moral precepts
and dance the Ghost Dance to bring about the new
order. Above all, he stressed the importance of avoiding
violence even in thought. Every other tribe absorbed
this commandment, but not the Sioux. The bitterness
engendered by the land agreement and the ration cut
left them with too much hatred toward the white man.
As described by the Sioux emissaries, the doctrine of
peace became a doctrine, if not of war, at least of vicious
antagonism to the whites. (underscore added) (pp. 72-73,
Utley, 1963)*

It appears more than reasonable to speculate that had the U. S. Government moved, even as late as mid-year of 1890, to restore the cut rations, and,
attempted to fulfill the provisions of the Crook Commission, that the Ghost
Dance Religion might have lost momentum among the Sioux. However, Agent
McLaughlin, like his counterparts throughout the Bureau of Indian Affairs,
continued to enforce treaty provisions that took the land, reinforced census
counts that resulted in cut rations and counted the effects of the drought on
the land as evidence that the Sioux had been reluctant to accept the white
ways.

Many writers have attempted to establish that it was through the influence and leadership of Sitting Bull that the Ghost Dance Religion was accepted
and spread among the Sioux at Standing Rock. It appears equally plausible
that the Sioux did look to Sitting Bull to see just how he would receive the new
gospel of deliverance and recovery. Sitting Bull's participation in the Ghost
Dance Religion is not altogether clear; however, it is more than evident that he
did not openly admonish his people NOT to dance if that is what they wished
to do.

So with much excitement, the Sioux painted their faces and formed the
slow shuffle of the Ghost Dance Circle. Like many others of the Native American People, the Sioux adapted the Ghost Dance to their own cultural aware-
nesses. Of special importance to the Sioux was the forming of the Ghost Dance
in a circle - a symbol of the Sacred Hoop of the People. As they danced, their
shuffled steps carried them around a central pole or tree -- the Tree of Life.
The Tree of Life had been the totem or emblem of the Iroquois League in the
Northeast nearly a 150 years before. The Tree of Life, strangely enough, was a
vision-legend described in The Book of Mormon as well. Other, more radical
forms of the Ghost Dance ritual began to take shape among the Sioux. Cradled
in the arms of many of the men were rifles. With calculated concern, the Indian
Agents looked with dismay at the weapons openly displayed and repeatedly
telegraphed their concern to their superiors -- all the way to
Washington. Seen through terror stricken eyes, the Sioux   150

Ghost Dance may well have taken on the apparition of a dance of war.

> *In 1890, the Sioux, under the influence of the medicine man, Sitting Bull, were greatly excited at the coming "return of the ghosts." The Great Spirit had sent the white man to punish the Indians for their sins. The Indians had now been punished enough and deliverance was at hand, but the whites had been bad ever since they had killed Jesus. Dancing would preserve the Indians from sickness, and the white man's bullets could no longer penetrate Indian skins. Red paint from the Paiute messiah was also widely used for this same protection. ...They must wear "ghost shirts" painted with the sun and moon and stars.[9](p. 230, LaBarre, 1972)*

Among the Sioux, the Ghost Dance was

> *...when in its infancy, purely of a religious character, and it was only when the medicine men and politicians in the nation began to enlarge upon the wrongs suffered at the hands of the whites, the scarcity of food, the presence of the military, that its general aspect was changed from a sacred rite to a warlike demonstration. Were it not for these complications and the lack of prompt action on the part of prominent officials, the craze might have been easily suppressed, and the dancers returned to their camps on the agency creeks without any trouble whatever. (p. 327, The Illustrated American, "Ghost Dance in the West," January 17, 1891)*

An observer of the history of the Sioux cannot help but wonder if not only the Ghost Dance, but another victory like the one at the Little Big Horn, would do much to restore the Sioux to their place of dominance upon the Plains. The conviction of rightness to the land was rekindled in the Ghost Dance whereas the hope in military supremacy appeared certain to the wearers of the new and mysterious Ghost Shirt.

To many of the Sioux, the hope of the future was strengthened by the acceptance of the Ghost Shirt and Dress. The Ghost Shirt was a "magical garment" which when worn would protect the wearer from harm especially harm in the form of the white man's bullets.

The Ghost Dance garment was, in the opinion of James Mooney, an adaptation of a garment worn by Mormons -- the Endowment Robe and

---

9   The Sun, Moon and Stars represent highly significant symbols to Mormons as well. The symbols represent the "glories" to which people will go after death. The "glories" differ in greatness even as the Sun, Moon and Stars differ in magnitude and light. Mormon belief; refers to the highest reward as that of the Sun, i.e., Celestial Glory. The Moon represents the Terrestrial Glory and Telestial that of the Stars.

Temple Garment. It was the Endowment Garment that if worn faithfully by the Mormon Elders and their wives, would have special powers of healing and protection. It was this same Temple garment that, it is said, protected Dr. Richards from the assassin's bullet in Carthage Jail on that fateful day of the murder of Joseph and Hyrum Smith in June of 1844. Thus, the Endowment Robe/Temple Garment of the Mormons and the Ghost Shirt of the Sioux were to share a strikingly similar role in the religious life of both cultures.

> The [Mormon] Church had its symbols, with all their
> emotional connotations, from the mystic embroideries
> on the temple garments to the beehive symbols of
> state industriousness. It had its uniform, the symbolic
> underwear known as "garments," worn by all married
> Saints, and so sacred that a really pious Mormon is
> supposed never to let his body be quite out of contact with
> them... (p. 97, Stegner, 1942)

Among both the Native American People and Mormon populations, the use of the Ghost Shirt and "Garments" was fairly well defined. Its use was never to be indiscriminate nor associated with any purpose that was not "religious" in nature. It was, after all, a sacred garment whose function was related to the faith and spiritual well-being of the wearer. Among the Mormons the special "garments" worn in the Temple may include:

> The man's garments include a special undergarment, a
> shirt and pair of white pants, a robe and girdle, a cloth
> cap like a baker's cap, cloth moccasins, and a green silk
> apron upon which are embroidered nine fig leaves. The
> woman assembles the same garments substitute a white
> blouse and skirt for the shirt and pants. (p. 165, Whalen,
> 1964)

> For a time, the appeal of the Ghost Shirt was nearly
> as strong among some of the Sioux as the endowment
> garments were and are among devout Mormons.
> Men and women who danced [the Ghost Dance] made
> themselves magnificently painted "ghost shirts," which
> were covered with prayer symbols. They expected these
> to protect them from harm by whites. (p. 586, Malis,
> 1972)

David Miller states that "overnight" the Ghost Dance became the topic of conversation in white settlements around the reservation and in each and every encampment of Sioux.

152

> *Mention of the cult was on the lips of people everywhere,*
> *and various newspapers across the country referred*
> *to it ominously as "The Dance of Death to Come."*
> *Unjustifiably regarded as a prelude to war, what little*
> *was known of its history was jammed into a jumble of*
> *accounts of previous raids and massacres of whites by*
> *Indians. Bloody tales of the Minnesota outbreak of 1862*
> *and Custer's stand on the Little Big Horn were revived to*
> *keep the journalistic pot boiling. (p. 140, Miller, 1957)*

At first, the "...Sioux agents had failed to take the Ghost Dance religion seriously, and none had received any hint of its militant trappings;" (p. 75, Utley, 1963) however, by June, "garbled" messages and rumors had begun to reach Washington.

The talk in frontier settlements and in smoke filled rooms in Washington spoke of a feared "uprising" being fomented by Sioux leaders such as Sitting Bull. Opinion was divided, however, as to what course of action should be followed in dealing with the Ghost Dancing. Some felt that it should be banned; others, however, like Colonel McGillycuddy, a former Agent among the Sioux, felt that it should be allowed to "run its course."

> *I [Colonel McGillycuddy] took charge of these people*
> *in seventy-nine. I organized the Indian police, had the*
> *troops removed, and for seven years we had no soldiers*
> *near us -sometimes during harder propositions than we*
> *have today -- and I won out. These Indians are not fools,*
> *I cannot but regard it as a mistake to have run troops*
> *in here. Were I still the agent I would let the ghost dance*
> *continue. After all, if the Seventh-Day Adventist get up on*
> *the roofs of their houses arrayed in their ascension robes,*
> *to meet the Second Coming of the Saviour, the United*
> *States Army is not rushed into the field to prevent them*
> *from doing so. Why shouldn't the Indians have the same*
> *privilege? (Underscore added) (pp. 147-148, Miller, 1957)*

The position that the Sioux should be allowed to continue to dance the Ghost Dance and even wear their Ghost Shirts, was by far, a minority opinion. The majority opinion, on the other hand, stressed the necessity of crushing the Sioux rebellion before it erupted into a full-scale uprising. The task of stamping out the rebellious dance form was, obviously, the responsibility of the army. This was, more than likely, just the excuse that the army needed to regain its own self-esteem after the humiliating defeat of Custer some 14 years previously.

"Apprehensive white authorities alerted the military and tried to stop the assemblies of the Ghost Dance adherents." (p. 511, Spencer, 1977) The army was mobilized, the day of revenge for the death of their fallen hero-chief, Colonel G. A. Custer, was now within their grasp. The Cavalry was to be redeemed at last!

Somehow, the words of Custer to his Arikara scouts before the Little Big Horn disaster echoed through the years. Custer had told Bloody Knife and Bob-tailed Bull:

> *If we beat the Sioux, I will be President of the United*
> *States -- the Grandfather. If you Arikaras do as I tell you*
> *and kill enough Sioux for me and capture many Sioux*
> *ponies, I will take care of you all when I come into power.*
> *(p. 13, Miller, 1957)*

Thus, it was that "Custer -- the great invincible soldier-chief, golden-haired hero of the East, self-styled swashbuckler of the Plains..." was to be vindicated at last. (p. 128, Miller, 1957)

The Sioux were intent that the rations and treaty payments be made. They too sought the vindication of a people whose honor had been broken by repeated encroachment by the Federal government. Agents like McLaughlin were equally intent upon breaking the political power of Indian leaders such as Sitting Bull. Events moved during the fall of 1890 to a tinder-box condition -- only a spark was needed to send the People into open rebellion.

> *...The Ogalala heard that the son of God had come upon*
> *the earth in the west. They said the Messiah was there,*
> *but he had come to help the Indians and not the whites,*
> *and it made the Indians happy to hear this. (p. 328,*
> *Olson, 1965)*

Peter Farb believed that the Ghost Dance "...took its most virulent form..." on the Rosebud, Pine Ridge and Standing Rock Reservations. (p. 283, Farb, 1968) It was in this geographical setting that the Ghost Dance Religion shed its pacifist nature and assumed an aura of resistance.

The Sioux had few weapons; however, the fervor of the Ghost Dance Religion armed the followers of the new religion with mightier weapons -- the conviction of the rightness of their cause and the added assurance that they gained through the wearing of the Ghost Shirt.

Yellow Bird had told the People through an interpreter: "I have made medicine of the white man's ammunition. It is good medicine, and his bullets cannot harm you, as they will not go through your ghost shirts, while your bullets will kill." (pp. 227-228, Nichols and Adams, 1971) At Pine Ridge, Weasel told observers: "We did not carry our guns nor any weapon, but trusted to the Great Spirit to destroy the soldiers." (p. 333, The Illustrated American, January 1981)

*Your correspondent asked the Weasel: "Did you ever see
the medicine-shirt worn?" "Yes, they wore the blessed
shirt that night. The Priests had said prayers over these
garments, and they were bullet proof. One girl tried to
gash herself with a butcher knife on the arm, but the
blade was bent and the edge turned, so powerful was the
medicine in the shirt." (p. 333, The Illustrated American,
January 1891)*

While it is evident that the historical record is not at all clear as to just
how strong Sitting Bull's leadership was in the Ghost Dance Religion; it is
clear, however, that he did not ask his people to stop dancing and to turn from
the Ghost Dance teachings even though Agent McLaughlin wanted him to do
so. It was clear to Sitting Bull that the agents at Standing Rock were even then
attempting to bring soldiers to halt the ceremonies. (p. 408, Brown, 1970)

Agent McLaughlin was openly in opposition to the Ghost Dance Religion. He feared the Indians new religion nearly as much as he disliked Sitting
Bull and Kicking Bear. It was largely through the sustained teachings of Kicking Bear that the Standing Rock Sioux were encouraged to take up the Ghost
Dance Religion; therefore, McLaughlin had soldiers remove Kicking Bear from
the reservation. This action, he hoped, would rid the reservation of the menace
of the new religion.

Rumors continued to sweep the reservation areas, each more intense
and more convincing than the last. "The Messiah had come. The Messiah
would come during the next spring." Some rumors told that the Messiah was
already on the reservation. On one occasion

*...fighting nearly broke out in Red Cloud's camp just west
of the agency settlement. A mysterious blanketed figure
had been making the rounds of the lodges claiming to
be the Indian messiah. Police came running to make an
arrest. Much to their chagrin and the astonishment of
the whole camp, they found the "messiah" was actually
a white man from Iowa, a harmless crank named Albert
C. Hopkins, self-styled "President Pro Tem of the Pansy
Society of America." (p. 209, Miller, 1959)*

To this charlatan, Red Cloud demanded: "You go home. You are no Son of
God." (p. 329, Olson, 1965)

The Ghost Dancing did not stop. On November 20, 1890, the Indian Bureau asked that a list be prepared that would give the names of all Ghost Dance
leaders. Sitting Bull's name was among those leaders who were reported to
General N.A. Miles. When General Miles saw that Sitting Bull's name was included on the list, he assumed, according to Dee Brown, that the medicine man

155

was the principle source of this Indian disturbance. The action that followed was the strengthening of the Army units throughout the Plains region. (p. 408, Brown, 1970)

In response to an invitation to look over the situation at the Pine Ridge Reservation, former Agent Valentine McGillycuddy recommended that the Sioux be allowed to continue dancing the Ghost Dance. McGillycuddy gave indication that it was his belief that nothing would result from the dancing if sufficient time were allowed for the muddied water to settle; however, by mid-November (1890), much of those activities considered "normal" -- schools, trading post activities, and work -- had come to a sudden and abrupt halt. At Pine Ridge, an alarmed agent reported that the Indians were "dancing in the snow" and expressed his fear that they had become "wild and crazy." The agent demanded immediate protection.

The dancing of the Ghost Dance continued on all of the South Dakota reservations during the next few days and nights. At Cheyenne River, Big Foot's band numbered, it is reported, 600. Elsewhere, Short Bull led his band of believers down the White River and into the Badlands, where the dancers' numbers swelled to a reported 3,000 persons. (pp. 410-411, Brown, 1959)

Agent McLaughlin had, as early as June of 1890, concluded that he had, by some means, to get rid of the troublesome Sitting Bull. McLaughlin had denied that the Sioux, as people, had any "hostile intentions;" however if Sitting Bull and other troublemakers -Circling Bear, Black Bird, and Circling Hawk -- were somehow "gone," then the action of "arrest" -- "...would end all trouble and uneasiness..."

> *He was doubtless correct, but the Indian Bureau quite rightly took no action, [then] for none of these man had committed any overt act to justify their removal. (p. 81, Utley, 1963)*

> *[Sitting Bull was] still the greatest chief and medicine man of the Sioux Nation, an elder statesman whose political, military, and religious triumphs of old had left him with a reputation and a demeanor of authority that few Hunkpapas or Yanktonais, even progressives, could resist when it came to a showdown. (p. 81, Utley, 1963)*

McLaughlin's troubles, it is reported, were minor when compared to those that were taking place on other reservations where spokesmen of the "old life" continued to preach and to gain a following among the Sioux. John Grass, Gall, and Crow King were spokesmen at Pine Ridge and Rose Bud, Hump and Big Foot at Cheyenne River. It had been Hump who had played an important leadership role in 1876 at the Little Big Horn, and who later had so distinguished himself with General Miles that Hump had been appointed, significantly enough, "Chief of Police" at the Cheyenne

River. (pp. 81-82, Utley, 1963) Hump, even as Chief of Police, continued to demonstrate his distrust of and contempt for the white government in Washington by leading his people to a location some 60 miles west of the Agency. Hump eventually -- unwillingly – had agreed to the Crook Commission recommendations and signed the land agreement; however, Big Foot had not! From Big Foot's encampment some 80 miles further West of the Agency, permanent cabins were constructed, and the people settled in to live as nearly as they could by the old ways. However, even from this remote region the watchful eyes of U.S. Army Captain Henissee and his troop saw the continuous trickle of Sioux cross into the newly ceded land. (p. 82, Utley, 1963)

It is true, beyond a shadow of doubt, that conditions were becoming potentially explosive!

The Sioux were disillusioned, terrified and at rebellions door. The Ghost Dance had come to them, and through their leaders the non-violent message of "recovery" was changed to meet the cultural demands of the Sioux to restore their old tribal ways of war and bravery. The Ghost Dance had altered the collective consciousness of the Sioux to include a magic garment that would make them safe from the white man's deadly aim. All they needed was the spark that would send a flame that in turn would ignite a nation. The spark came during December 12-15, 1890!

The spark that culminated in the battle at Wounded Knee was not the Ghost Dance, or any of its derivatives. The spark was not Mormonism or any of its teachings. The spark was not even the Ghost Shirt, or its failure to keep the Sioux safe from harm's way. The spark was that of which Helen Hunt Jackson spoke so well, in <u>A Century of Dishonor,</u> the many broken treaties by the white government in Washington, D. C. The fire raged in the hollow and broken promises of the white government to disallow the People to have their land, to have rations sufficient in quantity and quality to see them through harsh winters. The Sioux might well have continued to prosper as ranchers had they not been required by over-zealous Christian missionaries and agents to become farmers in an unpredictable land with uncertain rainfall.

The Sioux had long since learned that they could not trust the white man's word and they were not at all certain about the white man's God! In this final curtain call on this historic drama, the Sioux turned from the white man's God to the God of the Ghost Dance and invoked his protective power.

On December 12, Lieutenant Colonel William F. Drumm had received orders directly from General Nelson A. Miles that he was "...to secure the person of Sitting Bull." Several days later, on the 15th, Col. Drumm and his troop surrounded the cabin occupied by Sitting Bull.

> *[Agent]...McLaughlin and [Col.] Drumm [had] discussed*
> *the problem and agreed upon a course of action.*
> *McLaughlin would move the Grand River police into the*
> *Sitting Bull settlement at dawn on one of the*

*biweekly ration days, when most of the Indians would
be at the agency. Under cover of night, Drumm would
send a command from Fort Yates to take station within
supporting distance. The police would make the arrest,
and if anything went wrong the troops would charge
to the rescue. As their carefully laid plans might be
upset at any moment by General Miles, the two officials
immediately and quietly determined to seize the first
good opportunity. (p. 148, Utley, 1963)*

The determined and punitive nature of the McLaughlin -- Drumm march can be seen in an assessment of the tactical supplies that were brought simply to arrest one man: General Drumm's force consisted of F and G Troops of the famous Eighth Cavalry and G and H Company of the Twelfth Infantry. Detachments of cavalry were thoroughly drilled in the operation of the Hotchkiss and Gatling guns.

*...Rations, grain, extra ammunition, buffalo overcoats,
and horse covers were packed and set aside, ready
for instant loading into the spring escort wagon and
ambulance that were to accompany the command. (p.
148, Utley, 1963)*

The authority for this infamous arrest had come from the President of the United States in a series of messages that directed:

*...Secretary directs that you make no arrests whatever
except under orders of the military or upon an order of
the Secretary of the Interior. (p. 150, Utley, 1963)*

On December 10, General Miles had telegraphed General Ruger to "...arrest Sitting Bull." (p. 152, Utley, 1963)

*For some reason, Ruger delayed passing the word to
Colonel Drumm until December 12, then wired him in
cipher to "make it your especial duty to secure the person
of Sitting Bull. Call on Indian agent to cooperate and
render such assistance as will best promote the purpose
in view." (p. 152, Utley, 1963)*

For better or for worse,

*...Ruger and Drumm were still inclined to follow
McLaughlin's lead. Drumm took the telegram to agency
headquarters, and he and McLaughlin decided to
carry out their original plan. The next ration day was
December 20, and they set this as the date for the coup.
(p. 152, Utley, 1963)*

158

From the time that orders came for the arrest of Sitting Bull until the ration day, the Sioux continued to dance the Ghost Dance. Across the plains the plaintiff refrain of the dance songs resounded:

> *The people are coming home,*
> *The people are coming home,*
> *Saith my father, saith my father,*
> *Saith my father.*
>
> *The time cometh, I shall see him,*
> *The time cometh, I shall see him,*
> *Saith thy mother, saith thy mother.*
> *(pp. 88-89, Utley, 1963)*

As the dancing increased and as the desperation of the people reached new heights, to some the vision came clear and true. This is how Little Horse described his vision experience:

> *...two holy eagles transported me to the Happy Hunting*
> *Grounds. They showed me the Great Messiah there,*
> *and as I looked upon his fair countenance I wept, for*
> *there were nail-prints in his hands and feet where the*
> *cruel whites had once fastened him to a large cross.*
> *There was a small wound in his side also, but as he kept*
> *himself covered with a beautiful mantle of feathers this*
> *wound only could be seen when he shifted his blanket.*
> *He insisted that we continue the dance, and promised*
> *me that no whites should enter his city nor partake of the*
> *good things he had prepared for the Indians. The earth,*
> *he said, was now worn out and it should be repeopled.*
>
> *He had a long beard and long hair and was the most*
> *handsome man I ever looked upon. (pp. 89-90, Utley,*
> *1963)*

Given sufficient time, the Ghost Dance may well have run its course; however, it appears that agent, McLaughlin was as concerned about his own reputation as. "leader and Indian agent" as he was about ending the practice of dancing the Ghost Dance. Sitting Bull was much too powerful a leader among the Sioux. Sitting Bull was a threat to the role of the Indian agent. This threat was intolerable and could not be allowed to continue. So the die was cast. The excuse to get rid of Sitting Bull was the Ghost Dance. The reason to get rid of Sitting Bull appears to have been envy, jealousy and hatred -- values not altogether unlike those with which modern men, women and societies continue to struggle.

159

The arrest of Sitting Bull was no easy matter for a man as great as he is difficult to arrest, difficult to kill, and more difficult still, to let live. Some of the Indian police that came to arrest Sitting Bull handed in their badges rather than take him. Others were jealous of his power and they more eagerly took the implied order of McLaughlin to take Sitting Bull "dead or alive."

At one point, Sitting Bull offered to go willingly on his own to see agent McLaughlin. Sitting Bull resolutely refused to be arrested by Indian police who had served under his leadership. In the scuffle that followed he was shot by Lieutenant Bull Head and Sergeant Red Tomahawk. The tragedy was equaled only in the senseless killing of Crowfoot, Sitting Bull's young son. Six Indian police lost their lives as did seven of Sitting Bull's followers.

> *...The scene around Sitting Bull's house stamped itself on Captain Fechet's memory. "I saw evidence of a most desperate encounter," he later wrote. "In front of the house, and within a radius of 50 yards, were the bodies of 8 dead Indians, including that of Sitting Bull, and 2 dead horses. In the house were 4 dead policemen and 3 wounded, 2 mortally [Bull Head and Shave Head]. To add to the horror of the scene the squaws of Sitting Bull, who were in a small house nearby, kept up a great wailing." (p. 163, Utley, 1963)*

It is impossible, or nearly so, to begin to describe the scene: the anguish and grief of the wives and relatives of the dead were real enough to touch the heart of the most seasoned of troops and police. For some reason, best understood in the culture of the People, a relative (Holy Medicine) of an Indian policeman, Strong Arm, took it upon himself to smash in the face of dead Sitting Bull with a neck yoke, Sergeant James Hanaghan instructed that the body be removed for fear that it would freeze to the ground or that other mutilation would occur. (p. 165, Utley, 1963)

As soon as it was clear that Sitting Bull was dead, many of his followers began hurriedly to move into the woods and hills, fearful that a similar fate awaited them if they dared to remain in the vicinity of Sitting Bull's cabin. As soon as the flight had ended, the police and troopers began to tend their fires, prepare breakfast, and care for their horses. Suddenly a cry of alarm was sounded by one of the police.

> *From the timber only eighty yards distant bust a single Indian. Mounted on a black horse, brandishing a long staff, and signing a ghost song, he raced at full speed toward the soldiers. (This was Crow Woman, one of the most zealous believers in the new faith. He had donned a Ghost Shirt and was demonstrating to his people, who watched from the hills across the river, that it did in fact turn the bullets of the white man.) The police*

160

loosed a volley, and the horseman wheeled abruptly
back to the shelter of the timber. He emerged some
four hundred yards up the valley, and again the fire of
the police drove him back to the trees. A third time he
galloped into the open, this time passing between two
cavalrymen Fechet had sent out as pickets. They opened
fire, but the warrior escaped up the valley unscathed.
For many Hunkpapas, here was proof of the magical
qualities of the Ghost Shirt. (p. 163, Utley, 1963)

Regardless of the effect of this bold encounter, one fact could not be erased: Sitting Bull was dead, and his body was buried at the Standing Rock Reservation on the afternoon of December 17, 1890. The body was wrapped in a canvas and placed in a rough wooden box, a detail of four soldiers from the military prison began the task of covering the grave with dirt. (p. 166, Utley, 1963)

Robert Utley expressed the belief that the burial of Sitting Bull signaled the end of an era, "...not only for Standing Rock Agency but for the whole American west." (p. 166, Utley, 1963)

Utley was indeed, correct, or nearly so, for in truth the final sets in this drama were at that very time drawing to a close. Many of the Hunkpapas felt leaderless now that Sitting Bull was dead and buried. In their bewilderment they left the Standing Rock Reservation and made their way to live in the Ghost Dance Camp of Red Cloud at Pine Ridge. It may be that sufficient numbers of the Sioux had heard the words of the Ghost Dance Disciples that they should not fight the white man -- perhaps this is why they did not retaliate in anger at the death of their leader. But then again, perhaps it was because they lacked sufficient weapons and ammunition, or that they were simply too cold and too hungry. Perhaps it was that they were vastly overpowered by the new and deadlier weapons of the Government soldiers.

James Mooney estimates that by the fall of 1890, the entire Sioux nation numbered about 25,000 persons of whom it is thought that from 6,000 to 7,000 were warriors. However, it was Mooney's belief that none of the Sioux that had been converted to Christianity had taken part in either the hostilities or the Ghost Dance dancing; therefore, he concluded that at best 700 warriors were engaged -- including Big Foot's band. (p. 98, Wallace, 1965) Under the command of General Miles, nearly 3,000 troops were in the field in Sioux country. (p. 95, Wallace, 1965)

In an effort to keep the entire Sioux nation from panic or turning to war, the army and police sent out couriers again and again to urge the People to come in and to surrender their arms. It was believed that the majority of the Sioux were "loyal to the government" and would not fight. (p. 105, Wallace, 1965)

Couriers were again sent after the fleeing Indians by McLaughlin, warning them to return to the agency, where they would be safe, or suffer the consequences if found outside the reservation. Within a few days nearly 250 had come in and surrendered, leaving only about one-third still out. Most of these soon afterward surrendered with Hump on Cherry. Regardless of the effect of this bold encounter, one fact could not be erased: Sitting Bull was dead, and his body was buried at the Standing Rock Reservation on the afternoon of December 17, 1890. The body was wrapped in a canvas and placed in a rough,, wooden box, a detail of four soldiers from the military prison began the task of covering the grave with dirt. (p. 166, Utley, 1963)

After the death of Sitting Bull, Hump was considered the most dangerous leader among those still hoping to retain their traditional ways. With Hump traveled a band of about 400 persons camped in the neighborhood of Cherry Creek and the Cheyenne River. For several weeks they had been dancing, and were thought to be extremely hostile to the whites. However, Captain E. P. Ewers and Lieutenant Hale approached Hump with a message that General Miles wished for Hump and his people to return to Fort Bennet, where he would be safe and his people cared for. Hump accepted the invitation of General Miles, and later served as a scout with Captain Ewers as the remainder of Sitting Bull's followers were sought.(p. 108-109, Wallace, 1965)

With the enlistment of Hump into the army scouts, the only powerful leader outside reservation boundaries was Sitanka or Big Foot. Big Foot and his followers had been camped on the mouth of Deep Creek, a few miles below the Cheyenne River. The task of watching Big Foot was assigned to Lieutenant Colonel E. V. Sumner of the Eighth Cavalry. His troops were camped, on Deep Creek as well. Each knew that the other watched, and on several occasions they visited in a friendly manner until about the middle of December when Big Foot announced that he was going to return to the agency to pick up his annuities. (p. 111, Wallace, 1965)

Several days later Sumner communicated with General Miles and informed him that the band of Big Foot was on its way to the reservation and that plans should be made to carry out his arrest. Sumner assured General Miles that he would "get him" if Big Foot attempted to return to his camp.

During the intervening days, Big Foot had stopped at Hump's previous camp ground, and there he met others of the followers of Sitting Bull. The Sitting Bull followers had found Hump's camp empty and the People gone. Hungry, tired and cold, they were unable to go further. It was in this condition that Big Foot found them and immediately began to share what food, clothing, and shelter that he had. It was this act of natural care and sharing – this act of social and communal concern typical of

Indian People that caused Lieutenant Colonel Sumner to challenge Big Foot for his having taken in and cared for the so-called "hostiles" from Sitting Bull's camp. (p. 111, Wallace, 1965)

A forced march brought Lieutenant Colonel Sumner into contact with Big Foot and his band. Much to Sumner's surprise, however, Big Foot had turned his people around and was returning to their lodges on Deep Creek. With Big Foot were an additional 38 Sioux from Sitting Bull's camp. These were added to the 100 reported members of Big Foot's band. Considerable confusion filled Sumner's mind as to just who the 138 persons were. Warriors? Men and boys, or the total number of persons in the combined band? (The actual count of followers of Big Foot numbered 340.) Colonel Sumner directed Big Foot, on December 21, 1890, to "come in" under a white flag of truce. (p. 113, Wallace, 1965)

The situation at this crisis is thus summed up by Indian Commissioner Morgan:

> *Groups of Indians from the different reservations had*
> *commenced concentrating in the Bad Lands upon or in*
> *the vicinity of the Pine Ridge reservation. Killing cattle*
> *and destruction of other property by these Indians,*
> *almost entirely within the limits of Pine Ridge and*
> *Rosebud reservations, occurred, but no signal fires were*
> *built, no warlike demonstrations were made, no violence*
> *was done to any white settler, nor was there cohesion*
> *or organization among the Indians themselves. Many of*
> *them were friendly Indians, who had never participated*
> *in the Ghost Dance, but had fled thither from fear of*
> *soldiers, in consequence of their friends. The military*
> *gradually began to close in around them and they offered*
> *no resistance, and a speedy and quiet capitulation of all*
> *was confidently expected. (p. 113, Wallace, 1965)*

Nearly 3,000 federal troops were deployed throughout Sioux lands in such a way as to encircle the People. Special strengthening of the northern deployment of troops was undertaken to ensure that the Sioux would not attempt to escape further north and into Canada. The northern cordon was commanded by General Brooke, whose orders included the slow, deliberate and gradual movement to the south, thus forcing the Sioux back to the reservation. The historic record indicates that the intent of the Army was to "...bring about a surrender by peaceful means" rather than to attempt any form of annihilation. (p. 113, Wallace, 1965)

Repeatedly the Sioux were told that "rights and interests would be protected;" however, the Sioux were long since accustomed to the willingness of the Government to break its word -- even under a flag of truce. Once again, however, the Sioux trusted the military to keep its word and on December 27, 1890, "...the entire force broke camp and left their stronghold in the Bad Lands and began moving in toward the agency at Pine Ridge." (p. 113, Wallace, 1965)

Regardless of the knowledge that Big Foot was moving in the direction of the reservation and that units of the army were even then biting at his heels, orders were given to "intercept Big Foot's party in its flight from Cheyenne River..." (p. 114, Wallace, 1965) The actual interception of Big Foot's band may have been made easier by the general poor condition of health that gripped most of the Sioux. Big Foot, himself, was no exception. He suffered greatly from pneumonia and was in an extremely poor condition. Big Foot was in such poor health that he could no longer ride horseback but was required to lay in a wagon bed.

Sioux Ghost Dance Dress of cotton cloth, ca. 1890
Courtesy Texas Tech University Museum

Thus, it was that on December 28, 1890, Big Foot's band met Major Samuel M. Whiteside of the Seventh Cavalry under the command of Colonel James W. Forsyth. Forsyth's command consisted of a regiment of 413 enlisted men and 25 officers for a total of 438 men. In addition Forsyth was reinforced by an artillery group manned by 20 men and two officers. The artillery unit was divided into batteries of two platoons with two Hotchkiss Breech-Loading Steel Mountain Rifles. Each gun having an effective range of 4,200 yards. Five hundred men of the 7th Cavalry faced on December 28th and 29th the 340 men, women and children of Big Foot's band. (pp. 200-201, Utley, 1963)

As Whiteside approached the wagon in which Big Foot lay, he looked in only to find:

> *...a small part of his face showing from the blankets that swathed him from head to foot. Blood dripped from his nose, staining the blankets and collecting in small pools that froze on the floor of the wagon. The warriors, still in line, milled around nervously. (p. 194, Utley, 1963)*

Significantly, the white flag of truce that had been raised by the band " ...was refused by Major Whiteside, who demanded an unconditional surrender, which was at once given, and the Indians moved on with the troops to Wounded Knee Creek..." (p. 114, Wallace, 1963) At this point in time the Big Foot band was still under the impression that they would be taken to the Pine Ridge Reservation; however, the orders of the Army were much more comprehensive and potentially fatal to the People.

> *Forsyth's orders from Brooke were to disarm the Miniconjous and send them, under escort of the First Squadron, to the railroad for movement to Omaha. Neither he nor any of his officers considered armed resistance to such overwhelming force anything but a remote possibility. His plan, therefore, was to place the troops of the Second Squadron, mounted, in positions on three sides of the Indians, and hold his First Squadron, dismounted, in reserve close by on the fourth side for any special task that the actual disarming might require. Such a display of might would reinforce the already obvious fact that resistance invited destruction. (p. 204, Utley, 1963)*

As the Sioux began the task of erecting their tepees, they did so in the form of an arc covering a distance of some 250 yards from the road to the agency, across the ravine, to the base of Cemetery Hill. The camp was well in the open and was in no way designed to be in an attack position. The band simply had not considered this option at this point in their travels. After the Sioux camp was made, Whiteside "promptly posted

165

Hawthorn's two Hotchkiss guns on top of Cemetery Hill, their muzzles pointed in enfilade at the Indian camp." (p. 198, Utley, 1963) The strategic and deadly placement of the Hotchkiss guns would unleash a rain of death and terror into both the Indian gathering and upon the troops as well.

Robert Utley reported that the "...officers of the Seventh Cavalry had a jolly time that night." (p. 199, Utley, 1963) The gay and festive time was occasioned by a keg of whiskey that James Asay, trader from Pine Ridge, had given to the officers. Then too, the officers felt this auspicious time as proper to celebrate the capture of Big Foot. Sometime during the night additional soldiers were brought in to those already in position.

> *Throughout the night the Indians, uncertain about the morrow and deeply suspicious of the soldiers, grew steadily more uneasy. With fear and foreboding, they greeted the chill dawn. (p. 199, Utley, 1963)*

Robert Spencer and Jesse Jennings (The Native Americans) suggests that the Big Foot band had gathered at Wounded Knee to "perform Ghost Dance rituals." (p. 511, Spencer and Jennings, 1977) It is fairly obvious that Big Foot's band had been forced to move to Wounded Knee, and that the very fact that they raised a white flag over this encampment was evidence that they were concerned in reaching an agreement with the army that would allow them to continue to exist as a people. Out of this agreement, they must certainly have reasoned that in the future they might be able to continue to worship and dance as they saw proper. Just how many of the band were adherents of the Ghost Dance is not known. It is known that "some" of the nearly 300 persons making up Big Foot's band were Ghost Dancers.

Regardless of their numbers, the Ghost Dancers in Big Foot's band were outnumbered, out maneuvered and materially captured by the superior force of arms that surrounded them. At best 106 warriors were all that stood in defense of their way of life. (p. 114, Wallace, 1963) With a force of 470 men, including light artillery, the army made preparation to disarm the Indians prior to taking them to the railroad.

At shortly before 8:00 a.m. on the morning of the 29th of December, the Indian men were ordered to come out of their teepees and to bring their weapons with them. Twenty men returned but with only two weapons. It was reasoned, perhaps correctly, that the People must certainly possess additional weapons so a teepee to teepee search was ordered. (p. 115, Wallace, 1965)

Soldiers were moved within ten yards of the place where the Sioux men were directed to stand while another detachment of soldiers was directed to each of the teepees. This effort yielded an additional 40 guns "...most of which, however, were old and of little value." (p. 115, Wallace, 1965)

The search took considerable time and in the process of

166

discovery many of the teepees were left in disarray by the soldiers efforts to probe the contents of every bed and blanket roll. Even more significant, perhaps, was the abusive nature of a search: women and children were rudely pushed and shoved while the men stood helplessly by. Such activities are rarely undertaken with respect and dignity.

A high degree of tension began to grip the encampment as husbands, sons and brothers desired to protect their families but were forcibly held apart from their loved ones. To add to the general state of fear and excitement, Yellow Bird, a religious leader of the Ghost Dance Religion, walked among the men urging them to trust in the power of their Ghost Shirts and to resist the whites.

While the soldiers had been looking for the guns Yellow Bird, a medicine-man, had been walking about among the warriors, blowing on an eagle-bone whistle, and urging them to resistance, telling them that the soldiers would become weak and powerless, and the bullets would be unavailing against the sacred "ghost shirts," which nearly every one of the Indians wore. (pp. 115-118, Wallace 1966 and p. 211, Utley, 1963)

Big Foot, still too ill from pneumonia to lead his people, lay helpless in his teepee. Somehow, as strange as it now seems, the role of leadership appeared to have passed to Yellow Bird at whose feet would be laid the blame of the massacre at Wounded Knee. The blame was laid upon Yellow Bird for his urging of the men to have courage, and to trust in the power of the Ghost Shirts to protect them from the deadly accuracy of the white man's bullets. Then, too, there was the matter of the handful of dust that Yellow Bird threw into the air...

> Meanwhile, an Indian named Black Coyote had
> been stalking around holding his rifle in both hands
> overhead....[Black Coyote] ...was also deaf. Black Coyote
> shouted that this gun belonged to him; he had paid much
> money for it; and he would not give it to anyone unless
> he received pay in return. Two soldiers approached from
> behind and seized him. There was a brief struggle. Black
> Coyote brought the rifle down. Pointing to the east and
> upward at a 45-degree angle, it went off. As Turning
> Hawk innocently observed, "Of course the firing of a gun
> must have been breaking of a military rule of some sort."
> 212, Utley, 1963)

During the next few moments, attention was redirected to the stooping figure of Yellow Bird, his fingers clutching a handful of dirt. Either by reflex or design, Yellow Bird hurled the dirt into the air. History is nearly silent as to the meaning and significance of this gesture: was it an act of defiance? A signal for an attack? An act merely to show disgust? Whatever its real meaning, it served according to the testimony of white soldiers, as a signal 167 for other young men to throw off their blankets and aim at least one rifle at soldiers in K-Troop.

> ...*Whiteside, glanced toward the scene of the disturbance.*
> *"By God they have broken," he exclaimed. To Lieutenant*
> *Mann, the warriors seemed to hesitate an eternal*
> *moment. "I thought, 'the pity of it! What can they be*
> *thinking of?' " He drew his revolver and slipped through*
> *the ranks of the front. The volley crashed into Troop K.*
> *"Fire! Fire on them!" screamed Mann. (p. 212, Utley,*
> *1963)*

A hundred carbines of both K and B Troops opened fire. The artillery was poised only ten yards -- a mere 36 feet away.

> ...*At the first volley the Hotchkiss guns trained on the*
> *camp opened fire and sent a storm of shells and bullets*
> *among the women and children, who had gathered*
> *in front of the tepee to watch the unusual spectacle of*
> *military display. The guns poured in 2-pound explosive*
> *shells at the rate of nearly fifty per minute, mowing down*
> *everything alive. The terrible effect may be judged from*
> *the fact that one woman survivor, Blue Whirlwind, with*
> *whom the author conversed, received fourteen wounds,*
> *while each of her two little boys was also wounded by*
> *her side. In a few minutes 200 Indian men, women, and*
> *children, with 60 soldiers, were lying dead and wounded*
> *on the ground, the tepees had been torn down by the*
> *shells and some of them were burning above the helpless*
> *wounded, and the surviving handful of Indians were*
> *flying in wild panic to the shelter of the ravine, pursued*
> *by hundreds of the maddened soldiers and followed up*
> *by a raking fire from the Hotchkiss guns, which had been*
> *moved into position to sweep the ravine. (p. 118, Wallace,*
> *1965)*

Wounded Knee has often been described as a massacre; and perhaps this is true. Realistically, however, it was more than a "massacre" -- it was carnage at its worst. It was in many ways, as dreadful as that which the Mormons had experienced at the hands of a mob at Hauns Mill in Missouri, or that of the Jews in the Warsaw Ghetto. It was without a doubt, senseless slaughter that took the lives of men -- but worse, the lives of innocent women and children.

Big Foot lay dead and with him many of his people.

> *Authorities differ as to the number of Indians present and*
> *killed at Wounded Knee. General Ruger states*
> *that the band numbered about 340, including*

168

about 100 warriors, but Major Whiteside, to whom they
surrendered, reported them officially as numbering 120
men and 250 women and children, a total of 370. (p. 120,
Wallace, 1965)

The whole number killed on the field, or who later died
from wounds and exposure, was probably very nearly
300. (pp. 120, Wallace, 1965)

There seems little reason to justify such wanton death and destruction
on a people. The unnecessary and brutal clubbing to death of defenseless wom-
en and children will undoubtedly stand as one of the most hideous acts ever
perpetrated by one group of humans upon another. Wounded Knee was an act
of genocide that will forever haunt the American Nation.

A long trench was dug and into it were thrown all the
bodies, piled one upon another like so much cordwood,
until the pit was full, when the earth was heaped over
them and the funeral was complete. Many of the bodies
were stripped by the whites, who went out in order to get
the "ghost shirts," and the frozen bodies were thrown into
the trench still and naked. They were only dead Indians.
(p. 130, Wallace, 1965)

The acts of brutality were, as one member of the burial party is recorded to have said, "...a thing to melt the heart of a man if it was of stone, to
see those little children, with their bodies shot to pieces, thrown naked into
the pit." (pp. 130-132, Wallace, 1965) Many bodies were found up to two miles
from Wounded Knee, their life flow having been clubbed from them -- women
and children alike.

All the Indians fled in these three directions, and after
most all of them had been killed a cry was made that
all those who were not killed or wounded should come
forth and they would be safe. Little boys who were not
wounded came out of their places of refuge, and as soon
as they came in sight a number of soldiers surrounded
them and butchered them there. (pp. 139-140, Wallace,
1965)

The Sioux have been criticized for the thoroughness of their will to
fight back and to kill the soldiers. The People fought with knives, clubs, even
rocks and their hands. In most instances the will to survive as a person and as
a people was too strong and too basic to the will of humankind to allow the destruction of the lives of loved ones to go on without some efforts to save themselves. These were not <u>hostiles</u> to the American Government,
they were patriots to their own land, people, and heritage.   169

The "Battle" of Wounded Knee -- ended in a hollow victory for the whites. The Sioux were defeated by a mightier military force than they. The army won at Wounded Knee not as a result of superior tactics, nor from a superior cultural base. They won because they possessed deadlier weapons -- weapons possessed by men who desired, in a large part, to avenge the death of their folk hero, Custer, and to restore the dignity of the 7th Cavalry.

Philosophically it might be concluded that regardless of the event or however base and hideous the act, some lesson can be learned that will in some way benefit future generations. Perhaps, this point of view is best left to those with greater reflective insights; nevertheless, it is certain that lessons can be learned. Wounded Knee is no exception.

SUMMARY

To the victims of Wounded Knee, both white and Indian, the ravages of war were very real and devastating. To observers in the East, Wounded Knee was a "newspaperman's war." (p. 167, Miller, 1959) The New York Times ran a series of articles in the latter half of 1890, that did much to negatively color the imagination of Easterners. It is David Miller's suggestion that the fear and anticipation of a whole-scale Indian uprising had been created to a large extent by the press. The reports in the press had been sensationalized and even glamorized by persons attempting to find their place in the journalistic sun.

> *...In many ways the Sioux outbreak in the Dakotas was a newspaperman's war. Perhaps no previous conflict in American history was so well covered by the press. Six correspondents remained at Pine Ridge Agency through the entire trouble, filling a maw of sudden reader interest across the country with a welter of anecdotes and observations as well as carefully censored blow-by-blow accounts of the sporadic fighting. (p. 167, Miller, 1959)*

> *(Footnote #1, page 167, Miller, 1959): "The press contingent at year's end at Pine Ridge alone included... Jack Kelly, the Lincoln (Nebraska) Journal; Crissy, Omaha Bee; Smith, Omaha Herald; Charles Seymour, Chicago Herald, Brackett, Chicago Inter-Ocean, Clark, Chicago Tribune; Warren K. Moorehead, Philadelphia Press, Charles Allen, New York Herald; O'Brien, Associated Press.*

Both in the mid-West and in Nevada's West, the image of the Ghost Dance as a form of resistance movement was generated and kept alive by the press. No real effort, other than that by James Mooney of the Bureau of American Ethnology, had begun to make an assessment of what the Ghost Dance Religion really was, i.e., an Indian revival movement that had at its source the desire only to recapture a lost way of life.

The sensationalism of the Indian war was further exaggerated by such persons as Buffalo Bill Cody, whose association with Sitting Bull had been in the Wild West Shows that had toured the Eastern United States and Europe. One scheme for the arrest of Sitting Bull had involved a plan whereby Buffalo Bill, a supposed friend, would arrest Sitting Bull. Artists and newspapermen followed with journalistic excitement this type of sensationalism and were pre-pared to "make the most of it!"

The power of the press in shaping public opinion was, indeed, an im-portant weapon and remained so throughout American history, up to and in-cluding the Spanish-American War. In many respects the Indian Wars set the tone of journalistic sensationalism that reached a climax in 1898. Here was, after all the expression of Manifest Destiny in its bravest example.

The press failed the attempt to evaluate where the real blame for the massacre at Wounded Knee began. In this sense the press was guilty of helping to create the war rather than to attempt in any way to say what the real causes were. While it may be true that the press was responsible for reporting the "facts" to the nation, it is equally true that truth was distorted in an attempt to place the blame for the Indian's resistance on desire for war rather than to address the broken promises and diminished rations that reduced the Sioux to levels of near starvation.

The influence of the Ghost Dance Religion on the outcome of Wound-ed Knee can be assessed; and such an assessment is necessary if the historical facts and victims of the war are to be vindicated. This much we know...

Among the Indian People living on the Plains, and especially among the Sioux, the Ghost Dance Religion began to decline rapidly after Wounded Knee. The death blow that was dealt to the Ghost Dance Religion was due nearly as much to the setting of a date for the return of the Messiah as it was to the bullets of the Hotchkiss guns. It is entirely possible, and highly probable, that the Ghost Dance Religion could have continued even after Wounded Knee had not the apostles of the religion set the date of "spring of 1891" as the time of return of the Messiah and the end of the white domination of the land.

Christianity itself has survived for nearly 2,000 years based on the ma-jor tenet that the Messiah, the Risen Lord, will return to the earth -- soon. It is the <u>soon</u> that has been the catalyst that has helped to hold the congregations of Christian believers through the ages.

Sects of Christianity, such as the Jehovah's Witnesses, look forward to the day when the elect, some 144,000 will be caught up in righteousness to meet the Risen Lord. The Seventh Day Adventist, too, looked forward to the return of the Lord as an event that was to occur "as quickly as the twinkling of an eye."

Followers and believers of Mormonism referred to within the body of Mormonism as Millenialist, too, looked forward to the   171 immediate return of Jesus as the Messiah -- the date December 23, 1890. It was in this year that Joseph Smith was purported to have told his followers that "IF" he remained on earth until his 85th year, i.e., 1890, the Messiah would return. It was this statement that caused James Mooney to believe in his appendix "The Mormons and the Indians," that the entire Mormon Church had believed and accepted the notion that Jesus was believed to be on the earth in 1890.

It appears that numerically only a part of the Mormon Church came to believe that Jesus was to return to earth and to the Mormons in 1890. This apparent minority was referred to as "Millenialist" and did not appear to express the majority view of the Mormon Church leadership on such issues as the Return of Jesus in 1890 and the Polygamy issue. The Three Nephites were personalities that emerge from the pages of <u>The Book of Mormon</u> and represent men of such extraordinary righteousness that they were given the choice of "not accepting the taste of death" but were translated from human to spirit forms. It was according to present day Mormon belief, the spiritual manifestation of the Nephites that returned in 1890.

The year 1890 was an auspicious one for the Mormons in several ways: The Millenialists were proclaiming the return of the Messiah and the Church hierarchy was proclaiming, with equal fervor, that the Church was renouncing the doctrine of polygamy. Bernard O. Walker, a Mormon, and former student of Brigham Young University, suggests strongly in an unpublished research paper that the question of Mormon belief in the return of the Messiah was perpetrated in a large degree by Mormons who had withdrawn membership from the Church and who were actively criticizing the departure from what they believed were the original teachings of Mormonism. Walker states:

> *The official declaration, referred to as the Woodruff Manifesto, was issued October 6, 1890, which renounced the practice of polygamy and indicated that no such marriages had been sanctioned for at least a year prior to that date (D & C, Official Declaration). As a result of this declaration, many of the members of the Church who had entered into the practice of polygamy and those who continued to believe this doctrine separated from the Church (Documentary History of the Church). It is believed that the document referred to by Mooney under the appendix "The Mormons and the Indians" is that written by such a person, A. McDonald, who labels himself a Free Thinker... The statement that heads the article, "The Mormons have stepped down and out of the Celestial Government. The American Indians have stepped up into Celestial Government" would be in consonance with such a philosophy since the Indians were known to espouse more than one woman.*

172

The argument is thus made that many former members of the Church, whether Indian or Whites, still believing that plurality of wives was a commandment of God, realizing that the Three Nephites were still upon the earth (3 Nephi 28:7-9, 36-40, Book of Mormon) and firmly convinced that Joseph Smith had indicated the approximate time of the second coming of Christ (D & C 130:15-17; History of the Church Vol. II, p. 182; Doctrine and Covenants Commentary, p. 693), and aware of the teachings with respect to the role the Indians were to play in the final scene before the Millennium did in fact give moral if not more tangible support to the Ghost Dance craze.

So prevalent was the thought of Christ's second coming among the people that President Wilford Woodruff, George Q. Cannon and many others took to the pulpit during the semi-annual Church conference of October 1980 to refute this notion. (Coates) (pp. 23-24, Walker, undated)

The notion or belief that Jesus had not returned was easy enough to place at rest; however, the hierarchy of the Mormon Church made no effort to discourage the belief that the work among the Indian people (Lamanites) was essential to the fulfillment of The Book of Mormon promise that the establishment of the City of Zion would be accomplished by the Indian People. Larry Coates, a Mormon historian, states in an unpublished paper, "The Mormons, The Ghost Dance Craze, and the Massacre at Wounded Knee," that:

...By increasing their work among the Lamanites, the Mormons fully believed they were working hand in hand with the three ancient Nephites who according to Mormon scripture had been preserved to aid in the redemption of the Lamanites. The nature of this cooperation was spelled out by the influential theologian and Apostle, Orson Pratt, when he, while relying upon many Book of Mormon scriptures, said:

"The Lord made a promise to these three [Nephites] that they should administer as holy messengers in the latter days, for and in behalf of the remnants of the house of Israel, which should fall into a low and degraded condition in consequence of the great wickedness and apostasy of their ancient fathers; that they should be instruments in his hands in bringing these remnants to the knowledge of the truth. We hear that these messengers have come, not in one instance

173

*alone, but in many instances. Already we have heard of
some fourteen hundred Indians who have been baptized.
Ask them why they have come so many hundred miles to
find Elders of the church and they will reply -- "Such a
person came to us, he spoke in our language, instructed
us and told us what to do, and we have come in order to
comply with his requirements."*

*Pratt further explained that the visit of these messengers
to the Lamanites was a sign the time-table leading to
Christ's millennial reign was rapidly unfolding. (p. 12,
Coates, undated)*

Mormon belief regarding the last days, the Jews, members
of the "Lost Tribes" of the House of Israel, and the Lamanites taught that:

*...the Jews would be gathered to the Holy Land and
a remnant of the Indians from both north and south
America would join the Mormon Church and they along
with a few faithful Saints, not of Indian ancestry, would
gather to Jackson County, Missouri, receive their land
inheritance and build the New Jerusalem in preparation
for the second coming of Christ. (p. 12, Coates, undated)*

As early as May of 1889, Mormon missionaries had encountered Indian People who had experienced the Ghost Dance Religion, or some other form
of "revival" and had approached the Presidency of the Mormon Church asking
them to assist in their efforts to understand just what it was that appeared to
be taking place among the Indian people:

Being puzzled by this "spiritual" movement, the Mormon Elders asked
the first Presidency for their advice and President Woodruff responded by saying:

*"We fully expect that the Lamanites...will receive
many manifestations in the last days ...It is probable
that they will receive the ministrations of perhaps the
Three Nephites...But the description which you have
of the narrative of these Indians who have seen these
supernatural things, does not inspire us with much
confidence.. .Great care has to be taken not to allow
a wrong spirit to prevail among those people; for
their tendency, as we understand, is to accept alleged
supernatural manifestations with a good deal of
credulity." (p. 16, Coates, undated)*

Throughout the early summer of 1890 reports of visitations of Jesus to
the Indians continued to be filtered through to the Mormon Church

officials. These reports were discussed in the work of Larry Coates in a very splendid piece of yet unpublished research into Mormon history. Coates revealed that President Woodruff sent a resident of Thistle Valley, a purported Cherokee Indian and an Elder in the Mormon Church, John King, to search out the truth of the rumors that had come to his attention.

Professor Coates stated the Elder John King had traveled to Fort Custer (Montana) in July of 1890 and there he is said to have learned of the visitation of Christ to the Indians from "...Porcupine and two of King's uncles who had all visited Wovoka in Mason Valley, Nevada." (p. 18, Coates) Just how Elder King's Cherokee relatives had come to be in Montana at the precise moment of the nephews visit is not known; however, Porcupine told Elder King of the marvelous things that he saw and heard while in Mason Valley, Nevada. Porcupine proclaimed that Jesus had appeared to the Indian People and that He had shown them the scars in his hands, feet and in His side. Jesus told them, so Porcupine said, that the dead would soon be resurrected.

> *Since many of the ideas in Porcupine's account agreed*
> *with the doctrines that King had accepted from the*
> *Mormons, he not only believed Christ had appeared*
> *to the Lamanites on earth, but he thought Porcupine*
> *had been appointed as one of Christ's "disciples to go*
> *forth and preach his sayings to all people." As a result,*
> *King, upon his return to Utah, reported his findings*
> *to President Woodruff, who assumed the heavenly*
> *visitor had been one of the Three Nephites instead of the*
> *Messiah. Nevertheless, Woodruff, convinced that the*
> *Church had a special responsibility to the Lamanites,*
> *requested King to serve the Church as a missionary to*
> *the "wild tribes: and after considerable deliberation he*
> *accepted the call." (pp. 18-19, Coates, undated)*[10]

During the summer of 1890 and into the fall, controversy continued to grip the Mormon communities. The Millenialists continued to look forward to the date of Joseph Smith's birthday, December 23, 1890, as the day that the Millennium would begin. Others of the Mormon faith, like Apostle Anthony H. Lund, pronounced that the events and stories of heavenly manifestations were but signs that a "spiritual awakening" had gripped the Mormon and Indian community and that this revival was an indication that the second coming was near.

Coates states that Apostle Lund addressed the San Pete Stake Conference and explained the surge of revivalism among the Indian People in this account:

---

10   Porcupine was often referred to as the "Messiah Preacher." He lived in the upper Rosebud Valley and died in 1929 at the age of 81. His "nobility of character" was considered to be an "inherent trait."

> *We need not say – 'Our Lord delayeth his coming!...*
> *We can be sure it is in the near future, because the Lord*
> *told Joseph Smith...that if he lived to be a certain age,*
> *he should see His face, which points to 91...Zion will be*
> *redeemed, but there are still many things to be done*
> *before that event takes place. Temples will be built - and*
> *the prophecies with regard to the Lamanites, and the ten*
> *tribes, will be filled. (p. 19, Coates, undated)*

The October General Conference of the Mormon Church was indeed, a memorable event for it put to rest the idea that Jesus had not returned and that it was one – or all – of the Three Nephites that had visited the earth again; and at the same time related an experience with the dead Joseph Smith that was designed to restore the faith in the Church in the words Joseph as Prophet and spokesman for the Lord:

> *I do not think anyone can tell the hour of the coming*
> *of the Son of Man ...We need not look for the time of*
> *the event to be made known. I will say here that in my*
> *dreams I have had a great many visits with the Prophet*
> *Joseph Smith since his death ...(In one interview I) asked*
> *the question, why are you in such a hurry here? He said...*
> *time nor opportunity to prepare to go to the earth with*
> *the great bridegroom...he said the time was at hand for*
> *the coming of the Son of Man...(but it was) not revealed*
> *to us, nor never will be until the hour comes. (p. 20,*
> *Coates, undated)*

A second member of the First Presidency, George Q. Cannon, further echoed the call to put at rest the concept that Jesus had returned to the earth:

> *We need not expect that 1891 will bring any such thing*
> *as the coming of the Lord. It was said yesterday that no*
> *man knoweth the day or the hour-but I will tell you what*
> *men can know. They can know that such and such a time*
> *is not the time.. .there are a great many events to take*
> *place that have not yet occurred; and the Savior will not*
> *come until they do take place. (p. 20, Coates, undated)*

Thus, a new wave of conservatism swept over the Conference and over the Mormon Church. Joseph Smith had been vindicated! The Millennium will await another time, another place and another people. The voice of dissent -- had there been one -- too, was silenced by the Mormon Prophet's declaration that he had spoken to the dead Joseph Smith, and it had been Joseph himself who had said Jesus was not going to return. Mormonism, like the Ghost Dance Religion, had been founded on the belief that a Prophet of the people had been in the presence of spirit persons and that truth had been   176 delivered through them to humankind. Mormons are few in number that question the authority of: "God told me so."

The Woodruff Manifesto quieted the uncertain waters of the polygamy issue and silenced forever the belief that Jesus had returned; nevertheless, a gnawing suspicion and yearning lingers in the human psychic:

> ...*Three years later, March 1890, the people of God, who were notified by the Three Nephites, met at Walkers Lake, Esmeralda County, Nevada, where a dispensation of the Celestial Kingdom of God -- the gospel in the covenant of consecration, a perfect oneness in all things, temporal and spiritual -- was given unto them. Twelve disciples were ordained, not by angels or men, but by the Messiah in the presence of hundreds, representing scores of tribes or nations who saw his face, heard and understood his voice as on the day of Pentecost. Acts 2, also fulfilling sec. 90:9, 10, 11 of Doctrine and Covenant. Ezk. 20:33-37. (Underscore added, p. 36, Wallace, 1965)*

> *Mormonism, too, had instructed its people...in the mouth of two or three witnesses, shall every word be established. (p. 24, Doctrine and Covenants, L.D.S. Doc. 6:28, p. 10, 1967 edition)*

A second lesson learned at Wounded Knee was that the Ghost Shirts had not been of sufficient power to turn away the bullets of the Seventh Cavalry. Yellow Bird had encouraged the wearers of the Ghost Shirt to stand at Wounded Knee and to demonstrate to the world that the power of the Ghost Dance garment would sustain the people. The dead bear no false witness!

It appears strange that people will trust to fate the wearing of an amulet, a rabbit's foot, an endowment robe, or a Ghost Shirt. Invincibility of a person, a community or a cause has been a frequent belief and hope throughout human history. In a sense, the belief in the invincibility of the People of God and His promise to Abraham has been a recurrent theme of Judaism. Then too, there had been the invincibility of the Nauvoo Legion, for the Invincible Dragoons were a common sight on the parade grounds of the City by the Mississippi. Dr. Richards testified of his deliverance from death in Carthage jail that he, too, had been delivered from harm's way because he was shielded by the protective power of the endowment robe. For whatever reason Joseph and Hyrum Smith had not however been so fortunate. Hubert H. Bancroft, in his 1890 work, the <u>History of Utah</u>, cites a footnote reference (317), p. 357, relating to Joseph Smith as follows:

> *This garment protects from disease, and even death, for the bullet of an enemy will not penetrate it. The prophet Joseph carelessly left off this garment*

177

*on the day of his death, and had he not done so, he would
have escaped unharmed.*

Somehow, the Ghost Shirt with its protective power had been derived
from the Ghost Dance Religion. It is nearly as much a mystery that the Mormon endowment garment became vested with protective properties!

The Indian's "magical garment" was, in the opinion of James Mooney,
an adaptation of a garment worn by Mormons and was said to have special
powers of healing and protection. The Endowment Robe of the Mormons and
the Ghost Shirt of the Indian share a strikingly similar role in the religious life
of both cultures.

Benjamin Ferris describes the Mormon Endowment robe:

> *In their initiation into the church, the novitiates
> are invested with a mysterious garment called the
> endowment robe, to which many virtues are ascribed...
> it is believed that Doctor Richards had on one of these
> robes, and thereby escaped unhurt at Carthage jail...
> The person thus invested is supposed to be safe against
> the arts of the devil to bring harm upon him, and in a
> condition to escape danger from shipwreck, bullets,
> disease, etc. (pp. 311-312, Ferris, 1854)*

It was James Mooney's belief that the "endowment robe" represents
the "most sacred badge of their faith," and is "supposed to render the wearer
invulnerable." (p. 790, Mooney, 1892)

Mooney maintains that the Indian prophet Wovoka, "disclaimed any
responsibility for the ghost shirt, and whites and Indian alike agreed that it
formed no part of the dance costume in Mason Valley." (p. 790, Mooney, 1892)

Paul Bailey stated the belief that after the news of the massacre at
Wounded Knee reached the Walker River (Nevada) Reservation, the Ghost
Dance Prophet became aware of the trouble that might come to him if it were
established that he had encouraged the use and belief in the Ghost Shirt. This
would be especially true if it could be demonstrated or proven that he had
encouraged the use of the shirt for purposes of making war upon the whites.
Thus, from this time forward, Bailey asserts, Wovoka denied that he had
taught the use of the Ghost Shirt for any purpose but peace.

> *But with the death of Sitting Bull and the Sioux blood-
> letting at Wounded Knee, the Messiahs, pretenders and
> real, now either sought complete anonymity or went
> underground. Not even a divine personage would want
> to head up a religious movement that had brought so
> insufferable and far-reaching a tragedy upon its people.
> (p. 174, Bailey, 1957)*

178

> *But now continued to confirm the fact that his Ghost
> Dance had been the very core of the Sioux troubles, and
> that a concerted effort by the United States Government
> was everywhere being made to suppress it. When finally
> he came to realize the enormity of the tragedy that had
> come out of the once simple religion he had preached,
> and the fact that he faced the possibility of having to
> answer for it all, he was shaken to the marrow. At
> every opportunity he explained that the eastern tribes
> had perverted the meaning of the doctrine, had made a
> thing out of it that it had not taught, and that the ghost
> shirts and their war implications were things concocted
> by them and added to the ritual without his consent.
> (Underscore added, p. 175, Bailey, 1957)*

Just how Wovoka came to incorporate the concept of invincibility into his beliefs is subject to considerable speculation. It is true that James Mooney suggested the Mormon invulnerability; however, Mooney also recognized that Wovoka's father, "...was not a preacher, but was ...a dreamer and invulner-able." (p. 13, Wallace, 1965) It is highly probable that the influence of Wovoka's father was as great, if not greater, than that of the teachings of Mormonism. This is especially important since Wovoka appears never to have entered the waters of Mormon baptism. The concept of invulnerability was by no means an exclusive belief of the Paiute, or the followers of the Ghost Dance Religion.

Paul Bailey asserted that Paiute Mormon Elders were in Mason Valley during a time of the Ghost Dance and that these same elders talked to Wovoka and

> *...he was cognizant of the holy garment they wore,
> and which was accepted by them as an actual physical
> protection against disease and death. (p. 123, Bailey,
> 1957)*

Bailey stated that Wovoka was "irked" by the exclusiveness of the Mormon endowment garment and was especially distressed that one must go through a Mormon Temple in order to wear one. Bailey expressed his belief that Wovoka continually stressed to the delegates of the many tribes that came to visit him that he "...was inviolate."

> *Those who had traveled so far to stand in awe before
> him, were under the natural assumption that ...he was
> immune from death; that the bullets of the enemy had no
> effect upon him; that he had long since been lifted from
> the menaces of disease and pain. (p. 123, Bailey, 1957)*

Ruth Underhill wrote that Wovoka

> *...had a garment of that sort, which he had said would*
> *turn away any bullet, though he averred that no fighting*
> *would be necessary. (p. 260, Underhill, 1974)*

As in the case of Mormonism, new disciples of the Ghost Dance Religion began eagerly to share the new found happiness with their friends and relations. It is singularly significant that considerable missionary effort was taking place at this time by both the Indian disciples of the Ghost Dance Religion and by Mormons. It would be easy to speculate as to just how the stories of the end of the age, the restoration of the earth, the return of the Messiah, and marvelous saving qualities of garments, should sweep across the country. In very little time the Mormon and Indian messages might well have become blurred as they melded more and more into a single story of deliverance.

The research conducted by Larry Coates revealed that "...thousands of Indians throughout the Basin came to the Mormons requesting baptism during the 1870's."

> *On the Fort Hall and Wind River Reservations, hundreds*
> *of Indians heard their shamans recount their vision*
> *and advise their people to locate the Mormons and as*
> *a result many traveled to Utah where they listened to*
> *the Mormon message and joined the faith. In eastern*
> *Nevada, hundreds of Indians gathered at Ruby Valley to*
> *join the church and in southern Utah, the whole tribe of*
> *Shivwits gathered near St. George and were baptized. In*
> *Grass, Thistle and Skull Valleys and Deep Creek, Nevada,*
> *the same process was reenacted. So many reported*
> *baptisms among the Lamanites occurred during this*
> *period, that the editor of the JUVENILE INSTRUCTOR*
> *stated that by within just a short time some two thousand*
> *Indians had embraced Mormonism. (pp. 10-11, Coates,*
> *undated)*

Bernard 0. Walker stated that Professor Coates

> *"...found that thousands joined the Church by his search*
> *of membership records and corroborated Mooney*
> *in that a considerable number were invested with*
> *the endowment robe through his search of the "live"*
> *endowment records. "(p. 21, Walker, undated)*

Walker, writing from the vantage point of his own Mormon beliefs, stated that

> *It is doubtful that those who did receive their own*
> *endowments understood fully the meaning*
> *or significance since these were conducted*

> *in the English tongue which might account for the*
> *misunderstanding with respect to the protective idea and*
> *its subsequent perversion if this in fact is where the idea*
> *stemmed from. (pp. 21-22, Walker, undated)*

> *...the Mormons tried to prepare their Lamanite converts*
> *to be ready for their prophetic calling to build a temple in*
> *New Jerusalem to be located in Jackson County, Missouri*
> *by taking them through the Mormon temples where they*
> *received the holy rites associated with the endowment.*
> *(p. 11, Coates, undated)*

It is highly likely that the "misunderstanding" of the purpose and the use of the endowment garment by the Indians, was, as Walker suggests, a natural result or consequence of the Temple ceremonies having been conducted in English. Undoubtedly, the imperfectness of language contributed greatly to the Indian's understanding or misunderstanding of the use of the endowment garment; however, it should be remembered that not only were the converts to Mormonism told of the protective nature of the endowment robes in the Temple, some were also undoubtedly told by Wovoka that his new religion had made him invulnerable as well. It appears more than certain that considerable confusion existed in the minds of converts to both Mormonism and the Ghost Dance Religion as to the protective nature of the holy garments.

Walker wrote:

> *It is true that every devout Mormon believes that*
> *the garment is a shield and protection; however, its*
> *protection is conditioned on one's faithful adherence to*
> *the Gospel of Jesus Christ ...While there are some who*
> *do credit the garment with unusual protective powers*
> *in cases of threatened physical danger, no universal*
> *or official claim is made as to its making the wearer*
> *invulnerable to bullets or knife. (p. 10, Walker, undated)*

In a strangely similar way, the concept of invulnerability of the Indians and invincibility of the Mormons moved from Illinois to Utah and from Nevada to the Dakotas and to the Plains. The Ghost Dance and, in time, the magical garment -- symbol or badge of the faithful followers -- appeared among the Sioux. The use of the garment, as well as its socio-religious significance, was, as was the Ghost Dance itself, a curious blend of native beliefs and traditions, with selected Christian, probably Mormon, practices and ceremonies. Both Mormonism and the Ghost Dance Religion began as a response of a "prophet" who saw and talked with God, who carried His message to earth, and whose message, once delivered, was modified with time and varying cultural awareness. The Ghost Shirt and Endowment Robe may well represent such an amalgamation and diffusion.[11]

Regardless of source, the Ghost Dance Religion and the use of the Ghost Shirt appeared among the Sioux sometime during the summer of 1890.

> *The slow, shuffling circle dance was foreign to them,*
> *but they made it more drastic by placing a dead*
> *cottonwood tree in the center to be hung with offerings.*
> *The cottonwood, the only tall tree of the Plains, was a*
> *symbol of life, ever renewed. Then one of their number*
> *began making ghost dance shirts -- long garments of*
> *white sheeting decorated with symbols in red and with*
> *eagle feathers at the elbows. (p. 260, Underhill, 1974,*
> *underscore added)*

Just which one of the Sioux's number introduced the concept and the first Ghost Shirt to the Sioux Reservations is not known. This missing knowledge stands between mere speculation and a positive association of the Mormon Endowment Garment and the Ghost Shirt especially among the Sioux.

Among those speculations as to how and by whom the Ghost Shirt arrived among the Sioux is that of Professor Larry Coates who postulates that a Sioux girl, Isabel, had been cared for in a Mormon home in the Council Bluffs region of Iowa about 1852. Coates theorizes that after several years away from Iowa and her Mormon benefactor -- Mary A. Powers -- the Sioux maiden returned for a visit. It was during this visit that Isabel came into contact with Elder E. H. Pierce, who taught her the tenets of Mormonism, whereupon she was baptized into the Mormon Church and then returned to her people. A short while after her return she is purported to have written to Mrs. Powers "...that many Sioux, if not all, might be soon converted by an elder speaking the Sioux language." (pp. 13-14, Coates, undated)

Coates does not attempt in his unpublished work to establish if a Mormon mission was sent to the Sioux; nor does he state that Isabel married a Mormon Elder for without this additional advantage she could not have been eligible to wear the endowment robe or take it to her people. Coates speculated that the message and testimony that Isabel bore to her people had a lasting impression on such persons as Spotted Tail.

---

11   To what extent the Ghost Dance Shirt and doctrine was believed or practiced among the Oklahoma Cheyenne (Southern Cheyenne), Kiowa, and Arapaho has not been established in this research design. It is highly likely, and even probable, that the doctrine was known in Oklahoma; what is not established is the influence of Mormonism among these tribes. It is hypothesized that the Kiowa may have stressed the more militant use of the Ghost Shirt. It has been suggested by Sam Chapman, Jr., that the Southern Cheyenne warned the Cheyenne and Sioux camps at Little Bighorn that Custer was making his way from Ft. Sill, Oklahoma in what would become a pre-emptive and punitive action. This hypothesis could serve as a significant research project.

*For one thing, Spotted Tail had apparently been
impressed with Joseph Smith's treatment of the conflicts
that existed among the Protestant Church, for near the
end of his life he repeated the essence of Joseph Smith's
story to Captain G. M. Randall. But more impressive
than Spotted Tail's account was Sitting Bull's vision
which included the Christian concepts of a Messiah and
the resurrection and an idea similar to The Book of
Mormon notion that one day the Indians shall possess
this chosen land again. (p. 14, Coates, undated)*

The historical record is not clear as to the nature and extent of Mormon missionary activity among the Sioux. The work of Professor Larry Coates
may contribute much to the task of clarifying this point; however, until that research is forthcoming, statements like those made by General Nelson A. Miles
continue to attempt to connect Mormonism to the Ghost Dance Religion in a
very narrow and extremely negative manner.

*...General Nelson A. Miles reported that Indians on the
Utah, Montana, and Cheyenne Reservation believed
the Messiah would restore them to their former glory,
bringing back the buffalo and driving the whites from
the land. When asked who he thought "responsible for
this imposition upon the Indians," General Miles replied,
it is my belief that the Mormons are the prime movers in
it. This is not a hard statement to believe, for there are
200,000 Mormons and .., they have had missionaries at
work among the Indians for many years and have made
many converts. (p. 158, Arrington and Britton, 1979)*

Regardless of the charges and counter charges made that attempt to
assert positively that the Mormons were responsible for the restlessness and
atmosphere of resistance and even rebellion in the Ghost Dance and the wearing of the Ghost Shirt, to date, NO conclusive evidence exists that gives time,
date, persons and locations that were responsible for bringing Mormons into
Indian camps with the intent of inciting them to rebellion.

It is entirely probable that those Indian People, either Sioux, Ute, Paiute, Shoshone or whatever tribe, that entered the waters of Mormon baptism
and received the Mormon priesthood as Elders, also received the endowment
robe; it is equally probable that they misunderstood the nature and significance of the garment and could have identified it, in the case of the Sioux, with
their earlier war shirts. The evidence may be circumstantial -- it is not conclusive and irrefutable.

In a similar manner, the statement by General Miles that the Mormons
were responsible for the unrest associated with the Ghost Dance,
is simply a statement--and probably highly biased -- and as

such is merely conjecture. General Miles failed to give documentation or supporting evidence to prove his point.

Likewise a frustrated white woman and devotee of Sitting Bull wrote in a letter to Agent McLaughlin at the Pine Ridge reservation that:

> *I believe that the Mormons are at the bottom of it all*
> *and misuse the credulity of the Indians for their own*
> *purposes... (p. 115, Miller, 1959)*

Supporting evidence as to who the Mormon Elders were, where they were from, and when they arrived at the Pine Ridge Reservation remains a mystery.

The Ghost Shirt and Ghost Dance Religion was an upwelling of the Indian spirit to be free and rid forever of the oppressive yoke of white culture. The form that it took may well have been a blending of Indian and White...even Indian and Mormon; however, the use of the dance and garment arose out of a perceived need of the Native American community to be rid of the whites and their culture. The Ghost Shirt may well have been invented to accomplish just this goal, or so may have reasoned the Sioux.

David H. Miller declares that Black Elk, the Sioux holy man made famous by the works of John G. Neihardt, was the "...inventor of the ghost shirt..." (p. 137, Miller, 1959)

> *Late summer breezes were rolling out of the distant*
> *Nebraska sand hills off to the southwest when Black Elk*
> *journeyed to the camp on Cut Meat Creek. With him he*
> *brought six of the holy ghost shirts like those he had made*
> *at Big Road's camp on Wounded Knee Creek. Dancers*
> *at Wounded Knee and White Clay Creek had kept Black*
> *Elk busy all summer leading their dances and fashioning*
> *"bulletproof" garments for them. Now he had brought*
> *immunity from bullets to the Brules. (pp. 85-86, Miller,*
> *1959)*

> *Years later, old, feeble and blind, Black Elk recalled his*
> *own mystical experience that day: "As I danced with*
> *Kicking Bear and Good Thunder, a queer feeling came*
> *over me. My legs seemed to be crawling with ants. Then*
> *I felt a strange power swinging me off the ground. I*
> *seemed to be gliding and swooping like a huge soaring*
> *bird, floating through the air with outstretched wings.*
> *Far in front of me I saw a single eagle feather dancing.*
> *The feather became a spotted eagle fluttering ahead of*
> *me, screaming for me to follow its dizzy flight. I floated*
> *over a high ridge. Beyond lay a beautiful green land*
> *where a throng of happy Indians lived in an*
> *old-time camp of tall cow skin lodges. On every*

184

*hand meat racks were heavily loaded with fresh buffalo
meat, while fat ponies grazed on neighboring hillsides.
Off in the distance the wild game ran thick. From every
direction came happy, singing hunters carrying fresh
meat into camp. Everything glowed with a bright living
light! (p. 78, Miller, 1959)*

*Suddenly I found myself in the midst of this happy
village. Two men wearing strange painted shirts
approached me. They said: "It is not yet time for you to
see your father. But he is happy. For you, much work
is still to be done. We will give you a gift to take back
to your people." I was then lifted into the air again and
came floating back to the camp on Wounded Knee Creek.
(pp. 78-79, Miller, 1959)*

*Soon I found myself sitting on the ground with dancers
crowding all around me, eager to know if I had seen a
new vision. Knowing that the sacred shirts had been the
gift for my people, I told the Dancers of my dream and
described the holy garments to them. (p. 79, Miller, 1959)*

*Of all who heard Black Elk tell of this vision, no one was
more impressed than Kicking Bear. It reminded him of
his own vision of the spotted eagle the time the sun died.
Moreover, when Black Elk told of meeting the holy men
who wore the strange shirts, Kicking Bear recalled that
Wovoka far in the west had worn just such a garment. (p.
79, Miller, 1959)*

Of all the followers of the Ghost Dance Religion, Black Elk is the <u>only</u>
person who is quoted as having spoken out that he was the originator of the
Ghost shirt. Whereas Wovoka, as Prophet of the Ghost Dance, sought to deny
his involvement in the spread and use of the Ghost Shirt, Black Elk openly
claimed its origin, use and purpose.

The claim of Black Elk is singularly important for several reasons: In
vision Black Elk received and gave the sacred shirt as a "gift" to his people. The
sacred shirt had been a gift of the "spirit" and had not come from a Mormon
Elder or even the Paiute Prophet, Wovoka. Its origin, therefore, was spiritual
and as such, it transcended time and the material culture of the white. The receipt of the sacred shirt of Black Elk was not altogether unlike the receipt of the
golden plates by Joseph Smith or the voice of Allah peaking to Mohammed or
to Wovoka.

To Black Elk, his "sacred shirt" was to become a symbol of his people's
desire to recover the completeness of the "Sacred Hoop." It was to
be, then, a symbol of the unity of the people. It was a symbol of   185

their desire to live in harmony with the earth and nature.

As a youth, Black Elk had seen, in his vision, the breaking of the Hoop of his people. This experience had greatly troubled Black Elk throughout his life until he had come into contact with the Ghost Dance religion. To Black Elk, the Ghost Dance Religion had come to the Sioux as a means whereby the Sacred Hoop could once again be complete and restored. Wounded Knee seemed, for awhile, to cripple the dream, but it did not destroy the vision; the vision of the returned Messiah and a restored earth was kept alive during even he darkest hour of life of the human family. This is the lesson that the Hopi's Blue Star Kachina seeks to teach. This is the lesson of the Jews crying from the ashes of a score of death camps. This is the same lesson taught in the Polish Solidarity Movement. The hope of the oppressed lies in their faith in the ideal, the principle, the vision of an earth living in complete harmony.

The failure of the Ghost Dance, if indeed it was a failure, is to be observed in the willingness of both the Whites and Indians to accept the notion that the fulfillment of the Ghost Dance prophecy would take place -- in a day, a week, or even a year. This simply was not to be the case; however, without dates, the Ghost Dance Teachings are as relevant to the earth in this day as they were in 1870, 1890, or 2012. The moral teachings of the Ghost Dance Religion, like those of Christianity, are ageless and transcend time, people, and races.

So it was that the year 1890 ended much as it had begun. The Mormon President had been correct in his prediction that 1890 would long be remembered in the life of the Mormon and Indian People.

> *President Wilford Woodruff...closed his 1889 diary with*
> *the following interpretation: "Thus ends the year 1889*
> *and the word of the Prophet Joseph Smith is beginning to*
> *be fulfilled that the whole nation would turn against Zion*
> *and would make war upon the Saints. The nation has*
> *never been filled so full of lies against the Saints as today.*
> *1890 will be an important year with the Latter Day*
> *Saints and the American Nation." (p. 249, Larson, 1971)*

President Woodruff had directed the Mormon missionaries to end, for the time, missionary work in those areas in which the Ghost Dance was taking place and warned the Saints to avoid conflict with the Indians.

In December of 1890, at Wounded Knee, "..the vision of the peaceful Paiute dreamer, Wovoka, had come to an end. And so had all the long and bitter years of Indian resistance on the western plains." (p. 229, Nicholas and Adams, 1971)

In point of history, that gathering up, those last days
which the Mormons expected within a few years had
been delayed. Good Mormons still look forward to the
restoration of Zion and the building of the miraculous
City on the site of the former Garden of Eden near
Independence, Missouri... (p. 26, Stegner, 1964)

In Utah, a more conservative wind had begun to blow, carrying with it the hope of the Mormon Millenialists and redirecting the missionary outreach away from the Native American People. The Temple in Jackson County, to be built by the Indian people, would of necessity, await another age, another prophet, and another people "whose author and finisher would be God."

The year 1890 ended in a tragedy for the Indian People and the Mormons as well. The vision of each people was blurred; nevertheless, a haunting melody of the inner soul of the people seems to cry out over the Plains and Basin. Short Bull, one of the delegates to Wovoka is reported to have said: "Who would have thought that dancing could make such trouble? For the message that I brought was peace. And the message was given by the Father to all the tribes." (p. 251, Utley, 1963)

The Sioux sang:
The whole world is coming,
A nation is coming, a nation is coming.
The Eagle has brought the message to the tribe.
The father says so, the father says so.
Over the whole earth they are coming,
The buffalo are coming, the buffalo are coming.
(p. 223, Nichols and Adams, 1971)

Wallace Stegner wrote:

...the sun had dipped behind the sharp skyline of
the Omaha hills. Silence was then called, and a well
cultivated mezzo-soprano voice ...gave...a little song: By
the rivers of Babylon we sat down and wept. We wept
when we remembered Zion. (p. 82, Stegner, 1964)

The religious experience of aspiration to a new order
grows amid the trials and sufferings of those who endure
it. Harry Paige, in his Songs of the Teton Sioux, *describes*
how the old people still see hope, even after the first
battle of Wounded Knee, in the wind that blows over the
grass every spring. The very landscape, too, has become
a part of the impatience for divine help that pervades
the temperament of the Plains Indians. As one studies a
section of the Wind River Mountains, he will
observe the outline of a profile which, say the

187

Indian People, represents a sleeping Indian. He has slept for a long time now, they say, but someday he will rise again. (p. 121, Carl Starkloff, 1974)

Cheyenne youth near Canton, Oklahoma, 1915

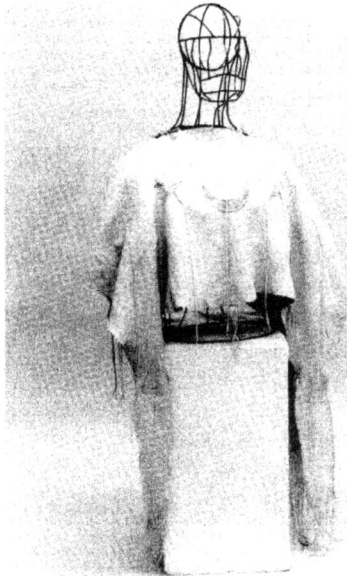

Kiowa Ghost Dance Cape in buckskin, 1894
Courtesy Texas Tech University Museum

188

BIBLIOGRAPHY

Adams, Alexander B. <u>Sitting Bull, An Epic of the Plains</u>. New York: Capricorn Books, G.P. Putnam's Sons, 1974.

Alexander, Hartley Burr. <u>The World's Rim.</u> Lincoln, Nebraska: The University of Nebraska Press, 1967.

Allen, James B., and Leonard, Glen M. <u>The Story of the Latter-Day Saints</u>. Salt Lake City, Utah: Deseret Book Company, 1976.

Alter, J. Cecil, ed. "State of Deseret." <u>Utah Historical Quarterly</u>, Volume VIII, (State Historical Society) Salt Lake City, Utah, 1940.

Anderson, Nels. <u>Desert Saints: The Mormon Frontier in Utah.</u> Chicago, Illinois: The University of Chicago Press, 1942.

Armstrong, Virginia Irving. <u>I Have Spoken: American History Through the Voices of the Indians</u>. Chicago, Illinois: The Swallow Press, Inc., 1971.

Arrington, Leonard J.   <u>Great Basin Kingdom: An Economic History of the Latter-Day Saints, 1830-1900</u>. Cambridge, Massachusetts: Harvard University Press, 1958.

Bailey, Paul. <u>Jacob Hamblin: Buckskin Apostle</u>. Los Angeles, California: Westernlore Press, 1948.

Bailey, Paul. <u>Sam Brannan and the California Mormons</u>. Los Angeles, California: Westernlore Press, 1942.

Bailey, Paul. <u>Walkara: Hawk of the Mountains</u>. Los Angeles, California: Westernlore Press, 1954.

Bailey, Paul. <u>Wovoka the Indian Messiah.</u> Los Angeles, California: Westernlore Press, 1957.

Bataille, Gretchen M.; Gradwohl, David M.; and Silet, Charles L. P.: eds., <u>The Worlds Between Two Rivers: Perspectives on American Indians in Iowa</u>. Ames, Iowa: Iowa State University Press, 1978.

Billington, Roy A., editor. <u>The Far Western Frontier, William Clayton's Journal</u>. New York: Arno Press, 1973.

Blouet, Brian W, and Merlin P. Lawson. Images of the Plains: The Role of Human Nature in Settlement. Lincoln: University of Nebraska Press, 1975.

Boller, Henry A., editor. Milo Melton Quaife, Among the Indians: Eight Years in the Far West -1858-1866. Chicago, Illinois: Lakeside Press, R.R. Donnelley & Sons Co., 1959.

Briggs, Marion F. and Sarah D. McAnulty. The Ghost Dance Tragedy at Wounded Knee. Washington, D.C., The Smithsonian Institution, Office of Printing and Photographic Services, 1977.

Brodie, Fawn M. No Man Knows My History. New York, New York: Alfred A. Knopf, 1945.

Brooks, Juanita. John Doyle Lee: Zealot – Pioneer Builder - Scapegoat. Glendale, California: Arthur Clark Company, 1962.

Brooks, Juanita, editor. On the Mormon Frontier: The Diary of Hosea Stout. Vol. 1 and 2, Salt Lake City, Utah: Utah State Historical Society, University of Utah Press, 1964.

Brooks, Juanita. The Mountain Meadows Massacre. Stanford, California: Stanford University Press, 1950.

Brooks, Juanita, editor. Journal of the Southern Indian Mission. (Diary of Thomas D. Brown). Volumes I - II. Western Text Society Number 4; Logan, Utah: Utah State University Press, 1972.

Brown, Dee. Bury My Heart at Wounded Knee. New York: Bantam Book Publications, 1970.

Brown, Thomas D., Journal of the Southern Indian Mission. Salt Lake City, Utah: Deseret Book Company, 1972.

Burton, Richard F., ed. The City of the Saints and Across the Rocky Mountains to California. New York, New York: Alfred A, Knopf, 1963.

Carson, Gustive O. The 'Americanization' of Utah for Statehood. San Marino, California: The Huntington Library, 1971.

Catlin, George. Episodes From the Life Among the Indians and Last Rambles. Marvin C. Ross, ed. Norman, Oklahoma: University of Oklahoma Press, 1959.

Catlin, George. North American Indians - Volume I. Edinburgh: John Grant, 1926.

Catlin, George. North American Indians - Volume II. Edinburgh: John Grant, 1926.

Catlin, George. O-KEE-PA. New Haven and London: Yale University, 1967.

Chafe, Wallace L. Meaning and Structure of Language. University of Chicago Press, 1970.

Coates, Larry.   "The Mormons, the Ghost Dance Craze, and the Massacre at Wounded Knee," Unpublished paper by Dr. Coates, Ricks College, Rexburg, Idaho, undated.

Debo, Angio. A History of the Indians of the United States. Norman, Oklahoma: University of Oklahoma Press, 1970, p. 128.

DeVoto, Barnard. The Year of Decision: 1846. Boston, Massachusetts: Houghton Mifflin Company, 1942.

Dobyns, Henry F., and Euler, Robert C. The Ghost Dance of 1889 Among the Pai Indians of Northwestern Arizona. Mississippi: Prescott College, 1967.

Eastman, Charles A. (Ohiyesa). From the Deep Woods to Civilization. Lincoln, Nebraska: University of Nebraska Press, 1916.

Egan, Ferol. Sand in a Whirlwind: The Paiute Indian War of 1860. Foreword by A.B. Guthrie, Jr. New York, New York: Doubleday and Company, 1972.

Farb, Peter. Man's Rise to Civilization. New York, New York: E.P, Dutton, Inc., 1965.

Ferris, Benjamin G. Utah and the Mormons. New York, New York: Harper and Brothers, 1854.

Fife, Austin and Fife, Alta. Saints of Sage and Saddle. Bloomington, Indiana: Indiana University Press, 1956.

Fite, Gilbert and Reese, Jim E. An Economic History of the United States. (2nd Edition) New York, New York: Houghton Mifflin Company, 1965.

Flanders, Robert Bruce. Nauvoo: Kingdom on the Mississippi. Urbana, Illinois: University of Illinois Press, 1965.

Furniss, Norman F. The Mormon Conflict! 1850-1859. New Haven, Connecticut: Yale University Press, 1960.

Gatschet, A.S., "Report of an Indian Visit to Jack Wilson, the Paiute Messiah," Journal of American Folklore, Volume 6 (April, 1893) pp. 108-11.

"Ghost Dance in Arizona," Journal of American Folklore, Volume 5 (January, 1892) pp. 65-68.

"Ghost Dancers in the West - A Report of two articles from the Illustrated American Magazine," Illustrated American Magazine (January 17, 1891; February 7, 1891).

Glover, William. The Mormons in California. (Foreword, notes and selected bibliography by Paul Bailey), Los Angeles, California: Glen Dawson, 1954.

Haberly, Lloyd. Pursuit of the Horizon. New York, New York: the MacMillan Company, 1948.

Hagan, William T. United States - Comanche Relations: The Reservation Years. New Haven, Connecticut: Yale University Press, 1976.

Hamblin, Jacob. A Narrative of His Personal Experience as a Frontiersman, Missionary to the Indians and Explorer. Salt Lake City, Utah: Juvenile Instructor Office, 1881.

Harris, Marvin. Cows, Pigs, Wars, and Witches: The Riddles of Culture. New York, New York: Vintage Books, A Division of Random House, 1978.

Haverstock, Mary Sayre. Indian Gallery - The Story of George Catlin. New York, New York: Four Winds Press, 1973.

Hickman, Bill. Brigham's Destroying Angel. Salt Lake City, Utah: Shepard Publishing Company, 1904.

Hittman, Michael. Wovoka and the Ghost Dance. Lincoln, University of Nebraska Press, 1990.

Hollon, W. Eugene. The Great American Desert: Then and Now. New York, New York: Oxford University Press, 1966.

Hopkins, Sara Winnemucca. Life Among the Paiutes: Their Wrongs and Claims. Horace Mann, ed. New York, New York: G.P. Putnam & Sons, 1883.

Howard, Helen Addison and McGrath, Dan L. War Chief Joseph. Lincoln, Nebraska: University of Nebraska Press, 1941.

Howard, James H. Shawnee! The Ceremonialism of a Native American Tribe and it's Cultural Background. Athens, Ohio: Ohio University Press, 1981.

Hyde, George E. A Sioux Chronicle. Norman, Oklahoma: University of Oklahoma Press, 1956.

Jacobs, Wilbur R. Dispossessing the American Indian: Indians and Whites on the Colonial Frontier. New York, New York: Charles Scribner's Sons, 1972.

Johnson, Edward C. Walker River Paiutes: A Tribal History. Salt Lake City, Utah: University of Utah Printing Service, 1974.

Jones, Daniel Webster. 40 Years Among the Indians. Los Angeles, California: Westernlore Press, 1960.

Jones, W. Osakie. "Legend of the Ghost Dance," Journal of American Folklore, 12 (October, 1899) pp. 284-6.

Jorgenson, Joseph G. The Sun Dance Religion (Power for the Powerless). Chicago, Illinois: The University of Chicago Press, 1972.

Josephy, Alvin M. Jr. The Indian Heritage of America. New York, New York: Bantam Books, 1968.

Kennedy, Thomas J. "Crow-Northern Cheyenne Selected for Study," Journal of American Indian Education, 11:1 (October, 1971) pp. 27-31.

Kersey, Harry A., Anne Keithley and F. Ward Brunson. "Improving Reading Skills of Seminole Children." Journal of American Indian Education, 10:3 (May, 1971) pp. 3-7.

Kroeber, A.L. "Ghost Dance in California," Journal of American Folklore, 17 (January, 1905) pp.32-5.

Kroeber, et. al., editors. American Archaeology and Ethnology. (Volume XXVIII) Berkeley, California: University of California Press, Kraus Preprint Corporation, New York, 1965.

Kroeber, A.L. Handbook of the Indians of California. Bureau of American Ethnology, Bulletin 78, Smithsonian Institution. Washington, D.C.: U.S. Government Printing Office, 1925.

Kulckhohn, Clyde and Leighton, Dorothea. Children of the People. New York, New York: Octagon Books, 1969. (Reprint of the 1947 edition.)

La Barre, Weston. The Ghost Dance - Origins of Religion. Delta, 1970. Also: London: Allen and Unwin Ltd., 1972.

La Barre, Weston. The Peyote Cult. (4th edition) New York, New York: Schecken Books, 1975.

La Pointe, James. Legends of the Lakota. San Francisco, California: The Indian Historian Press, 1976.

Larson, Gustive O. The 'Americanization' of Utah for Statehood. San Marino, California: The Huntington Library, 1971.

Lauben, Reginald, and Lauben, Gladys. Indian Dances of North America. Norman Oklahoma: University of Oklahoma Press, 1976.

Leitka, Gene. "Search for Identity Creates Problems for Indian Students." Journal of American Indian Education 11:1 (October, 1971) pp. 7-10.

Leone, Mark P. Roots of Modern Mormonism. Cambridge, Massachusetts: Harvard University Press, 1979.

Lesser, Alexander. The Pawnee Ghost Dance Hand Game. (A Study of Cultural Change) New York, New York: Columbia University Press, 1933.

McCarty, Darene. "An Indian Student Speaks." Indian Historian 4:2 (Summer, 1971) pp. 10, 20.

McCraken, Harold. George Catlin and the Old Frontier. New York, New York: The Dial Press, 1959.

McGavin, E. Cecil. The Nauvoo Temple. Salt Lake City, Utah: Deseret Book Company, 1962.

McKern, Sharon and Thomas. "The Peace Messiah," Mankind, (September, 1970) p. 60.

McPhee, John.Basin and Range. New York, New York: Farror, Straus, and Giroux, 1980.

MacEwan, Grant. Sitting Bull: The Years in Canada. Edmonton, Canada: Hurtig Publishers, 1973.

Mails, Thomas E. <u>The Mystic Warriors of the Plains</u>. Garden City, New York: Doubleday and Company, 1972.

Marriott, Alice and Rachlin, Carol K. <u>American Indian Mythology</u>. New York, New York: A Mentor Book from New American Library, 1968.

Marriott, Alice. <u>The Ten Grandmothers</u>. Norman, Oklahoma: University of Oklahoma Press, 1968.

Mashbir, Sidney Forrester. <u>I Was An American Spy</u>. New York, New York: Vantage Press, 1953.

Matthiessen, Peter. <u>In the Spirit of Crazy Horse</u>. New York, New York: The Viking Press, 1980.

Mayhill, Mildred P. <u>The Kiowas</u>. Norman, Oklahoma: The University of Oklahoma Press, 1962.

Medicine, Beatrice. "The Anthropologists and American Indian Studies Programs," <u>Indian</u> <u>Historian</u> 4:1 (Spring, 1971) pp. 15-18.

Meighan, Clement W. and Riddell, Francis A. <u>The Maru Cult of the Pomo Indians (A California Ghost Dance Survival).</u> Los Angeles, California: Southwest Museum, Highland Park, 1972.

Merk, Fredrick. <u>History of the Westward Movement</u>. New York, New York: Alfred A. Knopf Company, 1980.

Mertz, Henriette. <u>Gods From the Far East: How the Chinese Discovered America</u>. New York, New York: Ballantine Books, 1952, 1973.

Miller, David Humphreys. <u>Custer's Fall: The Indian Side of the Story</u>. New York, New York: Duell, Sloan, and Pearce, 1957.

Miller, David Humphreys. <u>Ghost Dance</u>. New York, New York: Duell, Sloan, and Pearce, 1959.

Milligan, Edward A. <u>Dakota Twilight. The Standing Rock Sioux, 1874, 1890</u>. New York, New York: Hicksville, Exposition Press, 1976.

Mooney, James. "The Ghost Dance Religion and the Sioux outbreak of 1890," <u>14th Annual Report of the Bureau of American Ethnology</u> Vol. 14 (18921893) GPO, 1896.

Moore, John L.S. "Study of Incentives and Attitudes in the Motivation of Navajo Indian Children in B.I.A. Elementary Schools," Unpublished dissertation George Peabody College 1971, Ann Arbor, Michigan, University Microfilm No. 72-3816.

Morgan, Dale. "The Administration of Indian Affairs in Utah, 1851-1858," <u>Pacific Historical Review</u>, 17 (1948) pp. 383-409.

Morgan, Dale, ed. <u>Overland in 1846: Diaries and Letters of the California-Oregon Trail</u>. (Volumes I and II) Georgetown, California: The Talisman Press, 1963.

Morgan, Otis. "Indian Education - A Cultural Dilemma," <u>Indian Historian</u>, 4:3 (Fall, 1971) pp. 23-26.

Morris, Richard B., ed. <u>Encyclopedia of American History</u>. New York, New York: Harper & Bros. 1953.

Nibley, Preston. <u>Brigham Young: The Man and His Work</u>. Salt Lake City, Utah: Deseret Book Company, 1970.

Nichols, Roger L. and Adams, George R., eds. <u>The American Indian: Past and Present</u>. Lexington, Massachusetts: Xerox College Publishing, 1971.

Olson, James C. <u>Red Cloud and the Sioux Problem</u>. Lincoln, Nebraska: University of Nebraska Press, 1965.

Ortiz, Alfanso. "An Indian Anthropologist's Perspective on Anthropology," <u>Indian Historian,</u> 4:3 (Fall, 1971) pp. 23-26.

Oswalt, Wendell H. <u>This Land Was Theirs (A Study of North American Indians)</u>. Third Edition. New York, New York: John Wiley and Sons, 1978.

Parker, Z.A. "Ghost Dance at Pine Ridge," <u>Journal of American Folklore</u> 4 (April, 1891) pp. 160-2.

Patch, Kenneth. "Leadership Training Program at Phoenix Indian High School." <u>Journal of American Indian Education</u>, 10:3 (May, 1971) pp. 14-17.

Pecoraro, Joseph. "The Effect of a Series of Special Lessons on Indian History and Culture Upon the Attitudes of Indian and Non-Indian Students." Unpublished dissertation, Boston University 1971; dissertation abstract, 32:4 (October, 1971) pp. 1757-A.

196

Peterson, Charles. Take Up Your Mission: Mormon Colonizing Along the Little Colorado River 1870-1900. Tucson, Arizona: University of Arizona Press, 1973.

Porter, C. Fayne. Our Indian Heritage: Profiles of Twelve Great Leaders. New York, New York: Chilton Book Company, 1964.

Pratt, Parley P. Autobiography of Parley P. Pratt. Reprint. Salt Lake City, Utah: Deseret Book Company, 1973.

Regan, Timothy F. and Pagno, Jules. "The Place of Indian Culture in Adult Education." Adult Leadership, 20:2 (June, 1971) pp. 53-55.

Reno, Thomas R. "A Study of the Knowledges and Attitudes of Navajo Indians in Two Communities Toward Navajo Reservation Schools." Dissertation - Michigan State University, Dissertation Abstract 32/6 (December, 1971) pp. 2975-A.

Rich, Russell R. Ensign to the Nations. (A history of the Church from 1846 to the present) Provo, Utah: Brigham Young University Publications.

Robinson, Doane. A History of the Dakota or Sioux Indians. Minneapolis, Minnesota: Ross and Hanes, Inc., 1956.

Roehm. Mariorie Catlin. The Letters of George Catlin and His Family. Berkeley and Los Angeles, California: University of California, 1966.

Sanford, Gregory. "The Study of Nez Perce Indian Education." Unpublished Ph.D. dissertation, University of New Mexico, 1970; dissertation abstract 31:11 (May, 1971) p. 5816-A.

Schimmelpfennig, Dorothy. "A Study of Cross-Cultural Problems in the L.D.S. Indian Student Placement Program in Davis County, Utah." Unpublished dissertation, University of Utah, 1971; dissertation abstract 32:4 (October, 1971), p. 1811-A.

Schmitt, Martin F. and Brown Dee. Fighting Indians of the West. New York, New York: Charles Scribner's Sons, 1948.

Schindler, Harold. Orrin Porter Rockwell: Man of God, Son of Thunder. Salt Lake City, Utah: University of Utah Press, 1966.

Smith, Rex Alan. Moon of Popping Trees. New York, New York: Readers Digest Press, 1975.

Spencer, Robert F. and Jennings, Jesse D., et al. The Native Americans. New York, New York: Harper and Row, Publishers, 1977.

Spier, Leslie. The Prophet Dance of the Northwest and Its Derivatives: The Source of the Ghost Dance. Menasha, Wisconsin: George Banta Publishing Company, General Series in Anthropology #1, 1935.

Starkloff, Carl. The People of the Center. New York, New York: The Seabury Press, 1974.

Stegner, Wallace Earl. The Gathering of Zion: The Story of the Mormon Trail. New York, New York: McGraw-Hill Book Co., 1964.

Stegner, Wallace Earl.   Mormon Country. New York, New York: Duell, Sloan, and Pearce, 1942.

Stensland, Anna L. "American Indian Culture and the Reading Program." Journal of Reading, 15:1 (October, 1971) pp. 22-26.

Taylor, Samuel W. Nightfall at Nauvoo. New York, New York: Avon, 1971.

Tunley, Roul.   "Smooth Path at Rough Rock." American Education, 7:2 (March, 1971) pp. 15-20.

Underhill, Ruth. Red Man's Religion. (Beliefs and Practices of the Indians North of Mexico) Chicago, Illinois: The University of Chicago Press, 1974.

Utley, Robert M. Assisting John Stands in Timber, and Margot Liberty. Cheyenne Memories. Lincoln, Nebraska: The University of Nebraska Press, 1967.

Utley, Robert.   The Last Days of the Sioux Nation. New Haven, Connecticut: Yale University Press, 1963.

Vestal, Stanley. New Sources of Indian History 1850-1891, The Ghost Dance - The Prairie Sioux. Norman, Oklahoma: University of Oklahoma Press, 1934.

Vestal, Stanley. Sitting Bull: Champion of the Sioux. Norman, Oklahoma: University of Oklahoma Press, 1969.

Walker, Bernard O. Were Sitting Bull and the Mormons Rightly Accused in the Wounded Knee Massacre? Unpublished research paper presented to Dr. Fred R. Gowans, Brigham Young University, undated.

Wallace, Anthony F,C., ed. The Ghost Dance Religion. Chicago, Illinois: University of Chicago Press, A Phoenix Book, 1965.

Wallace, Robert, et al., The Miners. New York, New York: Time-Life Books, 1976.

Waters, Frank. The Book of the Hopi. New York, New York: Penguin Books, Inc., 1977.

Waters, Frank. Mexico Mystique: The Coming Sixth World of Consciousness. Athens, Ohio: Ohio University Press, 1975.

Wauchope, Robert. Lost Tribes and Sunken Continents. Chicago, Illinois:The University of Chicago Press, 1962.

Weitfish, Gene. The Lost Universe. New York, New York: Basic Books, Inc., 1965.

Wellman, Paul I. The Indian Wars of the West. Garden City, New York: Doubleday & Company, Inc. 1954.

Werner, M.R. The Life of Brigham Young. New York, New York: Harcourt Brace, 1925.

West, Ray B., Jr. Kingdom of the Saints. New York, New York: The Viking Press, 1957.

Whalen, William J. The Latter-Day Saints in the Modern Day World. Notre Dame, Indiana: The University of Notre Dame Press, 1964.

Widtsoe, John A., ed. Discourses of Brigham Young. Salt Lake City, Utah: Deseret Book Company, 1961.

Withycombe, Jeraldine S. "An Analysis of Self-Concept and Social Status of Paiute Indian and White Elementary School Children in Nevada." University of Connecticut, 1970, Dissertation
Abstract 31:12 (June, 1971).

Yost, Nellie Snyder. Medicine Lodge. Chicago, Illinois: The Swallow Press, Inc., 1970.

Young, Brigham, President. Journal of Discourses, Vol. I. London, England: Liverpool, 1956.

Young, Brigham, President. <u>Journal of Discourses, Vol. II</u>. London, England: Liverpool, 1956.

Yudof, Mark G. "Federal Funds for Public Schools." <u>Inequality in Education</u> 7, (1971) pp. 20-30.